The Man with Many Lives

Department of State portrait - November 1958
(credit to United States Department of State)

THE MAN WITH MANY LIVES

Best Wishes To Anne,

Robert W. Day

12/10/19.

Robert W. Day, FSO, Retired

Copyright © 2019 by Robert W. Day, FSO, Retired.

Library of Congress Control Number: 2019917033
ISBN: Hardcover   978-1-7960-6739-2
            Softcover   978-1-7960-6738-5
            eBook   978-1-7960-6740-8

All rights reserved. No part of this book may be reproduced or transmitted in any form or by any means, electronic or mechanical, including photocopying, recording, or by any information storage and retrieval system, without permission in writing from the copyright owner.

Print information available on the last page.

Rev. date: 10/30/2019

To order additional copies of this book, contact:
Xlibris
1-888-795-4274
www.Xlibris.com
Orders@Xlibris.com
801464

DEDICATION PAGE

To past, present, and future Foreign Service officers and staff who spend years at our embassies working to develop friendships and good relations with the diplomats and citizens of foreign countries.

DISCLAIMER

I have related the stories and adventures of my life as I remember them. I hope that I have faithfully rendered the essences of cultures, customs, and religions I have had the pleasure to experience. In order not to cause offense, I have in many cases substituted the names of the actual person with a facsimile name. Any slight or misrepresentation of individuals, cultures, countries, or religions is wholly unintentional; and I hope I have not offended anyone. So here is my story as I remember it and as supported by my notes.

CONTENTS

Dedication Page v
Disclaimer vii
Acknowledgments xi
Biography xiii
Chapter 1   Early Teenage Years 1
Chapter 2   Adventures In Scouting 15
Chapter 3   Disillusioned 37

Chapter 4   Middle Teenage Years 40
Chapter 5   Later Teenage Years 53
Chapter 6   Moving On 95
Chapter 7   The Beginning Of A New Career 107
Chapter 8   Military and World War II Service 110
Chapter 9   A New Assignment: Traveling Auditor 117
Chapter 10   Assignment: Wendover, Utah 123
Chapter 11   Government Assignments 133
Chapter 12   Arriving In Baghdad, Iraq 137
Chapter 13   Baptism Under Fire 142
Chapter 14   A Serious Accident 146
Chapter 15   Mistaken Identity 154
Chapter 16   Accident On The Babylon Highway 158
Chapter 17   A Family In Distress 162
Chapter 18   Leaving Baghdad, Iraq 167
Chapter 19   Short Stories 170
Chapter 20   Assignment: Washington DC 185
Chapter 21   Assignment: Tehran, Iran 187
Chapter 22   A Man In Distress 192
Chapter 23   A Night To Remember 194
Chapter 24   R & R Trip To Paris 203
Chapter 25   Hijacked 212

Chapter 26	Medical Attention In Tehran, Iran	219
Chapter 27	A Lady Called Spider	221
Chapter 28	Assignment: Munich	230
Chapter 29	The Rescue	235
Chapter 30	A Lucky Miss	243
Chapter 31	Celebrations In Germany	246
Chapter 32	A Tragedy To The Nation	249
Chapter 33	Leaving Munich	252
Chapter 34	Assignment Change	254
Chapter 35	Assignment: Ghana, West Africa	256
Chapter 36	The Ambassador's Get-Acquainted Visit	258
Chapter 37	Rescue of The Monthly Food Shipment	264
Chapter 38	The Revolution	268
Chapter 39	A Shocking Story	274
Chapter 40	Hunting In Africa	276
Chapter 41	My Dad's Passing	279
Chapter 42	What Price My Daughter	284
Chapter 43	Assignment: Washington, DC	293
Chapter 44	Retirement	297

ACKNOWLEDGMENTS

A book is not the product of one mind. In my case, my three wives all contributed greatly. My first wife, Charlotte, was planning to write a book of our travels in the Middle East, but the accident that led to her death prevented her from accomplishing this. My second wife, Dottie, was with me on most of the adventures you will find in this book and was a great inspiration. My third wife, Eloise, encouraged me and started working with me on this book before her untimely death.

I am indebted also to my older sister, Hazel B. Anderson, who was an author in her own right, completing twelve books of our parents' and grandparents' memoirs. In order to bring alive these memoirs, she and her husband Ralph traveled many miles within the United States gathering data over a period of years. During the six years before her death, she kept constantly reminding me that I had a book to write. I am confident that if it wasn't for her push, I would not have proceeded to finally complete my memoirs.

I would like to acknowledge Betsey Leonard and Shaula Noonan, my daughters, and their husbands Jack D. Leonard, II, and David Noonan, and my grandson, Jack D. Leonard, III, for being my inspiration and for courageously sharing many of the experiences I will write about.

Also, I wish to thank Mary K. Head and Faye Smith, editors; Sylvia M. Gregory Kelley, who devoted hours typing these memoirs, and offering other suggestions to the completion of this book, Donna J. Hunt, who also edited the book, gave computer support, and helped keep us on track, and others who contributed to my efforts.

Subsequently, Donna J. Hunt and Sylvia M. Gregory Kelley were made editor and co-editor in finalizing the book, which is most appreciated. This book would never have been completed without their assistance.

I am indebted to my family and friends who listened patiently while I told my stories.

Finally, I wish to thank my many friends and others who will be purchasing this book to learn more about the duties and requirements of a Foreign Service officer at our many embassies abroad. Many individuals do not realize the efforts and the life-threatening dangers the Foreign Service Officers experience maintaining diplomatic relations and protecting American citizens as they travel abroad.

In addition, I wish to thank the six presidents, from President Roosevelt to President Nixon, who served as our country's leaders during this period. I am grateful for the opportunity to serve them as well as my country while fulfilling my duties as a federal employee, a member of the military, and a Foreign Service Commissioned Officer of the Diplomatic Service.

Robert W. Day, FSO, Retired

BIOGRAPHY

Robert William Day was born in Leavenworth, Kansas, on April 16, 1919, to a middle class family. His parents were Minor H. and Anna Jane Day. He was the third child from this marriage. Robert was an average student in school, and his dad thought he should go into engineering, as he performed very well on engineering aptitude tests in school.

His father owned a medium-sized electrical and battery business which catered to the public of Leavenworth County, in Fort Leavenworth and many farmers of eastern Kansas. Prior to going into business for himself, Minor was wire chief (supervisor) for the Bell Telephone Company in Kansas City, Missouri, and later owned several telephone exchanges in small cities in western Missouri and eastern Kansas.

The electrical business did very well until the Great Depression, when his father reluctantly closed his business and worked for private firms until America's entrance into WWII. At that time, he devoted his engineering experience to winning the war by being employed in the electrical field at Fort Leavenworth. He was later employed as chief electrical engineer at the patrol torpedo (PT) boat factory in Leavenworth, which was constructing PT boats. Then he worked as a civilian engineer for the US Navy, as a chief inspector of heavy guns on US warships in San Francisco, California. He served in this capacity for the last fifteen years of his working life. Perhaps it was from watching his father as he worked throughout his life that Robert developed his never-ending work ethic.

When Robert graduated from high school, he wanted to go on to college in the engineering field as his dad had hoped; but, like 90 percent of his graduating classmates, he did not have the financial means to continue his education at that time, so his higher education would have to wait a few years before it could be achieved. Soon after graduation, as a result of a Civil Service exam he had taken, Robert was offered a position with the US government in the accounting field.

His first position was as an accounting clerk for the US Treasury Department in Kansas City, and after two years, he advanced to the position of accountant for the Department of Agriculture in Lincoln, Nebraska. On December 7, 1941, when America entered WWII and declared war on Japan, he was solicited for a defense position with war housing. Unknown to Robert, because of the high-security classification, it was not revealed that he was actually employed and working as part of the Manhattan Project for the development of the atomic bomb and the method for delivery.

After completion of this assignment, he was subsequently offered a position with the US Department of State and assigned to his first post in Baghdad, Iraq. He served in overseas positions at American Embassies in the Middle East, Europe, and Africa, as well as in Washington DC for diplomatic assignments. His title varied from Budget and Finance Officer at his first post to Consular of Embassy for Administration and Security. His last diplomatic assignment was as Deputy Budget Officer in Washington DC for financial operations for all worldwide American Embassies.

After thirty-two years, Robert left the Federal Diplomatic Service and retired to Florida, where he took a job with the State of Florida in Tallahassee, where he was appointed by the governor to various positions. His last assignment was as a member of the Florida Board of Professional Engineers. He retired from the State of Florida after approximately twenty four years.

After retirement, he traveled extensively within the US and abroad for pleasure. Now at the age of one hundred, he thinks back on his long life and the good times he shared with the three intelligent and wonderful ladies who were his wives, and considers himself blessed and most fortunate to have had these three wonderful marriages. In addition, he has shared his life with two great daughters, Betsey and Shaula, and his grandson, Jack D. Leonard, III, along with some wonderful, dear friends. He has enjoyed friendship with many individuals, including a wonderful lady, Sylvia M. Gregory Kelley, during the last several years.

When asked to what he attributes his longevity, Mr. Day replied, "I've been blessed with a very wonderful life: three very happy and loving marriages, staying healthy, having a positive attitude, accepting responsibilities, and setting goals, which have kept me active and busy."

He continued with, "Once, my daughter asked me why I didn't just sit down and relax and enjoy retirement. I remember telling her, 'I'm afraid if I sit down for too long, I won't be able to get up! Staying as active as you can for as long as you are able keeps you going.'"

One goal of his retirement years has been to complete his memoirs, which he began fifteen years ago with several short stories. These have now blossomed into a book of forty-four chapters, which are based on his life's experiences growing up in Kansas, his years during WWII, his adventures living overseas, and his later years. "Some events were frightening, others challenging, and many rewarding, but they were always exciting," he said.

Here now are some of those stories in Bob's own words.

CHAPTER 1

Early Teenage Years

The year was 1931, April had finally arrived, and I would be twelve years old on the sixteenth. I had been waiting for many months, not always patiently, for my twelfth birthday, as my life was about to change in many ways. For a long time, it had been my great desire to purchase a new Hawthorne Flyer bicycle. I knew that upon reaching the age of twelve, this became a real possibility.

After shopping around at several bicycle shops, I settled for a blue Hawthorne Flyer that had twenty-eight-inch wheels, a built-in toolbox, a tire pump and a little seat above the rear wheel strong enough to carry a second person. This purchase required a great deal of thought and planning on my part, as I was going to spend most of my savings from selling magazines since the age of nine.

After some discussion and a little negotiation with a Mr. Brown, who was of the owner of George Brown's Bicycle Shop, one of the leading bicycle stores in town, the $32.50 purchase was completed, and I was the proud owner of a brand-new bicycle. I then decided that I needed a wire basket for the front of my bicycle if I was going to be selected for a paper route. My two buddies, Stanley Wade and Kenneth Wittig, both of whom had paper routes with the *Kansas City Journal-Post*, had talked to the route manager, Mr. Sam Gibson, and had put in a good word on my behalf. However, it would be another year before a suitable paper route was offered to me.

A few days later, my mother asked me if I would go to the grocery store to pick up a few items. The Gonzer Grocery Store was only a block from our house, but that gave me another opportunity to ride my new bicycle. I readily agreed, and she gave me a short list of items that were needed. As I sped off down the street, I thought, *how wonderful it is to be the owner of such a great bicycle.*

When I approached the intersection where Gonzer's Store was located, I noticed they were painting a building just across the street, and there was a sign in the window giving notice that a new drugstore was opening soon and delivery boys were needed. I thought I could earn some money as a delivery boy since I no longer had a magazine route, so I parked and locked my bicycle and went to the front door. It was unlocked, and as I opened the door, I was greeted by a very nice-looking man, probably in his mid to late forties, in a white coat, and was asked if he could help me.

I told him my name, mentioned the sign in the window, and told him I would like to apply for the position of delivery boy. He introduced himself and said his name was Al Derzinski and that he was starting a new neighborhood drugstore. As I recall, he asked me my name again, where I lived, my age, and then handed me a sheet of paper with a few questions on it.

He said, "Bob, here is an application. If you are interested, please fill it out and have your mother or dad sign it. I am about ready to hire a couple of boys, so please get the application back to me soon."

I thanked him and went on to the grocery story, purchased the items for my mother, and headed for home. I showed my mother the application and told her my story and asked her if I could complete the application and if she would sign it. She agreed, with the stipulation that I would keep my school grades up. I also remember her reminding me that I was just twelve years old and probably would be working some at night, so I had to be very careful riding my bicycle on the streets during the day and at night. Mr. Derzinski had suggested that I install a head-light and a tail-light that were bright enough for people to see me. I had reassured my mother that I would keep my grades up to par and would be careful on the streets; I would ask my dad if he could install a head-light and a tail-light on my bike.

Later that day, I delivered my application to Mr. Derzinski, and after handing it to him, I thought he would say, "Well, Bob, if I need you, I will give you a call." But instead, he said, "Bob, let's sit here and talk for a little while. How about having a coke with me?"

I replied, "Sure, Mr. Derzinski, if you have time."

He then said, "Bob, just call me Al. By the way, I want you to meet my pharmacy assistant, Dave Smith, who is working his way through the University of Kansas, as he is going to be a doctor."

As we sat there sipping our cokes, Al was reading my application and smiling, and I thought, *Do you suppose I am going to get the job and earn some real money?*

Shortly, he put my application aside and said, "Bob, I like your application, your neatness, and your character. You live near here, and it looks like you have a good bicycle for deliveries. By the way, do you know anything about a soda fountain?"

I said, "No, Al, I don't, but I am certainly willing to learn."

Dave was working behind the fountain, cleaning the shining silver levers on the syrup containers, and said, "Don't worry, Al, I will teach him everything he needs to know."

Al then said, "Bob, the job will be as a delivery boy, curb hop, and sometimes fountain man. It pays ten cents per hour, plus tips, to start with. All of my boys get a free soda or milkshake after work of an evening. You will work every other night including Saturday and Sunday and should wear dark pants and a white shirt and a jacket as needed. Until summer, the weekday hours will be from 6:00 p.m. to 10:00 or 10:30 p.m. When you work on Saturday or Sunday, the hours will be from 1:00 p.m. to 10:00 or 10:30 p.m. In the summertime, we may stay open longer, depending on business. Are you interested?"

"Yes, Al," I responded. "When do you want me to report for work?"

Al replied, "Well, today is Saturday—our opening day is next Monday. So be here Monday evening at 6:00 o'clock. Let's shake on it."

I shook Al's hand, not knowing then that I would be working for Al and Dave, either part-time or full-time, for the next three years; I would eventually have doubled my salary to twenty cents per hour, plus tips; and our long friendship would end in a tragedy.

That evening, I asked my dad if there was any way he could install a head-light and a tail-light on my new bicycle. After dinner, we went to check my bike, and I remember him saying, "Bob, this sure is some bicycle you have. I wished for a bicycle when I was a boy, but never was able to buy one. You may remember the many stories I have told you. We lived on a farm, and I did have an Indian pony that my dad purchased for three dollars, which was a lot of money in those days, from an Indian family who had a small farm about ten miles from our farm. Well, enough talk. Let's take a look to see what we need to do to get you all lit up."

After checking out my bike, he decided what was needed, so he said, "Bob, if I can have your bike one afternoon in a few days, you will have a good head-light and tail-light so you will be able to drive at night and cars will be able to see you front or back."

My dad was an electrical engineer and owned his own business, known as Day's Battery and Electric Service, which included a small battery-manufacturing plant. A few days later, he told me that anytime I could spare my bike for a few hours, he was ready to install my lighting equipment. As I was anxious for my new lighting system, the following day, I left my bike with him for the afternoon; and when I returned after school, my dad had built a single-cell wet rechargeable battery that was installed in a flat metal box clamped to the bicycle bar between my knees. I now had very bright head-lights and tail-lights; all I had to do was plug it into the charger every other night or so. Now I had the only bicycle in town that had a rechargeable battery for my lights.

When I reported for work the following Monday in early June 1931, I found that Al had employed a second boy, Bill Harris, who also lived in our area and went to my school. In the summertime, I frequently worked full-time during most of the day, and also of an evening, making deliveries on my bike or working the soda fountain. During this three-year period, I made hundreds of deliveries of prescriptions or other merchandise and rode my bike hundreds of miles. This was in 1931, and the Great Depression had begun, and many boys my age, as well as men, did not have jobs or any source of income. I felt very fortunate.

During the summer months, the drugstore did a remarkable soda fountain business, as we were known for great milkshakes, ice cream sodas, and banana splits. Frequently in the evenings, there would be ten or fifteen vehicles at the curb waiting for or getting curb service. This required four or five boys, called gutter pups, to be available to provide service to these patrons and make deliveries. We had a long wooden bench backed up to the wall of the drugstore, where we all sat when we were not busy waiting on cars.

Late one Saturday night in 1933, I was fourteen years old and on curb hop duty with four other boys. One of the boys, who I will call Richard, had been waiting on a very attractive single lady in a late-model vehicle. When he returned from placing her tray at the door of her vehicle, he said, "Fellows, this gal in the new car, which I just waited on doesn't have any clothes on. She does have a little towel on her lap. I will sell the right to pick up her tray when she is finished to the highest bidder."

One of the boys said, "OK, Richard, I will give you ten cents." Another one said, "I will give you fifteen cents."

Even though I had three sisters, I had never seen a nude female, so I said, "OK, Richard, I will give you twenty-five cents."

Richard said, "OK, Bob, sold to the highest bidder."

As the highest bidder, I then gave Richard twenty-five cents, equal to two and a half hours' pay. After about fifteen minutes or so, Miss Bare-breasted honked her horn for tray pickup, and I answered the call. I walked up to the driver's door thinking maybe Richard was pulling one of his jokes on me, but he wasn't! There sat Miss Bare-breasted, as bare as a skinned rabbit.

She said, "Hello, young man, I am lonesome. Will you talk to me for a little while?"

I said, "Sure, miss. My name is Bob. What is yours, and what shall we talk about?"

She said, "My name is Sally, and let's talk about the beautiful moon that is shining tonight."

I stood there with my foot on the running board, with my eyes wide open, and my eyeballs hanging out, and we talked for a good ten minutes or more. When I told her that I was sorry but I had to go back to work, Sally said, "Bob, it was so nice meeting you, and I do hope to see you again."

I said, "Thank you, Miss Sally, and I do hope to see you again."

As I picked up the tray, she placed a dollar bill on the tray as a tip, which was unheard of in those days, and blew me a kiss. Miss Sally made my day!

When I returned to my seat on the bench and Miss Sally had driven away, I showed the boys my dollar bill and said, "Fellows, not only did I increase my knowledge, but it looks like I made a very good investment."

Unfortunately, I never did see Miss Sally again.

A year had passed since I started working at Al's Drug Store. One evening, one of my buddies, Stanley Wade, came by the drugstore and told me that Sam Gibson, route manager for the *Kansas City Journal-Post*, wanted to see me the following day after school at his office as he had a paper route available that might be of interest to me. I thought, *this is great! I asked myself, can I go to school and hold down two part-time jobs at the same time? Think of the money I will be making.*

I was at Sam Gibson's office the next day after school. He mentioned that one of the boys had become ill, and there was a route available on the west side of town if I was interested. He told me the requirements for being a *Journal Post* carrier: pay my monthly paper bill in full when due, be at the route manager's office when the delivery truck arrived, and deliver my papers promptly to my customers. The delivery truck arrived at 4:00 p.m. on weekdays, at 5:00 a.m. Saturdays, and 1:00 a.m. on Sundays. All papers had to be picked up by 5:00 a.m. This route was on the west side of town, and the territory was one square mile, consisting mainly of residences, with just seventy-six customers, but it was expected for the new carrier to build up the route considerably.

I was familiar with the area of the city he mentioned, which consisted mainly of older homes, but there was a group of new homes being built. Many employees of the federal penitentiary and the military post at Fort Leavenworth were moving into the area, as it was a convenient location for their work. I knew what carriers had to pay for the papers, so I could quickly calculate my monthly commission, which would not be too great with only seventy-six customers. However, I could see the possibility of route expansion, so I told Mr. Gibson I was interested in the route. He said I could take over the route the next day, if it was convenient for me. He would give me a list of customers and would drive the route with me in his car for three days, so I could become familiar with the area and where the customers lived.

At that point, I became a carrier for the *Kansas City Journal-Post*. I worked hard making house calls, and in four months or so, I had increased my route to 150 daily customers. It then became a very good-paying route, but it was difficult to get up some Saturday or Sunday mornings in the winter when the temperature was below freezing and there was snow on the ground. Most of the time, I would ride my bike; but if there was too much ice or snow, I would have to walk my route, which was seven or eight miles round trip from my home.

Returning to the subject of my job with the drugstore, I was now just fifteen years of age. I had been working for Al Derzinski for three years, and we had, in my opinion, an excellent relationship. Some of the boys Al had hired did not last too long, as some left if the pay was not sufficient or for other reasons. A few Al fired, as he caught them stealing merchandise or shorting the cash register when making change. He found that I did not mind working long shifts and was very honest, so we got along very well.

During my years at Al's Drug Store, I had worked as curb hop, delivery boy, fountain boy, and drug clerk, but now I worked mostly in the store stocking shelves, as a fountain boy or drug clerk. Some of the new or younger boys were required to make the deliveries.

Each Fourth of July, Al would have a shipment of fireworks delivered, and they would arrive probably three or four days before the Fourth of July. He would then have a fireworks stand moved from behind his building to the curbside near the street in front of the drugstore. He would then select one of his delivery boys to operate the fireworks stand for about three days before and including on the Fourth of July. It was always an honor among us boys to be selected by Al to operate the fireworks stand during this time. Al had selected me as the operator the year before; and he was pleased with my service, so he appointed me as fireworks manager for the second year, which pleased me very much.

It was the morning of the Fourth of July. I had arrived early, about 8:00 a.m., to get the stand set up and ready to go, because we expected business to be very good that year. By about 9:00 a.m., I had the stand completely set up. A car pulled up to the curb just in front of my stand about three or four feet from me with two men in the front seat. The passenger in the car, a young man who seemed very friendly, asked me how I was and wanted to know how much a firecracker known as a "red salute" would cost. This was a firecracker that was round, had about a three-inch fuse, and was very powerful. It was so powerful that if it exploded in your hand, it could easily blow a couple of fingers off.

I had just set a box containing seventy-five or a hundred of these "red salutes" on the counter in front of me. Suddenly the man, who had said his name was David, took his lit cigarette out of his mouth and flipped it into the box of these "red salutes" and then they quickly drove off.

I could see that the fuses on a number of these "red salutes" had picked up a spark from the cigarette and would be going off within the next few seconds and would probably ignite many of the other fireworks in the stand if they exploded.

There was no traffic on the street at that time, so I grabbed the box of "red salutes" and threw them out of the stand into the street and then immediately left by the back entrance of the fireworks stand. Suddenly, there was a series of very loud bangs as many of the "red salutes" exploded. No one was injured, and none of the fireworks in the stand caught fire. My boss Al came running out of the drugstore asking me what happened. I explained, and he said, "Bob, thank you for that quick thinking. No one was injured, and we did not lose the fireworks stand. Thanks again. Now, next year, you can operate the fireworks stand again."

It was a Sunday afternoon in late May 1934, about 4:00 p.m. I had been working the soda fountain all afternoon, and Al's wife, Virginia, had been at the store most of the afternoon, stocking shelves and talking to some of the customers.

When the customers had all left the store, Virginia came over to the fountain, sat down on one of the fountain stools, and said, "Bob, how about fixing me a cherry coke?"

I said, "Sure, Virginia. A short one or a tall one?"

"Well," she replied, "as we are not too busy, I would like to sit and talk with you a little while, so make it a tall one."

We talked for about half an hour, just about school, football games, and when she was a teacher—nothing special, just passing the time.

About that time, Al came over, sat down on one of the fountain stools next to Virginia, and said, "What are you drinking, dear?"

She said, "Bob just fixed me a cherry coke. Do you want a taste?"

He said, "No, I don't think so. But, Bob, will you fix me a tall root beer with a dip of ice cream in it?"

"OK, Al, one root beer float coming up."

After I served the drink to Al, he and Virginia sat at the fountain and talked for a little while. I was doing a little cleanup on the fountain and checking the syrup containers.

Shortly, I heard Al say, "Virginia, let's go downstairs and talk a little while and finish our drinks."

They got up, saying, "See you later," and headed for the stairway leading down to the basement area. Al had renovated one of the basement rooms of the drugstore into a nice area similar to a living room. Rather frequently, some of his friends would come by, and if business was slow, they would retire to his basement hideout with a pot of coffee and play cards or chess.

By then, I got busy serving some customers at the fountain; and when they left about thirty minutes later, Dave, the assistant pharmacist, came over, sat down, and said he had just finished doing some work in the pharmacy room. We had been talking only a few minutes when we heard Virginia coming up the steps from the basement.

As she came by the fountain, she said, "See you all later," and went out the front door. Usually, she stopped and talked a little, so David and I wondered if she had a problem.

After about ten minutes, Al came up from the basement, and we heard him in the prescription room. Then he came to the door and checked to see if we were alone. He said, "Dave and Bob, come back here for a minute."

This was not unusual, as many times, he would ask us to work on something in the prescription room. When we arrived, he said, "I want to show and tell you something."

He opened a drawer, took out a .38 caliber revolver, and said that when he and Virginia went down to the basement to visit and finish their drinks, she opened her purse, took out the revolver, and showed it to him. He said, "Virginia, why are you carrying this revolver in your purse?"

She said it was for protection, and he told her that since she had not been trained in the use of a weapon, he would appreciate if she would give him the revolver until she received some appropriate training. She handed him the revolver, and they talked a little while longer before he gave her a big hug, told her he loved her, and she left. He said he was telling us so that if we saw a revolver in the safe when getting petty cash, we would understand. Al asked us not to say anything about the revolver to anybody, and Dave and I both agreed not to mention it to anyone else and then started to leave.

Then Al said, "Bob, I have four prescription deliveries that are some distance from the store, so give two to each of the delivery boys on duty and tell them to take off right away because the customers want them this evening. It's nearly 6:00 p.m., and I want you to work tonight. Go home, get your supper, and return when you can."

Then he said to Dave, "I need two of Homer's large hamburgers with lots of mustard and pickle from Homer's Hamburger Store down the block. Dave, you get whatever you want to eat. Here is a ten-dollar bill. That should cover the cost."

Dave said, "OK, Al, but that will leave you here at the store by yourself."

Al replied, "That is OK. I can handle all the business."

Dave and I followed Al's instructions. Dave headed for Homer's, I gave the prescriptions to Richard and James, and then I headed home for my dinner.

When I arrived home, my mother had just placed our evening meal on the table, and she, my Dad, my three sisters, and I sat down to eat. We always had a light supper on Sunday evening, as usually our noon meal on Sunday was a full-spread dinner.

Afterward, we sat and talked a little while before I decided it was time for me to get back to the drugstore. I excused myself from the table, and as I got on my bicycle, an ambulance and two police cars with their sirens blasting passed by our house. I thought there must be a bad accident on the main highway.

Before I arrived, I saw the three emergency vehicles parked in front of the drugstore. I parked my bike and noticed a crowd was gathering near the front door of the store. I ran through the small group to enter the building where a police officer was standing guard in the doorway.

As I started through the door, the police officer said, "Young man, you can't go in there," and placed his arm across the doorway. I told him I worked there, and he let me in the door. No one was in the front section of the store, which was usually quite busy, but I heard talking in the prescription room. Moving on to the back of the store, I saw Dave, one police officer in uniform, and two other large men dressed in business suits looking down. I knew these two men were detectives, and friends of my dad's.

As I walked in, the police officer said, "Kid, what are you doing here?"

I replied that I worked there as a clerk and fountain boy, and then I realized why they were looking down at the floor. There was something on the floor covered in a white sheet.

One of them said, "Young man, do you know who this person is?" He pulled the sheet back, and there was Al, lying very still with a big red bloody spot in the middle of his chest on his white shirt and coat. I replied, "Yes, that is Al, my boss."

As I stood there looking at Al's motionless body, I immediately noticed three things: he had what appeared to be a smile on his face, his eyes were wide open, and the revolver was lying on the floor at his side. One of the detectives told us not to touch anything, as the photo lab had not arrived yet.

I said, "Dave, his eyes are still open, and Al is dead."

As Dave was in medical school, no doubt he had previously encountered death. He looked at one of the detectives, who nodded after a brief moment and Dave stooped down over Al's body and, using his right hand, carefully closed Al's eyes. As he did so, I saw tears rolling down Dave's cheeks, and I started to cry as well. As Dave and I stood there with tears running down our faces, he put one hand on my shoulder and softly said, "This is tough on both of us, Bob."

The three police officers had turned away to give us a moment of privacy and were looking at a piece of white paper lying on the prescription counter. One of the detectives told Dave it was a note from Al, and Dave reached for the note before stopping suddenly as he realized he should not be touching anything in the room that might be considered as evidence.

The detective bent over the note without touching it and said, "I will read it to you. It says, 'To Virginia and my friends, sorry to go out this way, but life is too much for me. I hope you all will forgive me. Al.'"

I never did read the note, so I do not know if the detective was reading exactly what Al had written or if we were just being given a message made up by the detective in order not to divulge some evidence that should not be revealed at that time.

One of the detectives motioned for Dave and me to leave the room as the photo lab people had just arrived. As Dave and I went into the main part of the store, we noticed a large group had formed outside, and we could see that Richard and James had returned from their deliveries and were standing near the front door.

Dave said, "Bob, I need to take care of this situation, and I will talk to you and the boys after talking to the policeman out front."

As we left the store, I joined Richard and James, who wanted to know what was going on, and I told them that Dave would see us shortly.

The police officer said, "Folks, please listen to me. There has been an accident, and that is all I am permitted to tell you. Please go home, and you will read about it in tomorrow's newspapers."

The crowd slowly thinned out, and then Dave joined us. "As the policeman stated to the crowd, there has been an accident. Al has been shot. He is dead, and at this point, we don't know what will happen at the store, but I will be in touch with all of you to let you know." Dave then said, "Richard and James, give me the money you collected on those deliveries, and I will call you so we can wind up any outstanding items."

We all said good-bye to Dave and headed for home on our bikes. A tragic day was ending for all of us.

The following day, we were anxious to read the paper to learn more details about the accident. However, none of the news articles told us why Al decided to end his life.

At the funeral, which was held in the local funeral home, all the delivery boys and Dave sat together, but at the graveside service, there was no sufficient seating, so we all stood in a group.

During some cold winter nights, when only Al and I were on duty at the store and business was slow, we would have some very interesting discussions concerning any number of subjects. On several occasions, we discussed religion. I was a Protestant, Al was Catholic, and I was interested in knowing more about the Catholic religion.

Standing there, we listened to the priest's last prayers for Al's soul before his body was lowered into his grave. It brought back memories of those confidential talks we had on those cold winter nights. Al had told me that his church members believed that when a person dies, his soul goes to purgatory before it may go on to heaven or hell. I remember asking Al how long the soul stays in purgatory and when can it move on. His reply was, "Takes prayer to get the soul out, and it depends on how good a person has been on earth and if they have committed any crimes."

As I listened to the priest with tears in my eyes, I had questions in my mind. *Was suicide a crime in Al's faith, had the priests said sufficient prayers to move Al's soul on to its final resting place, or was his soul still in purgatory, and when would it move on to its final destination?*

Prior to leaving the cemetery, I saw Virginia talking to one of her friends. I approached her and expressed my condolences, and I remember she kissed me on the cheek and said, "Bob, thanks for everything. You are so sweet."

I never saw Virginia again.

A few days after the funeral, Dave called all the boys and asked us to be at the store at 4:00 p.m. the following day to get our final wages.

When we got there, the store was closed for business, so we all sat at the serving tables, and Dave settled our outstanding obligations. He then introduced us to a man who had been at the store when we arrived. His name was James Voorhees, and he was an attorney. Dave explained that Mr. Voorhees was representing Al's estate and turned the meeting over to him. Mr. Voorhees explained to us that he would be closing the store, paying off any debts, selling or disposing of all inventory, and selling the building. He thanked us for the service we had provided our customers and the time we had given Al, and also mentioned that Dave would be going back to medical school in a couple of weeks and wished him the best of luck in becoming a doctor.

Finally, he stated that there was a lot of frozen inventory that we needed to do something with, so he told me to get behind the soda fountain and make whatever the rest of the guys wanted, and requested a chocolate milkshake for himself.

"Fellows, I have checked, and there are plenty of quarts of ice cream in the freezer, so when you finish with your drinks, have Bob give each of you a quart or two to take home to your mother for dinner tonight."

After finishing our drinks, all the boys said their good-byes and left the store. I stayed to clean up the fountain, wash up the glasses, and pack a quart of chocolate ice cream to take home. Dave and I sat and talked a little while before we said our good-byes.

Dave graduated from medical school with honors and, to my understanding, later became a very prominent physician in the Chicago area. It would be sixty years before we would meet again at a class reunion breakfast back in Leavenworth. Five years later, I would meet James Voorhees again, and we would become very good friends. This three-year chapter in my life had reached a decisive closure.

Bob on his first bicycle
(with sister Frances) - 1931

CHAPTER 2

Adventures In Scouting

Back when I was nine years old, I had started a magazine route, selling the *Saturday Evening Post*, the *Country Gentleman*, and *Ladies' Home Journal* to my residential customers to earn a little spending money. I knew that when I reached the magical age of twelve, I would be old enough to make four different changes in my life: I could discontinue my magazine route and start a newspaper route with the *Kansas City Journal-Post*, I could give up my old bicycle that I had purchased two years earlier for ten dollars from a friend, and purchase a new Hawthorn Flyer bicycle using my savings. I could take a part-time job in my neighborhood if one was available, provided I kept my grades up, and then I would be old enough to join the Boy Scouts of America, which had been on my wish list for a long time.

In those days, the various Boy Scouts were permitted to march in the Independence Day Parade, Veterans Day Parade, and other special event parades that took place in many small towns. The Boy Scouts proudly marching with Old Glory and the troop flags in the lead with the Eagle Scouts marching nearby always made me feel very proud. That was when I decided that I was going to join the Boy Scouts when I reached the eligible age, and someday I would become an Eagle Scout. Shortly after my twelfth birthday, my dad and I visited three different Scout troops during their weekly meetings, and I decided to join Troop 73, which was sponsored by the First Methodist Church in Leavenworth, Kansas. At that time, Jim Trackwell was the Scoutmaster, and Edward Baker was the Assistant Scoutmaster. Jim was the owner of the New Way Restaurant, which made delightful hamburger sandwiches; and Edward owned the E. E. Baker Plumbing and Heating Company.

Frequently, two to four other men would attend our Friday-evening meetings to assist Scouts with their merit badge tests or coach them on many issues. Most of our coaches were professional men such as doctors, attorneys, teachers, or engineers, who provided the Scouts with some excellent advice and training. I was fortunate, as I gained the confidence of a counselor whose name was Jim Grey, and as I recall, he was an engineer and had taught engineering at a university. With Jim's assistance and guidance, I moved up the ranks from Tenderfoot to Second Class to First Class in about a year. Then Jim was transferred to another city, and I never heard from him again.

Boys who select scouting usually enjoy hiking, camping, the companionship of other boys, and the spirit of the pioneers. This was true in my case, and I was always ready for a weekend, or an even longer camping trip. I recall, in one instance, three of our fathers took about fifteen boys of our Scout troop out about twenty miles from town to a large forest area where Scouts frequently camped for the weekend. Our Assistant Scoutmaster stayed with us for the Friday and Saturday night campout. Our fathers said they or three others with their vehicles would be back Sunday morning to take us back to town.

We all had a great two days of camping and became more educated regarding Scouting and camping. However, there was a communication gap somewhere along the line, and by nine thirty Sunday morning no vehicles had arrived for transportation.

Assistant Scoutmaster Edward Baker, said, "OK, boys, let's break camp, and we will surprise your dads and meet them on the road. This will get some of you in shape for our next twenty-mile hike to earn another merit badge."

We broke camp, loaded our knapsacks and bedrolls on our backs, and headed for home. We walked and walked and walked, and by noon, transportation still had not arrived. We stopped to rest by a large apple orchard. Watching the group passing by, the farmer came out to the road and talked with us quite a while. Then he said, "Boys, when are you going to have lunch?"

We advised him that we did not have any lunch as we had eaten all our food at breakfast time. He said, "Boys, I don't have any lunch to serve you, but I will give each of you three apples for lunch if you are interested. The apples are not quite ripe and a little green, so they shouldn't give you too much of a stomachache."

We all had green apples with salt and water for lunch, which did fill the empty spot in our stomachs. After our green apple lunch, we started walking again, and by five o'clock, we had walked twenty-four miles and had arrived at the city limits of our hometown. There was a small country store open, and the manager let us use his phone.

Our Assistant Scoutmaster called our Scoutmaster and a couple of the fathers, with no answer, so I called my dad and explained our problem and told him we were all too tired to walk any farther. He said, "Bob, ask Edward and the boys to stay there at the country store, and I will get some transportation for all of you."

We all sat down at the side of the country store, and after about thirty minutes, here came my dad in his Studebaker sedan, followed by a large stake-bed pickup truck owned by Joe Smith, a friend of my dad's. The rescue team had arrived, and we were very happy to see them. We all piled our camping gear into the back of the truck. Some of the boys climbed on top of the camping equipment, some inside my dad's car, and the remainder on the running boards of the two vehicles. Of course, our Assistant Scoutmaster rode up front with my dad.

My dad and his friend Joe delivered all the boys safely to their homes, and I am confident that all the exhausted boys hit the sack with their sore feet early that Sunday evening. As a result of this incident, the Scoutmaster and the fathers always made sure everyone knew who was to drive the Scouts to and from the campsite.

A year had passed since I became a Scout. I looked forward to every Friday's Scout meeting, which usually began about 6:45 p.m. and always finished by 10:00 p.m. Several of us boys would walk home together, which was less than a mile, and frequently stop at a mom-and-pop hamburger shop and have a hamburger, chili, and possibly a cold drink. We were all somewhat disappointed that night as our Scoutmaster, Jim Trackwell, announced that he was resigning. He was expanding his business and would no longer have adequate time to devote to the Scout troop. Ed Baker had agreed to move up and become our new Scoutmaster. We knew he had been a captain in the US Army and was most disciplined, but always fair, so we knew we would have to behave ourselves and follow his orders.

Ed's promotion meant we would need a new Assistant Scoutmaster, and we wondered who it might be.

The following Friday, most of us arrived at the social room of the First Methodist Church a little early as we wondered if we had a new Assistant Scoutmaster. At 6:45 p.m., Ed blew his whistle, and we all took our seats, assembled by patrol. We noticed that there were three men sitting with Ed at the leaders' table, with the American and troop flags mounted on their staffs on each side of the table. By then, as a First Class Scout, I had become the leader of the Eagle Patrol and was quite proud of my accomplishments. As I recall, there were three other patrols in our troop—the Panthers, Tigers, and Wolves.

The first order of business was the Pledge of Allegiance, and then Ed introduced the three men sitting with him at the leaders' table. I do not recall their names, but I do recall that one was a doctor, one a teacher, and the third was an engineer. Ed said the men were professionals and had volunteered to devote a certain amount of their time to assisting and advising us as our counselors. He then announced that he had a very fine man lined up to be our new Assistant Scoutmaster, and if everything worked out, he would be with us next Friday evening.

"Now, as your new Scoutmaster," he continued, "I have decided to announce some revisions in our Scout program and meetings. I consider all of you boys fine young men who are anxious to move ahead in Scouting. As you are aware, I spent quite a number of years in the military service, where you must maintain discipline and the same policy will apply to our Scout troop. It is one of my objectives that Troop Number 73 will be the most outstanding troop in Leavenworth County, and if any of you boys do not follow orders or get too far out of line, there will be a penalty."

At that point, many of the Scouts looked at each other. When the word "penalty" was used, we knew the meaning. In those days, to discipline a boy for a severe misbehavior in gym or physical education class in junior high or high school, the instructor was permitted to impose what was then known as the "belt line" or some might refer to it as "the gauntlet." This consisted of a double line of boys facing each other with approximately six to eight feet between the two rows, with each boy holding his belt by the buckle. The boy being punished would have to run between the two lines, and the other boys would attempt to strike him. The rule was, you did not strike the boy above the shoulders or below the waist, you did not use the buckle of your belt, and all had to participate. If you violated any of these rules, you were then required to run the belt line.

I have no doubt this method of punishment developed from the style of punishment the American Indians used on members of their own tribe or prisoners, except, according to stories I have read, the American Indians used various weapons, not belts, and the individual being disciplined frequently did not survive. To my knowledge, no one in our troop was ever severely injured by this method of discipline, but it certainly would not be permitted today. I do not recall the offense, but I do remember one time in physical education, I was ordered to run the belt line. However, in the ninth grade, I held the record for the 100-yard dash, so I did not receive very many hits, but I do remember the strikes did sting.

At this point, Ed continued with his proposed program. We were to have the Scout Oath and Scout Laws memorized, as we could be called on at any time to recite those passages, and we were to also follow the Oath and Laws in our daily lives. We were to wear our full Scout uniform to all Scout meetings and functions, unless told otherwise. If we could not afford a full uniform, we were to discuss it with either Ed or the new Assistant Scoutmaster. In addition, first aid and safety were very important in our daily lives, so with the assistance of our physician counselor, an advanced first aid and safety course would be established for which we would earn a merit badge. Once we became a Second Class Scout, it would be the first merit badge to work on and earn. Scouts who had already passed the first aid and safety merit badge requirements would take a refresher course, as Ed wanted us all to know how to handle a medical emergency at home, while camping, and elsewhere.

"Now," he said when he was finished, "I would like for all of you to come forward by patrol and introduce yourselves to our counselors, then assemble by patrol and work on your merit badges. I will be meeting with each patrol before we close for the evening to give you more information on a camping trip we have planned for later this month."

Before we were dismissed that evening, our Scoutmaster announced that during the following month, we would be going on a three-night camping trip to the Leavenworth County Scout camp, which had one large camp building with 24 built-in bunks and a large fireplace. Our troop had camped there previously, and it was a great place to spend a few days, but troops had to reserve it due to the demand. He was making this announcement so we could get our camping gear ready.

In addition, he announced that Jim Trackwell had invited the full troop to a hamburger-chili get-together at one of his hamburger restaurants the following Friday after the Scout meeting, and transportation for all Scouts would be provided. Jim had told our leader that he was giving this hamburger party for the Scouts in memory of the good times he had spent with them and in honor of our new Assistant Scoutmaster. He was making this announcement so we could tell our parents about the party and that we would be home later than usual after that Scout meeting.

The following Friday evening, most of the Scouts arrived early for our meeting in the social room at the church, as we were all anxious to see and meet our new Assistant Scoutmaster. We were all sitting around talking, and it was nearly 7:00 p.m. and there was no Scoutmaster, but two of our counselors were present. Just at 7:00 p.m., our Scoutmaster walked in with a young man, probably in his mid-twenties, tall with a muscular build but shorter than our Scoutmaster, who was around six feet tall.

Ed Baker took his friend over to the two counselors who were sitting at the leaders' table and introduced the young man to them, after which they all sat down and talked for a short time. Then Ed blew his whistle, and we assembled by patrols. He then said, "Scouts, we will now recite the Pledge of Allegiance."

We all stood at attention with our right hands over our hearts and noticed that the new man snapped to attention and did the same. After the Pledge of Allegiance, our Scoutmaster introduced the new man as George McGee, our new Assistant Scoutmaster. George had been working for Ed in his plumbing shop for the last several months and had proved to a good worker, honest and reliable.

"I believe George will work out fine with you Scouts, assisting you with the merit badges, coaching you in your scouting activities, and being your leader on hikes and camping trips when I am not able to accompany you."

Then Ed asked George to stand over to one side and had each patrol come forward so the boys could introduce themselves to George. Afterward, we worked on merit badges or other projects, read, or tried to memorize some of our Scout manual. We also spent a little time with George, who told us he had been in the US Navy and had many experiences on the navy ships at sea. He appeared to be a very nice man, and I believe most of the boys liked him from the beginning.

Later that evening, we attended the hamburger-chili party at the New Way Restaurant and had a great time. I am sure most of the boys drank too many coke and ate too much chili and too many hamburgers; but fortunately, the following day was Saturday, and we did not need to go to school.

The following month, the troop did go on a three-night camping trip at the LCSC grounds, with George McGee as our leader and thirty-two boys attending the campout. As there were only twenty-four bunks in the large Scout cabin, a problem developed: which boys would get to sleep in the cabin and who would have to pitch their pup tents and sleep outside in their sleeping bags? The weather was still quite warm, so there was no problem with some of the Scouts sleeping in their pup tents.

George took inventory and found that more boys wanted to sleep in the cabin than in their pup tents. Therefore, he said, "Boys, the only fair thing to do is to draw straws for the cabin bunks."

George volunteered to sleep outside, and then he prepared the straws—twenty-four short straws and eight long straws. As luck would have it, my friend Paul and I both drew long straws, so we had to pitch my pup tent and sleep outside, which was OK with us. George pitched his larger tent at the head of the column and told the eight of us to pitch four two-man pup tents across from each other. In other words, his tent would be at the head of the column, and there would be two tents on each side of the column. That way, he could look out of his tent and see the front flaps of our tents.

At this point, I will mention that Paul and I had been buddies for several years, and he was in my patrol. Most of the time, Paul lived across the street from my parents with his grandparents, whose last name was *Hooper*. Paul's mother and dad lived in Tucson, Arizona but for some reason, he only spent a month or two with his mother and dad each year. I do recall Paul saying that his dad was an engineer and that he and his mother frequently traveled to South America.

George appointed two of the older Scouts as cabin captains to control activities in the cabin. Then he told everyone to team up with another Scout, build their fires, and cook their suppers. As this was the first camping trip for a few of the new Scouts, the older boys assisted them in getting their fires started and cooking their food. It all worked out quite well, and after everyone had finished, George gave the order to police up the camping area before dark and put out all fires except one, as after dark, we would have a campfire storytelling.

Later that evening, we all gathered around the campfire. And several of the older Scouts told stories. I recall one of the Scouts told a story about his family camping in the mountains in Colorado and his little brother getting lost, but fortunately, he was found after several hours. Another boy told a story about his family camping in Canada, and one night a large bear came into their camp and destroyed several tents looking for food. Then George told several stories about the experiences he had when he was in the navy and was on the pistol and rifle teams and had won several awards for his marksmanship.

Eventually, George told us it was time to turn in and get some sleep, as tomorrow would be a busy day with the counselors joining the group and doing some testing for merit badges. All Scouts had been issued whistles to carry on their uniforms to use in case of an emergency or to use if they got lost in the woods. George said, "OK boys lights-out in fifteen minutes." And then he jokingly added, "Don't forget to keep your whistles handy in case the bears arrive." That made us all feel good.

Around three or four in the morning, when everyone in camp was sound asleep, one of the boys, whose tent was next to mine, started blowing his whistle. All the boys sleeping in tents were up and out, shouting, "Where is the bear?"

George came running out of his tent shouting at the Scout blowing his whistle, "Stop blowing that thing! What is the problem?"

Bill said, "My tent buddy, Kenneth, is gone. He walks in his sleep, and he must have walked off into the woods."

George gave the order: "All Scouts get dressed, get your flashlights, and be at my tent in five minutes."

We reported to George's tent by patrol, and he gave instructions. "Scouts, these woods are still very dark, and I don't want any more men getting lost, so keep in touch with each man in your patrol, blow your whistles, and call out Kenneth's name. Check your watches, and if you do not find Kenneth, all Scouts report back here at camp in one hour. Bob, I am leaving John, one of your patrol members, here at camp. John, in forty-five minutes, you start blowing your whistle in one-minute intervals in order to guide us back to camp and build another fire. That should help. I will go with the Eagle Patrol, as you are one man short, and we will head due south. The Panthers will head west, the Tigers east, and Wolves north. Be sure all of you have your compass handy so you will know your directions. Remember, this is teamwork. Be careful. Do not fall off any rocky ledges. If you find Kenneth and you need help, blow your whistles in long, straight blows."

An hour later, all patrols reported back to camp. No Kenneth, and no injuries among the search teams.

George said, "Scouts, go back to bed, except the Eagle Patrol. We are going to keep a large fire going so if Kenneth sees it, he will know his way back to camp. We will call all of you at daylight. We will have coffee, drinks, fried eggs, and bacon ready for a quick breakfast. Then we will all head out in the same directions as last night, and we should be able to find Kenneth. He is probably just lost and doesn't know his way back to camp."

My patrol was sitting around the fire talking, some of the boys were dozing when George said, "Boys, it will be daylight before long. Let's get breakfast ready for everyone. A couple of you boys, come with me to my tent to help carry some items I brought along with me."

Paul and I jumped up and went with George to his tent, where he had several boxes of food items, which included a box with twelve dozen eggs, a side of sliced bacon, a half dozen loaves of bread, and several cans of coffee, in addition to two or three large skillets and a couple of coffeemakers.

I said, "George, where did you get all of this food? We brought our own."

He replied, "Well, you are a bunch of good boys, and I wanted to do my part." Then he added, "Bob, don't bother with that large brown case. There is no food in it."

I looked at the large brown case, which looked like a very large tennis racket bag I had seen in the sporting goods shop, but I thought to myself, *why would George be carrying a tennis racket on a camping trip?* I did not say any more. We all left the tent and started preparing breakfast. I remember how good the bacon and eggs smelled frying over the open fire, but I kept thinking about Kenneth out there in the woods somewhere, probably not able to find his way back to camp. At the same time, I realized why George called off the search until daylight, as there was a danger of some of the other boys being lost or hurt in the search for Kenneth.

George blew his whistle, and it did not take the boys long to get dressed and eat the breakfast that had been prepared. It was now daylight, so we could continue the search for Kenneth.

George said, "Boys, we will do the same search this morning that we did last night, but I want two boys to stay and watch our camp while we are gone. John, you and your buddy Bill, stay and guard the camp, as we may be gone several hours. If the two counselors arrive, ask them to just stay here until we return or send word. Boys, don't stay out more than three hours. Take water with you, and if we don't find Kenneth within this time limit, we will then notify the sheriff's office and get their help."

We all started out in the same direction we had taken earlier that morning, spreading out more than we had previously. We had traveled a good half mile through the woods, and one of my patrol members called out that he had found something. Several of us, including George, rushed over and we saw a pool of blood. We could see drippings of blood on down through the woods. We were sure Kenneth was lying hurt or dead in the dark woods. Suddenly, after following the blood trail for about fifty feet, we saw the remains of a large jackrabbit that had been killed by some larger animal.

We continued on and had traveled at least a mile from camp and we had been out over an hour. There was still no sign of Kenneth, and then suddenly, George, who was a short distance ahead of us, raised his hand high over his head.

As we slowly moved forward, George said, "Boys, there is something on the ground backed up against that tree over there to the right."

Sure enough, we could now see this brown object, partly on the ground resting against the tree. We all rushed over, and there was Kenneth, in his brown Scout uniform, barefoot, sleeping against the tree. We gently woke him, and as he opened his eyes and looked up at us, he said, "Gee, guys, it sure took you a long time to get here."

We looked him over and his uniform was torn, his hands and face were scratched, he did not have any shoes on, and his feet were bleeding.

George said, "OK, Bob, you are good at first aid—let's patch him up a little and get him back to camp. If our doctor friend arrives this morning as scheduled, he can do the rest."

George and I cleaned Kenneth up a little, using our water bottles and first-aid kit, and gave him some crackers and water; and soon he was feeling better.

Now the question was how to get Kenneth back to camp, which was over a mile away, with his cut feet. It was decided that we would all take turns and carry him on our backs. George sent one boy ahead, blowing his whistle, to let the others know that Kenneth had been found. As I recall, it took us quite some time getting back to camp, as it was tough going through the woods with Kenneth on our backs.

When we reached camp, we found the counselors had arrived, including our doctor friend. Kenneth was not seriously injured, just cuts and a few bruises. His wounds were treated, but he did not do too much walking during the remainder of this camping trip. Kenneth explained that in his sleep, he had gotten out of his sleeping bag, dressed himself, and without shoes or socks, walked off through the woods. When he woke, he knew what he had done, as he had previously walked in his sleep at home. He knew he was lost, so he just sat down against the tree and went to sleep.

I asked him if he was afraid of the snakes in the woods, and his reply was, "I sure was, but if I was asleep, I wouldn't be thinking about snakes."

After that incident, George got a ten-foot piece of rope; and anytime Kenneth was on a camping trip, we always made sure one end of the rope was tied securely to his leg and the other end to his sleeping buddy.

Shortly after Ed Baker became Scoutmaster of our troop, one Friday evening, just before closing, he announced that he would like to see eight boys after the meeting, and he called off their names. My name was included in the group. We looked at each other and asked ourselves, *what have we done now?*

After the other Scouts had departed, Ed Baker, George McGee, and our three counselors sat down at the leaders' table, and Ed said, "Boys, pull your chairs up close to the table."

Once again, we looked at each other, and I thought, *what is this, a court-martial?* I had read about such things, but at that age, I really did not know what to expect.

Ed explained that he had been contacted by some other Scout leaders concerning a new initiation program they wanted us to consider developing. Our troop would be traveling within the city, or to other cities within the state, to conduct this initiation program, which would involve a serious, inspirational candle-lighting service for Scouts moving up through the ranks. The other boys and I had been selected because of our stature, dress, conduct, and devotion to Scouting. Ed closed by asking if we were interested in becoming a member of the initiating team.

As I recall, we were all proud to be selected and accepted the assignment, and in my opinion, we developed a most interesting and impressive devotional initiating ceremony. For the next year or so, we traveled quite frequently with Ed Baker and George McGee, usually on Saturdays or Sundays, to various cities in eastern Kansas conducting this ceremony. As the program developed, other troops were so impressed with the program that they adopted it for use in their troops.

One Friday evening, possibly a month or so after George McGee became our Assistant Scoutmaster, George suggested that our Scout troop, dressed in full Scout uniform, attend the 11:00 a.m. church services together on the first Sunday of each month. Our Scoutmaster endorsed this suggestion, so most of our Scout members attended as suggested; and this practice continued for quite some time. My sister Hazel sang in the church choir for many years and said she remembered so well sitting in the church choir loft and looking down at the Scouts in full uniform with Assistant Scoutmaster George McGee.

When Ed Baker became our Scoutmaster, he stated that one of his requirements was that all Scouts be in full uniform for all Scout meetings and functions unless otherwise excused. These were the days of the Great Depression, and many families did not have the extra money to purchase Scout uniforms. I was fortunate as I had a paper route and worked some evenings and weekends at a neighborhood drugstore, which gave me some earnings. Therefore, I was usually able to purchase the necessary Scout clothing or equipment that was needed. I do not recall seeing Ed or George give money to any of the boys, but I do remember seeing them ask certain boys what size they wore, and the next meeting, a pair of pants or a shirt would be handed to them. George always had a number of extra Scout scarves, belts, and hats in a box, which he gave to boys who needed them.

Approximately a month had passed since our last camping trip when Kenneth got lost while sleepwalking. Our Scoutmaster announced we would be going on another two-night camping trip the next Friday and Saturday night if the boys were interested. Sufficient interest was expressed, and we planned to meet at the church at four o'clock on Friday afternoon. Cars would take us to a large farm west of town, where no one had lived for a number of years. Ed mentioned that he would be there Friday evening and night, but would have to return to town early Saturday morning due to a business meeting.

He said, "George will be with you all the time, so you will have a good leader and be in good hands. As there is no cabin or shelter house at this location, you will all need your pup tents and sleeping bags."

The following Friday, thirty members of our troop were waiting at the church with our tents, sleeping bags, and food when our transportation arrived. We loaded our gear into the six vehicles, and Ed and George rode in the first vehicle, leading the way for the others.

It took us about an hour to arrive at our camping ground—quite a large open space that may have been a field at one time. The old house, which had been vacant for many years, looked haunted, and was about a city block from our camping area. We unloaded our gear, and George marked off how we should set up our tents. As usual, it was in a U shape, with George's larger wall tent at the top of the U facing our pup tents that were on both sides of the U facing each other. That way, George could again see the front of all pup tents from the front of his tent. Many times, we would see George sitting in his tent with the flaps back, watching our main street and keeping an eye on the Scouts. The fathers had helped unload the gear and advised us they would all be back for sure early Sunday afternoon, and then they left for town.

George said, "Boys, we have a lot of work before it gets dark, so get your tents pitched, your fires built, and your suppers cooking. I want everything done before seven p.m., when we will have tonight's Scout meeting around the fire."

That Scout meeting was somewhat different from other meetings. Ed led the meeting, and we recited the Pledge of Allegiance, followed by a knot-tying contest that was a lot of fun. Then several boys were selected to read aloud passages from the Scout manual. Ed told us a story about when he was a youngster, George told a couple of stories about the US Navy, and a number of ghost stories were told. By 10:00 p.m., we put out all the fires and turned in for the night. George shared his larger tent with Ed, and we made sure Kenneth and his buddy had the rope tied to their legs so Kenneth would not walk off again in his sleep.

Saturday morning after breakfast, Ed left for his meetings in town, and afterward, we formed teams and the older boys helped the younger ones with a number of merit badges. Then we formed into two groups and had a tug-of-war, using a large rope George had brought in his car.

After lunch George said, "Boys, this afternoon we are going to do two things. First, we are going on about a five or six-mile hike. There is a large pond about a mile from here, so we will stop there on the way back and take a swim. Be sure to take your swimming shorts. Frank and John sprained their ankles playing football this week, so they are going to stay in camp, keep an eye on everything, and do some reading. If anyone else wants to stay and miss the fun, they are free to do so."

When we arrived back from our hike and swim that afternoon, all of us were tired, so George said, "Boys, you have one hour to take a little rest. Then we will have our supper and police up the camp. After supper tonight, I am going to show you something you may never have seen before. That is it for now. Let's get a little rest."

As Paul and I lay in our pup tent, he said, "Bob, what do you think George is going to show us tonight, some kind of a trick?"

I remember saying to Paul, "It sure beats me. Possibly he is going to show us something he did in the navy, or maybe he is a magician."

The boys were anxious to finish supper and police up the camp, as they had been thinking about what George had said about showing us something we had never seen before. Finally, supper was over, and George made a camp inspection. Everything was in good order, and George said, "Boys, you did a good job. Now I want all of you to go over there to that open area and sit down in a group. Bob, you and Paul go over to our trash can and find six cans and wait over there with the other boys until I return."

George walked to his tent and went inside, staying about ten minutes, and when he came out, he was strapping on two revolver holsters down to his thighs like a cowboy. No doubt, most of the boys had seen this in a movie, but I doubt if any of us had seen it in live action. George had his back to the boys sitting on the ground, and he said, "Bob and Paul, I want one of you on each side and a little behind me, and when I say go, throw those cans as fast as you can up into the field in front of me. All boys, stay where you are now sitting."

George said, "Go!" Immediately Paul and I each threw six cans forward as fast as we could. George dropped to a half squat, drew both revolvers at the same time, and started firing. As I recall, I do not think George missed a can. We thought he was the greatest!

We asked him how he learned to shoot like that, and all he said was, "In the navy." Then we asked him why he carried these two revolvers with him on Scout camping trips. His reply was, "Well, boys, not everyone is good, and it is for your protection if we should meet some of those individuals who are not so good. In addition, there have been several banks robbed in eastern Kansas in the last few months. So who knows, we might run into some of those guys." Then he laughed and said, "Who knows, we might even run into a bear."

I mentioned this incident to my dad, and I know several of the other Scouts told their fathers, but I do not recall that there was ever any issue made of the incident. I knew my dad had a permit to carry a weapon, and when he was traveling in the country at night, he always had a revolver under the front seat of his car.

The next day was Sunday, and we were all up at sunrise, ready for the events of the day. George said, "Boys, we are going to have breakfast. Then we are going to have a little church service, as this is the first Sunday of the month. As you know, we should be in church this morning, but I am in hopes the good Lord will forgive us. I have just one Bible and one songbook in my car, which I will get before it is time for church. I have some extra eggs and bacon, so we have plenty to eat. Let's get started."

George was always most generous this way, bringing extra food on camping trips and purchasing uniforms and equipment for the Scouts who needed some assistance.

After breakfast, we cleaned up the campsite, and then it was time for our church service. We all sat in a group on the ground, and George led us in several songs, which we knew quite well. He then told us a story about when he was a little boy and his mother would always read a

Bible story to him before he went to sleep at night. He then read several passages from the Bible, and the service was concluded with another church song. I think we all felt better knowing we had attended our own church service out in the open woods.

After church, George said, "Boys, let's break camp and get our gear together so it will be ready to load when our transportation arrives this afternoon. However, be sure to leave sufficient food out for our lunch, as we do not want to go hungry. I would appreciate it if a couple of boys will help me carry my gear and load it into my car."

As Paul and I had our gear in good shape, we headed for George's tent carrying his gear to his car. Paul reached in the back seat of the car and started to rearrange some of the items so there would be more space for the camping gear. There was the large brown tennis racket bag we had previously seen in George's tent. Paul reached out to move it just as George arrived with a load of gear.

He shouted, "Paul, what are you doing?"

Paul said, "George, I am just moving that brown tennis racket bag and some of the other stuff so we can get more gear into the back seat."

George said, "That is a very expensive tennis racket. Now keep your hands off it."

We had never seen George so upset or talk like that, so we just walked back to our campsite and let George load his own car. A short time later, George came over to Paul and me and said, "Boys, I am sorry I spoke to you like that, but I didn't sleep very well last night, and I am a little edgy this morning."

Paul said, "That is OK, George. Hereafter, we will not touch that old tennis racket bag if it means that much to you."

We then continued helping George carry his gear to the car, but we let George load everything into his car. By then, the boys had collected their camping gear in a central location, ready to be loaded when transportation arrived.

Suddenly, we heard a car coming up the road. As the farm was located at the end of the road, we had not seen a car in the two days we had been camping, and we knew it was too early for our transportation to be arriving.

We saw George look at his watch, and then he started running toward his car. When he arrived at the car, he jerked the back door open and just stood there waiting for the car to come within view. When the visitor's car pulled to a stop, George closed the back door of his car and waited until the visitor got out and walked toward him.

The two men shook hands, talked for a short time, and then started walking toward our group who were now sitting on the ground near our piled-up gear. As they came near, George said, "Boys, I would like for you to meet my brother, Walter McGee. He is a salesman for a large manufacturing company, and he stopped by to ask for my advice on a big deal he is working on."

We all shook hands with his brother, and as I recall, he asked if we were enjoying our camping trip, and we all said we were having a great time. Then Walter said, "Which one of you is Kenneth? I have heard a lot about you."

Kenneth jumped up and said, "I am Kenneth who walks in his sleep," and we all laughed.

The two men turned and walked toward Walter's car, where they stood and talked for about thirty minutes. It could be easily seen by their gestures that they were disagreeing on some subject.

When they finished their talk, Walter jumped into his car, turned around and peeled out of the farmyard with his rear wheels spinning and the dust flying in all directions. We knew there was a problem. One of the older Scouts said, "Boys, don't say a word to George when he gets here. You can tell he is in a bad mood."

When George joined us, he said, "Sorry, boys, for the interruption, but my brother wanted me to buy some stock in his company, and I am not interested. Let's have some lunch before our transportation arrives."

That was the end of that conversation, and everything returned to normal. We never did know why, or figure out why, George ran to his car and opened the back door when he heard a car approaching the farm.

Shortly after lunch, which consisted mostly of sandwiches, apples, and cold drinks, some of the fathers arrived with their cars for our transportation back to town. We all loaded our gear, and our drivers headed for our church, which was the pickup and drop-off point. Upon arriving safely at the church, we thanked George for the great camping trip and the fathers for the transportation. Placing our gear on our backs, Paul and I started walking home together, where we knew a good shower would be waiting for us. I had no idea that would be the last camping trip Paul and I would share.

In November 1932, I had an experience related to scouting that I will never forget. Our troop had been invited to usher at the Thanksgiving football game at University of Kansas (KU), in Lawrence, Kansas, which was the big event of the year for the Jay Hawkers.

I knew it would be very cold ushering in the large open stadium at that time of the year; no doubt the temperature would be below freezing, and I did not have a matching tan heavy jacket to go with my Scout uniform. If it was not too cold, I would frequently wear one or two sweaters under my Scout shirt to keep warm, but I knew it would be too cold in the stadium for just sweaters.

Therefore, my problem was what to do for a warm jacket. It looked as though I was going to have to cancel going to the game, as I did not have ten or fifteen dollars in my savings to purchase the necessary warm clothing. This was a special event that did not come often, and I really wanted to go with the group. Neither of my parents had extra cash as the Great Depression was still on, and it was most difficult to make ends meet; I had been buying my own clothing since I was twelve. I didn't have anything to sell, and I certainly was not going to sell my bicycle. *What should I do?*

I was not going to ask George for assistance, even though he always seemed to have plenty of cash. I was depressed. *What should I do?*

It was Saturday morning, just two more weeks before Thanksgiving. I had to tell my Scoutmaster within a few days if I could go with the group to the KU game.

My mother said, "Bob, are you going to town this morning? If so, I have a package for you to mail at the post office."

I said, "No, Mom, no plans to go, but I will be glad to mail it for you."

She gave me the package with the change for postage, and I hopped on my bicycle and headed for town. For some reason, I decided to go a different route past a small park. As I pedaled along, I noticed a small brown bag lying in the street. That seemed a little unusual, so I wheeled my bike around and picked up the bag. I could see no one around who might have dropped it. I opened the bag and could not believe my eyes. There was a new pair of expensive ladies' brown leather gloves, with no sales slip. But there was something else in the bottom of the bag. I reached deeper inside and pulled out a twenty-dollar bill. I looked around again, but there was no one near who might have dropped the bag.

I went on to the post office, mailed my mother's package, and headed home to show my mother what I had found. She said, "Bob, watch the newspapers for the next three or four days under the Lost and Found ads. If there is no ad regarding these items, I see no reason why you can't consider them yours."

I eagerly checked the Lost and Found ads for the next four days, but no ad appeared for the contents of the brown paper bag, so it seemed that the two items were now mine!

The following day, I went to the department store and purchased a heavy, warm tan jacket that matched my Scout uniform for fifteen dollars; and that evening, I called my Scoutmaster and told him I would be joining our group to usher at the Thanksgiving game at KU. My mother sewed new Scout emblems on my tan jacket, and I was ready to go.

I asked myself, *do I have a little angel that looks after me? If so, I bet she was sitting on my shoulder the day I found that brown paper bag.*

The beautiful brown leather gloves became a Christmas gift for my mother that year, as they were a perfect fit.

Spring of 1933 arrived, and we had not been on too many camping trips during the winter season. Most of the Scouts had been faithful about attending Scout meetings on Friday evenings and church on Sundays. During the winter months, I had studied hard and gained the necessary merit badges and requirements and had been promoted to a Star Scout. I was feeling quite proud of myself. Possibly one of these days, I would become an Eagle, which was my Scouting objective. Then came some very sad news.

During the Christmas vacation, Paul had gone back to Arizona to spend some time with his parents. In early January, I received a letter from him saying it had been decided for him to stay in Arizona until summer. He would then return to live with his grandparents and start school.

Sometime later on, while I was in the yard working with my mother, Paul's grandmother, Mrs. Hooper, came out of her house crying. My mother said, Mrs. Hooper, "What in the world is wrong?"

She said, "I just received a call from my son in Arizona, and little Paul, my only grandson, has died. He was bitten by a black widow spider and the hospital did not have an antidote."

That was tragic news for me, as Paul had been my buddy on most of our camping trips, and it was most difficult for me to pass this message on to our Scoutmaster and others the following Friday at Scout meeting.

The following month, tragedy struck our Scout troop again. Our Scoutmaster announced at a Friday evening Scout meeting that a special member, Kenneth, had suddenly died the previous day due to a ruptured appendix. As I recall, in those days, this was not unusual as sulfa drugs, penicillin, and other antibiotics to combat various infections were still unknown to the medical profession.

Due to Kenneth's love for the Scouts, his parents had requested our Scoutmaster to have a Scout funeral and to have eight Scouts as pallbearers. When Kenneth had moved from a Tenderfoot Scout to Second Class a year or so previously, he had been initiated through our Candle Lighting Service and his parents were most impressed by this ceremony. Therefore, our Scoutmaster decided that our eight Candle Lighting Members, which included me, would be the pallbearers and would participate in the funeral service. It was suggested that all other Scouts in our troop attend, and transportation would be provided. Kenneth was laid in a walnut coffin, dressed in his Scout uniform with his merit badge sash and his hat laid on his stomach. It was a very moving ceremony. There was also a graveside service at the cemetery; and at the end of the service, when a senior Scout bugler sounded taps, there were tears in the eyes of every troop member. Kenneth was always remembered as the *Scout who walked* in his sleep.

Bob in Boy Scout uniform - 1932

CHAPTER 3

Disillusioned

It was late May 1944, spring was ending and summer was just starting. I had been attending Scout meetings every Friday evening, but for the last couple of weeks, George had not been present. Many of us wondered about George, but we did not ask too many questions as Ed was conducting the meetings and everything was going along smoothly.

On Sunday, May 29, I was returning home from my early morning paper route. It was about six thirty, and my dad was sitting on the front porch reading the morning paper, waiting for my mother to call him to breakfast.

As I walked up, he said, "Bob, have you seen the morning paper?"

Joking, I replied, "I sure have—about 150, which I just delivered."

He laughed and then said, "Seriously, have you read the first page of the paper? It has the names of some people I think you know."

As I still had a couple copies of the paper, I sat down on the porch and started to read. I could not believe what I was reading! Here was the picture and Wanted notice for five men, including Walter and George McGee. The police, sheriff, US marshal, and the FBI wanted them.

I thought, *there must be some mistake. This cannot be true!* I read on, with my eyes glued to the morning paper. Law enforcement was looking for Walter McGee and George McGee, plus others concerning the kidnapping of Ms. Mary McElroy, daughter of the city manager, Henry F. McElroy of Kansas City, Missouri. The story developed with Ms. McElroy being taken from her home and held in a kidnapping scheme until a ransom of thirty thousand dollars was paid. It was learned that those participating in the kidnapping were Walter McGee, George McGee (our Assistant Scoutmaster), and three other men. It was reported that Ms. McElroy was not physically harmed during the time she was held.

Walter McGee, George McGee, and two others were eventually arrested, tried, and convicted of the kidnapping. Walter and George were both given life sentences and, to my understanding, died in prison. The fifth man was never found.

This incident affected me and no doubt a number of members of our Scout troop. We had trusted George McGee as our leader and friend, and now George had seriously broken the trust of us boys, and, I am sure, of our Scoutmaster, Ed Baker, who brought George into our troop.

I continued attending Scout meetings and participating in Scout activities, but the spark of scouting had been somewhat extinguished for me. Possibly I was to blame for this, and I should not have let this happen, but other interests developed, and I slowly dropped out of the troop.

Looking back I thought to myself, *how did George obtain the extra money he used to purchase food and supplies for camping trips, and uniforms for the Scouts who were short on funds? Did it come from his day job or from a robbery he may have committed?*

After George's arrest, a picture was shown of his firearms loot found in Lynchburg, Virginia. There appeared to be a brown tennis bag with a Thompson machine gun barrel protruding from the opening. I thought to myself, *was this the same large tennis bag that George carried on Scouting camping trips? Was this why he was upset with Paul during the loading of camping equipment into his vehicle?* On the camping trip where George's brother came to talk to him, *I asked myself, why did George run to his car and open the door while waiting for the other vehicle to come down the road? Was he afraid this could be law enforcement officers or someone else looking for him, and he wanted to be ready to use the object in the tennis bag?*

These questions will never be answered. No doubt other Scouts in our troop may have asked themselves the same questions over the years. Disillusioned, I knew I was not going to achieve my objective of becoming an Eagle Scout. My scouting career was ending, and it was time for me to turn the page and start a new chapter in my life. However, I have never forgotten my wonderful experiences during my scouting activities, and I would certainly encourage all boys who are interested in joining a Scout troop to take advantage of this wonderful opportunity.

No doubt, the actions of the McGee brothers in the kidnapping of Ms. McElroy led to disappointment for the leaders and members of our Scout troop. Near the end of this story, there were other tragedies. At that time, the parole commission decided to hear a final plea by George McGee seeking to be paroled. The hearing officer informed George that due to the number of hearings he had already had, there would be no more. Ms. McElroy and her father died while Walter and George were in prison.

CHAPTER 4

Middle Teenage Years

One very cold snowy night in January 1932, when I was in the seventh grade, the Leavenworth Senior High School caught fire around midnight. The school was only six city blocks from our house, so we were awakened by the sound of the fire trucks, but the fire hydrants and fire hoses were frozen and the school was destroyed.

My mother, dad, three sisters, and I gathered in one of the upstairs bedrooms to watch the great flames that stretched far into the sky that night. To my knowledge, the cause of the fire was never determined, but I do remember for a long time they considered it to be arson.

This fire created a real problem for the education directors and many others, including teachers and students; but in my opinion, the educational directors did a superb job of reaching a decision and resolving the immediate problem within a week. After several meetings, it was determined that the junior high school building would become the school for both junior and senior high school students. I would estimate the student enrollment of each school was 600–700 students, so all junior high students would attend class from 7:00 a.m. to 12:30 p.m., and all senior high students would attend class from 1:00 p.m. to 6:30 p.m.

As I was in junior high, I went to school in the mornings, and my sister Bessie attended senior high in the afternoon. My other sister Hazel had graduated in May 1931, which was the last class to graduate from the old senior high school. There were a limited number of lockers, which meant that all students were required to share lockers with other students. As I recall, this policy was followed for three years until a new high school could be completed at the same location as the old building.

In May 1934, school had been dismissed for the summer, and I was fifteen and unemployed except for my *Kansas City Journal-Post* paper route. It was a good feeling not to have any special responsibilities during the day, but I knew this freedom would not last long. I would be starting my ninth grade, and would need money for new clothes, and other items when school started in early September (I had been buying my clothes since I was twelve years old). The Great Depression still wreaked its havoc on the American people, and the economy had been extremely difficult for many families in our town for the last four years.

On a Saturday morning in early June, I was in my dad's home shop working on my bicycle. My mother called out to me, telling me I had a phone call from one of my buddies, Kenneth Hardman. In talking with Kenneth, he mentioned that there was an advertisement in the morning paper for a soda fountain boy at the Al Christ Drug Store, which was considered a top-of-the-line drugstore located in the downtown area. I asked him if he was interested in the job, and he replied he had a summer job delivering groceries for a large store, otherwise he would check it out. After we ended our call, I checked the morning paper and found the advertisement.

I changed my clothes and hopped on my bicycle to head for Al Christ Drug Store. Upon arrival, I asked for Mr. Christ and said that I wished to apply for the soda fountain job that was advertised in the morning paper. Mr. Christ came out from the prescription room. I was surprised when I met him, as he had attended Al Derzinski's funeral just a few weeks previous. He recognized me immediately and mentioned that he had heard good reports concerning my work at Al Derzinski's drug store. He asked me a number of questions concerning my previous soda fountain and drugstore experience, about my school subjects, and a little about my family.

After a short time, he said, "Bob, as mentioned, this will be a part-time job—a lot of evening and night work and some weekends. The salary is twenty-five cents an hour plus tips. How does that sound?"

I accepted and worked part-time for Al Christ for approximately two years. The first year, I rode my bicycle on most deliveries, but after that, I had gained Al's confidence and drove his automobile for deliveries.

Al was Catholic. I respected his religion, and he respected my Protestant faith. I recall that frequently, priests or nuns would come into the store for purchases. He would sit and talk with them over sodas or milkshakes, which I had prepared and served to them. Many times, when they had finished their talks and refreshments, he would call me over and ask me to drive Father Smith or Father Jones or the nuns back to the church or their residence.

At times, Al would say, "Bob, this a beautiful spring day, and you are not too busy, so just take our friends for a short drive in the country. I am sure they don't get out too often." I followed Al's instructions and took them for a drive, enjoying some of the stories and conversations we had during these trips.

The City Hall building was just across the street from the Al Christ Drug Store, so many of the city officials, including the mayor, chief of police, judges, attorneys, and others frequently visited the drugstore. Al was on a first-name basis with most of them. Quite often, many of them would stop at the soda fountain and order a soft drink or a milkshake. I recall that one prominent attorney would come in at least once a week and order a double chocolate milkshake with two raw eggs. He claimed those were the best milkshakes he had ever had, and he would always leave a twenty-five-cent tip, which was most welcome.

I have many fond memories working for Al during that two-year period. At nights, when business was slow, I was permitted to do my homework at a small table behind the soda fountain. Some nights, Al or Spencer, the assistant pharmacist, would ask me to come back to the prescription room and assist them with various projects. Spencer was a diabetic and had to have his insulin shot every night at about ten. He did not like to give the shot to himself, so he taught me how to give him the injection in his shoulder. I recall one night he told me he wanted me to work every night that he was on duty as I gave the best shots he had ever received. This made me think that I should consider becoming a nurse or a physician.

In mid-June 1934, I was working quite a number of evening hours at Al Christ Drug Store, in addition to my paper route. I heard that there were some local business firms looking for someone to deliver handbills to the residences in the city.

Handbills, compared to newspaper advertising, were a very convenient method for advertising, as they could consist of two to eight pages and provide a complete description of the items for sale. I contacted one of the business firms and worked out a favorable agreement to deliver approximately ten thousand handbills to residences and stores within the city. With the assistance of one of my buddies, Stanley Wade, it took us approximately a week to properly distribute the handbills and complete the contract.

The following week, I was contacted by two other business firms wanting handbills delivered, so I lined up a contract with them. Stanley and I delivered two handbills to each residence or business at the same time. This way, we distributed well over 20,000 handbills at the same time we delivered only one set, and thus doubled our income. I recall I was fortunate to arrange a number of handbill contracts, and we walked the entire city that summer at least six or seven times delivering 120,000 to 140,000 handbills, making a nice little nest egg for ourselves.

An amusing incident occurred during the course of our handbill deliveries. Stan and I were making our deliveries in a very affluent neighborhood, and I was about a half a block ahead of Stan. I stopped to rest for a couple of minutes, and an automobile drove up near where I was standing. A well-dressed man got out holding a large camera, and greeted me, saying his name was Jim. I introduced myself, then I asked Jim what he was going to do with the camera. He replied that he was with the local newspaper and usually covered action news or accidents, but this week, he had been assigned to the society page. Therefore, he had been assigned to take a special lady's picture who would be getting married in the near future, and she lived in a nearby house. Jim mentioned that he was a little early for the appointment and asked me if I had time to chat for a few minutes.

Just then, there was a large bang from the front of a house down the street and a tall, good-looking man came running out the front door, across the porch, and up the street toward us. All he had on was his underwear and socks. He was carrying his shoes in one hand, and his pants and coat were over his other arm. Suddenly, a second well-dressed man carrying a baseball bat came running out of the house after the first man.

I looked at Jim, and he was pushing the ON button on his camera. He shouted to me, "Bob, stand aside, I have got to get a picture of this action."

The last I saw of Jim, he was running behind the two men, still taking pictures. By then, the two men were only about ten or fifteen feet apart, and the ball bat was raised, ready to strike.

The next day, Jim's pictures appeared on the front page of the local paper. According to the article, one of the men, who had been out of town on business, came home unexpectedly and found a visitor in his bedroom. I do not recall if the article mentioned the ball bat being used. Both men were prominent businessmen in the city. I am confident that this was most embarrassing to both families involved. I later said to Stan, "It sure looks like Jim got his action shots."

September 1934 arrived, and I was back in school for my ninth-grade year. Our classroom hours were still 7:00 a.m. until 12:30 p.m. due to the previously mentioned fire that had destroyed the senior high school building. We had to get up early and be at school on time, but it did give us some extra time in the afternoons to complete our homework, of which there was plenty, due to our shorter school hours.

This would be my last year at junior high school. Even though I was not an outstanding scholar, I enjoyed school in many respects, as the subjects I was taking included mechanical drawing, government, science, math, and history, which were most interesting and a challenge. Athletics were not my greatest talent, as I was not heavy enough to play football, but I played some basketball, was on the track team, and ran the 100-yard dash and the mile relay. During my eighth and ninth grades, I earned a number of blue and red ribbons. I continued working three or four nights a week and some weekends at Al Christ Drug Store and still had my paper route. These activities kept me very busy, but it gave me the opportunity to earn a little money and kept me out of trouble.

I remember one basketball game we were playing against, as I recall, the Atchison team, from a town just north of Leavenworth. I had been asked to play on the first team for this game as several members of our first team had been injured in a previous game.

It was a very tight score in the 70s or 80s, and both teams were very tired. I had been in and out of the game as our coach rotated the team members; I usually jumped center as I was taller than most of the boys. We had only one or two minutes to play, and the Atchison team was one point ahead. I thought, *here we go. We are going to lose this final game of the season.*

One of the Atchison team members had the ball, and he came toward me, dribbling it very fast. Suddenly, the ball slipped, and he lost control. The ball came bouncing in my direction, and I grabbed it, knowing there were only a few seconds left in the game. I was near the center of the court and was aware that I did not have the power to do a two-handed shot. Instead, I did a one-handed shot with all my strength, and lo and behold, the ball hit the basket rim, bounced high in the air, then dropped to the other side of the basket rim, then bounced again into the air. There was a loud gasp by many of the players as well as the spectators. Then the ball slowly dropped through the hoop to the floor. At that moment, the whistle blew, and the game was over. Leavenworth had won the final game of the season over Atchison. The crowd cheered, and I was the star of the evening. This was my one day of fame!

There was another event near the end of the school year. In order to earn a passing grade in physical education, we were required to do a five-minute boxing round with one of our classmates. If a student refused the instructor's orders to go into the boxing ring, he was subject to a non-passing grade. I did not want to be given a failing grade for the course and was not really interested in trying to give one of my classmates a black eye or a bloody nose. However, I decided to accept this requirement and do my best.

The day arrived when I was scheduled for my five minutes in the ring and was to learn who had been assigned as my opponent by our instructor. I do believe our instructor was quite fair in his assignments, as he would try to assign two boys of about equal weight and height. I was assigned a boy by the name of Bill Johnson, who was about my height but probably outweighed me by possibly 10 pounds.

At this point, I will mention that any students who had a study hall class at the time of these boxing matches were permitted to sit in the gym bleachers to observe the boxing. It so happened that Bill's girlfriend, who I will call Nancy, decided she would attend some of the boxing events and was present during our scheduled match. Bill and I lived in the same general neighborhood, but we were not close buddies, so I decided if I had to give Bill a few extra punches or a black eye in order to win the match, I was ready.

Our physical education instructor assisted us in putting on our boxing gloves and tied the laces very tight so the gloves would not slip off. We began sparring, and I landed a few solid blows, and Bill gave me several good punches. We continued this action back and forth for possibly two or three minutes; then suddenly, Bill gave me a one-two up to the side of the head, and I went down. I lay there on the floor to the count of five or so; and when I got up, I saw Nancy jumping up and down cheering Bill, and he had turned around and was bowing to her. I walked over and gently tapped him on the shoulder. He may have thought it was the instructor, but he slowly turned around, still eyeing Nancy in the bleachers. I wound up with a haymaker and caught him in the chin, and he went down, flat on the floor.

Our instructor rushed over and started counting. Nancy was calling out, "Get up, Bill. Get up!" And Bill was trying to sit up but was having difficulty.

Our instructor was still counting, and suddenly he shouted, "Ten, and, Bill, you are out." He reached over and grabbed my hand and held it high in the air. "Bob, you are the winner of this match."

I went over and helped Bill back on his feet, and all he could say was, "What in the hell happened?"

When I received my grade card for the semester, it reported, *Physical Education – A*. After that, Bill and I became fairly good friends and graduated from high school in the same class. Bill joined the US Marines shortly after graduation. After WWII, we met again and had an evening of celebration together with friends, then went our own way. To my understanding, after a distinguished and heroic career in the Marines, Bill retired. We did not meet again until our fiftieth high school class reunion in June 1988. I realized we had all changed considerably, so I walked up to Bill and asked him if he remembered me. He said, "Sure, I do, Bob. You are the guy that knocked me down in gym and won our boxing match."

The months rolled by, and then it was May of 1935. I would soon be graduating from the ninth grade and moving on to Leavenworth Senior High School as a sophomore. The economy of the country was still depressed, and many individuals were unemployed; some working for very low wages. A number of my paper customers could no longer subscribe to the daily paper and had discontinued their subscriptions, and I decided it was time to give up my paper route, which I had worked on for nearly three years.

I had been offered two other summer jobs. My dad's electric and battery business had purchased equipment whereby he could manufacture new batteries in his own establishment. He asked me if I wanted to work for him most mornings during the summer manufacturing parts for the new batteries. Some of the manufacturing process consisted of making new lead grill plates. Most of the batteries he was making contained three cells, but some had six, and each cell had twelve grill lead plates, which he made. My dad would not let me work with the molten lead, as that was the dangerous part of the process; if the molten lead should spill, it was so hot that it would burn through the flesh to the bone. Therefore, my job started after the lead grill plates had cooled. This consisted of filling the lead grill with a special compound, similar to putty. The surface on both sides of the grill plate had to be very smooth. I worked out a system whereby I could fill twelve grill plates in one operation and place them in racks to dry. My pay was determined on a piece basis, and if I worked steadily, I could earn three or four dollars per morning.

My second job that summer consisted of delivering vanilla extracts. I answered an advertisement wanting a person to deliver a product. The extract firm would pay a set fee for the delivery of each pint-size bottle of vanilla extract. We were required to deliver at least one hundred bottles each afternoon. The extract firm had received all the orders, and the items were prepaid, so it was just a matter of making the proper delivery of the product. I recall that after a little negotiation, we agreed on a delivery price of twenty cents per bottle.

During the interview, I was informed that the person had to have an automobile, but I did not have one, and delivery was to start within three days. I called a friend, Joe Parker, who was a couple of years older than I was and owned a car and was in need of a summer job. Joe and I agreed that he would furnish the car and drive, and I would do the legwork of delivering the extracts to the purchaser. Joe and I agreed to split evenly the delivery fees. Some of the orders were for one bottle, but most were for three, six, or a case of twelve. At times, I wondered why anyone would want twelve bottles of vanilla extract; but before too long, the mystery was solved when I made a delivery of a case of vanilla extract to a residence in a very upscale residential district.

After ringing the doorbell, a very nice-looking lady came to the door very scantily dressed. She said, "Young man, I am so glad to see you. Several of us ladies are having a small party, and we are just ready to mix some drinks. Would you care to come and have a vanilla extract cocktail with us?"

I said, "Thank you. No, I have a driver waiting for me."

She replied, "That's great. Ask him to come in and join the party."

I asked her if she was drinking the vanilla extract, and her reply was, "Sure. It is 18 percent alcohol, and it makes great cocktails." Kansas was a dry state—no alcohol—and it was then I knew why this vanilla extract was in such great demand.

Joe and I worked most of the afternoons during that summer delivering vanilla extract and earned quite a nice sum. The following spring, I wrote to the extract company asking them if they needed any vanilla extracts delivered the following summer. A few weeks later, the letter was returned with a statement on the envelope, "No Longer in Business," so I considered Uncle Sam must have caught up with them and closed their doors. Some years later, I asked Joe if he remembered the summer we were unknowing bootleggers. He replied, "I sure do, Bob. We made quite a sum of money that summer."

As I was busy working, the summer passed very quickly. Before long, it was September 1935. I was back in school, now sixteen years of age, in the tenth grade. The school subjects had become more difficult. I was considered an average student. All boys were required to take the Reserve Officer Training Course (ROTC), and our instructors were assigned from the US Army Post at Fort Leavenworth and consisted of a major and a master sergeant. One or two days each week, we were required to wear our full military uniforms; and at least once a week, there would be inspection of uniforms and firearms. There were a number of student officers, mostly seniors. For a time, I enjoyed being on the rifle team, as we had the opportunity to travel to other ROTC schools for rifle competition. Many students did not like ROTC, but I considered it excellent training, and it gave me some advantage when I went into the military service during WWII.

I was still working at AL Christ Drug Store, usually on weekends and a few nights during the week. One evening, in early September, a man

walked up to the soda fountain and ordered a coke. As he stood there drinking it, he said, "I have been talking to your boss, Al, and he tells me your name is Bob Day, and that you work here just part-time."

I replied, "That's right. I have been working for Al for quite some time."

He then introduced himself as Ward Keeler, owner and editor of the *Chronicle* newspaper, and said he was looking for a young man to work part-time on his newspaper.

"Al mentioned that you are most trustworthy, and you just work here part-time. He also mentioned that you might have time to work for me in a part-time capacity."

I said, "Thank you Mr. Keeler, I attend senior high, but I do have some free time in the afternoons. As Al mentioned, I work here some evenings and weekends, but I would be interested in more part-time work if it does not interfere with my school activities."

He then handed me his card and asked me to come by his office the following afternoon to talk.

The following afternoon after school, I went to see Mr. Keeler to learn more about his part-time job. He was in his office when I arrived. He introduced me to his wife, who was their head bookkeeper, and to several others, then showed me around the office, including the operations of their printing presses. He offered me the job of working two afternoons and evenings each week, Wednesdays and Thursdays, from 4:00 p.m. until 10:00 p.m., and the salary would be forty cents per hour. He further mentioned that, at times, it might be necessary to work a little later in order to finish the work for the day. My job on Wednesday was to bring the mailing list up to date on the addressograph machine and on Thursday run the papers through the addressing and stamping machines for mailing. As I recall, they had a circulation of about ten thousand customers, and the papers had to be mailed early Friday morning.

I accepted the position, starting work that week, and worked at the *Chronicle* until May 1936, when I took a full-time position for the summer months. I learned a great deal about the newspaper business during this period, including setting up the printers and other equipment.

One day, a young girl my age came into the office and talked to Mr. and Mrs. Keeler for quite some time. Mr. Keeler then brought her back to where I was working and introduced her to me as his niece. She was a very attractive girl, with dark hair worn in a pageboy style, and her name was Marietta Walton. I thought she was the cat's meow!

Marietta lived in another city, so she would come into the office about once a month; but when she did come by, she would frequently come back and talk with me for a little while. After leaving the *Chronicle*, I did not see Marietta until after I graduated from high school. One evening, she called and said that she was in nurses' training at Cushing Memorial Hospital. I asked her out on a date, she accepted, and we dated off and on for about a year. Unfortunately, being in nurses' training, Marietta did not have a great deal of free time. Consequently, we were not able to see each other too frequently, possibly one or two evenings a week for only a couple of hours. I certainly enjoyed her company, but due to our limited time together, we slowly drifted apart.

I did not see Marietta again for seven or eight years until we met unexpectedly in Leavenworth. We were both very surprised, as we were both living in other cities. I invited her into a coffee shop for a snack, and we brought each other up to date on our activities. She was married and had become a very successful surgical nurse at a Kansas City hospital. I was also married and was working as Finance Director for the US Public Health Service in Baltimore. After our coffee and visit, we gave each other a hug, wishing the other the best, and then parted. That was the end of our relationship; we never met again.

One Thursday evening, I had been working later than usual. It was close to midnight when we finished addressing and stamping all the papers. We closed up the office to head for home. I started walking home, which was about a mile through a very prominent business district, then on into the residential area. I was walking quite fast, as I was anxious to get home and get some sleep, since I would be getting up early for school. There was little traffic on the street at that hour of the night.

I was probably about halfway home when I noticed a man walking possibly a hundred feet behind me. As I walked faster, he increased his pace as well. I crossed to the other side of the street, and he followed. Then I crossed back to the other side, and again he followed. I knew then that he was after me for some unknown reason. I did not have much money, but I wondered if he intended to try to rob me.

By then, I was within a city block of my home, so I started running; he did likewise. I ran down our street, through our side yard, toward the back porch of my house. I had a key to the back door, but my folks always left the door unlocked for me. By this time, the man was only about fifty feet or less behind me. I opened the screen door onto the back porch; and as I grabbed the kitchen doorknob, I discovered it was locked. *What do I do now?* The man was opening the screen door, and I heard him holler, "Boy, I have got you now!"

I looked around and saw my short-handled Boy Scout ax lying on the porch where I had left it the previous afternoon after cleaning and sharpening it. I grabbed the ax handle; and as the man made a grab for my throat, I swung the ax with all my strength and caught him in the side of the head, cutting one ear nearly off. He let out a scream and yelled, "You little bastard! I am going to kill you now!"

I drew my ax back one more time to strike him again, but before I could hit him, he turned, with blood running down his face and neck, his ear just hanging. He then placed his left hand against his head, as if trying to find his ear, and turned and ran out into the yard and down the street. I followed him with my ax raised for a short distance, then turned and headed for the back porch. I let myself in with my key, and, as everyone was asleep, I washed his blood off my hands and went to bed.

The next morning at breakfast, I told my dad what had happened, and he immediately got up from the breakfast table and went out and checked my ax. Upon returning, he said, "Bob, you should not have left your ax on the porch, but I am sure glad you did. You got your man!

There are several blood spots on the porch floor and a lot of blood on the ax blade."

My dad reported the incident to the police, and to my understanding, they conducted an investigation. As I recall, the police did not contact me again, and I did not hear anything further concerning the attempted assault. Apparently, the incident became a closed case.

Bob's home growing up in Leavenworth, Kansas

CHAPTER 5

Later Teenage Years

My first year at Leavenworth Senior High School as a sophomore seemed to be quite a normal year. Shortly after starting school, I had an accident on my bicycle, and sustained a couple of broken ribs and an injury to my chest. As a result, I had to give up ROTC and my sports activities, but I did attend many of the basketball and football games.

I was becoming interested to some extent in girls, but usually, a small mixed group of us would attend movies, dances, or other activities without being in a serious relationship with any one person. As mentioned earlier, I was still working part-time for the *Chronicle* newspaper and Al Christ Drug Store in addition, to working at times with my dad when he needed assistance.

My dad had acquired the dealership for the Delco-Light Plant and the Wind Charger Plant, which were electric generators that were frequently used on farms or ranches where the electric high line was not available. From the 1920s to the 1940s, these were two types of electric generators available in rural areas in the Midwest.

My dad had two small trucks with a Delco-Light Plant mounted on the bed of each truck. During the summer months, he would frequently receive calls from various country churches asking if he could bring one of his trucks out and light up their ice cream social or country picnic. He would usually agree and ask me if I wanted to go with him to assist in stringing up the electric lights. Many times, I would go, and we would arrive early, string up the lights in the trees, and set up his advertising signs, to let people know that the lighting was provided by Day's Electric Service. He would talk to the farmers about the power plants, and by the time the evening was over, we had consumed all the ice cream we could eat.

After each of these outings, my dad would always stay open late on Friday and Saturday nights, as frequently a number of farmers or ranchers would come in to look at the power plant. As I recall, the electric generators came in three sizes: the small one about two feet tall, the next one about three feet, and the largest four feet tall. Of course, the larger the plant, the more power it could generate.

Many times, the farmer would come in, sit down with my dad in his office, and go over his requirements to determine his estimated power needs. It would be necessary for my dad to visit the farm to know the exact electric demand, but he would give the prospective buyer a cost estimate and size of the power plant that was needed.

A number of times, I heard the customer say, "Mr. Day, it has been a good crop year, and I have the money, but I believe the power plant is too complicated for me to operate."

My dad would say, "Mr. Smith, do you consider you have as much knowledge and mechanical ability as a sixteen or seventeen-year-old boy?"

Mr. Smith would frequently say, "I sure do," or "You're damn right I do."

My dad would then say, "Mr. Smith, this is my son, Bob, and he will show you how to start and stop the generator."

I would then show Mr. Smith where the choke was and how to use it. Then I would throw the switch, and the engine would start immediately. Frequently, the prospective buyer would say, "Mr. Day, when can you come out to my farm and determine my exact requirements? And be sure and bring a contract."

When the prospective customer had left the store, my dad would say, "Bob, you just helped me make another sale."

Many times, my dad would receive calls from customers who had purchased Delco-Light Plants several years previous and indicated that it was time for a checkup on his generator or something needed an adjustment. My dad or his assistant usually made these service calls in the evening, and it was not unusual for my dad to ask me if I had time to go with him. When I rode with him, we would have some good talks, or he would tell me some of his many stories, as he was a great storyteller. Some nights, I might assist him with the problem, or just hold a light, or possibly sit in the car and do my homework by flashlight. I do not think we realized it then, but looking back, these were good father and son companionship evenings.

My dad was always out for a little fun, and sometimes it was rather risky. One night, we were out on one of the service calls about twenty miles from town on an isolated unpaved country road on our way home. We were probably traveling about thirty-five or forty miles per hour when a large black sedan came out from a side road in front of us, traveling very fast. The back seat and the trunk were loaded so heavily that the back of the sedan sagged.

My dad said, "Bob, there goes a bootlegger. Let's have some fun."

I am not sure why, but my dad was deputized and carried a sheriff's badge, and he always carried a .45-caliber revolver under the front seat of his car. He reached down, picked up the revolver, and checked to make sure it was fully loaded. After placing the gun between our seats where it would be handy if needed, he turned on his twin spotlights. Within seconds, the sedan must have been doing seventy miles an hour on those dirt country roads. No doubt, the driver of the vehicle thought the sheriff had him. We both got a big laugh as to how fast the sedan took off. I do not recall having asked my dad what he would have done if the fellows in the black sedan had shot at us. However, knowing my dad, without a question, he would have used his weapon and returned fire.

As I recall, in those days, a driver's learner's permit was not required or issued, so my dad had been teaching me how to drive on the country roads, and now this was my year. I had turned sixteen and was now eligible to apply for a driver's license and take the required driver's test, and I was anxious.

My birthday was on April 16, so the following day, I was at the Kansas State Driver's License Bureau to apply for a driver's license. I filled out the papers and paid my two dollars, and the desk clerk looked over the papers and told me the inspector was outside at my car waiting to administer the test. I had borrowed my dad's car that day, and the highway patrolman was standing next to the car. I got in the driver's seat, and he in the passenger seat. I was confident, but a little nervous sitting next to this husky man in uniform.

He said, "OK, young man, let's see what you can do. Drive out the highway about fifteen miles."

I drove very carefully, keeping my speed within the established speed limit. After reaching our 15-mile target, he instructed me to return to town and park on the main street, and I followed his instructions. He had me park several different times, asked me a number of questions concerning traffic regulations, then told me to drive back to the Driver's License Bureau. Up until then he had not corrected me or said anything about my driving, good or bad. I asked him how one becomes a Highway Patrolman and he explained the experience and age requirements.

When we arrived at the Driver's License Bureau, he said, "Kid, you did great. You passed. Come inside and pick up your new driver's license." Then he added, "Son, when you turn twenty-four and still want to be a patrolman, come see me."

I said, "Thank you, Officer. I will remember." When I walked out with a driver's license in my pocket, I was floating on air.

One afternoon, when I arrived home from school, my mother told me that Reverend John West, our Methodist minister, had called and wanted to talk with me and that I should call him. I wondered why he would want to talk with me, since I saw him nearly every Sunday at church and he had not mentioned anything special.

I called him, and he mentioned that he would like to see me sometime in the next few days, as he was considering a new church project and wanted to discuss it with me. We set up an appointment time to meet at his church office. When I arrived, three other boys my age were just entering his office. I asked my friends what was going on, but they had no idea.

Soon Reverend West arrived, greeted us, and advised us of his plan. He asked us if we would volunteer as altar boys to serve communion with him the first Sunday of each month. We all agreed, and he had used choir robes altered to fit each of us. He developed a procedure and a system, which we followed very closely in serving communion on the specified Sunday to the church members as they knelt at the altar. As a young boy, I felt rather special and very pleased to serve in this capacity as my sister Hazel sat in the front row of the choir loft. Our little group was present every designated Sunday to fulfill this commitment for approximately two years until Reverend West was transferred.

My sophomore year was ending, and I had just received my report card. Even though I had one C, I was pleased to see that I was still on the honor roll. A week or so prior to the end of school, I heard that Fleming Wilson Company, a wholesale food store, needed a person to work during the busy summer months. I applied for the job, and a couple days later, the manager called and asked me to come in to see him, if I was still interested.

I talked to Dave Jenkins, the manager, and was advised that the position was for a stockman, the office hours were from 7:00 a.m. to 6:00 p.m., and the salary was fifteen dollars a week. As jobs were few and far between, I accepted and worked the full three months until school started in early September. The work was difficult, as at times we would have to unload trucks that were carrying sacks of sugar or potatoes, each weighing a hundred pounds. During those years, I weighed only 150 pounds, but I did develop some new muscles. I do recall that at some point during the summer, my wages were increased to twenty dollars weekly, which at the time seemed like a substantial increase in pay.

Eventually, summer ended, and school began again. It was September 1937, and I was now a junior in high school. I had been offered a job with an investment firm as manager of a neighborhood apartment, a beautiful old mansion that had been restored and made into four large luxurious apartments. "Manager" was a glorified title, as I had no responsibility in the actual management of the apartments. However, it did give me the opportunity to earn sixty dollars a month to work one hour each morning at the apartments before school—cleaning the halls, porches, and walks, and removing the trash from each of the units. On Saturdays, I was required to clean one bachelor apartment, cut the grass, or keep the lawn neat and clean. The renters were all upscale business people and always very friendly.

I recall that one of the apartments was rented by Jim and Saundra Morrison, who were probably in their mid-forties. He was a general manager for a group of hardware stores and traveled considerably. Saundra was a rather stately, good-looking person, a musician who played the organ, and I believe she worked part-time in the public school system. Several times when I would be working in the yard on Saturdays, Saundra would bring out two soft drinks and invite me to sit with her in the backyard. We would talk about school or various other subjects.

One afternoon, I had been working in the yard, and Saundra came home from doing some shopping. After parking her car, she came over and said she had purchased some cake and wanted to know if I would like to come up to the apartment and have some hot chocolate and cake with her, also mentioning that she had to do some practicing on her organ.

I thought that sounded good, so I accepted and thanked her. A few minutes later, I finished my work, and I rang the Morrison's doorbell. Saundra came to the door and invited me in, and the hot chocolate and cake were ready on the table. I asked about Jim, and she said he was traveling this week, so we sat and talked, had our refreshments, then she sat down at the organ and began to play. To me, she appeared to be an excellent musician and played some very popular music.

After thirty minutes or so, I told Saundra that I had some other things that needed to be done, thanked her for the refreshments, and left her apartment. During the next month, when I was working at the apartments, Saundra invited me up for refreshments a couple of times, and I was always a little reserved.

One Saturday afternoon, I was on the way to town and found it necessary to go by the apartments to check on a couple of items. I met Saundra in the hall as she was just returning from an appointment.

Saundra said, "Bob, I need a cool drink. Will you come in for a short time? I will also play the organ to catch up on my practice."

As I recall, I said, "Sure, Saundra. I would love to hear you play, and I can use a cold drink."

Saundra fixed soft drinks, sat down at the organ, and began to play. She played for about five minutes or so, then stopped and turned to me and said, "Bob, I am unhappy. I had a call from Jim earlier saying he was in a meeting and would not be home until Sunday afternoon. He travels entirely too much of the time."

Then she turned and began to play again. After about fifteen or twenty minutes, she stopped playing, got up from the organ, excused herself, and left the room. I was sitting on the sofa, so I just picked up a magazine and started turning through the pages.

Saundra returned to the room, wearing only a brief negligee. She sat down beside me and said, "Bob, you are such a nice boy. I think it is time that we got better acquainted." Then she placed her hand on my knee and gave it a squeeze.

I am sure my temperature went sky high and my heart jumped to about 300 beats per minute. My immediate thought was, *here I am, sitting on a sofa with a beautiful lady, very scantily dressed, who is at least twice my age, and I have just been propositioned.* My sex education was very limited. I quickly asked myself, *how should I respond to this suggestion, and what am I supposed to do now?*

I took her hand and said, "Saundra, you are a very sweet lady, and I would like to get to know you better also, but right now, I have an appointment downtown, so I had better leave."

Saundra gave me a kiss on the cheek, escorted me to the door, and said, "Bob, I don't want you to forget we have an engagement at a later date."

I worked as manager at the apartments until the end of May, when school was out for the summer. I saw Saundra a number of times after that Saturday afternoon. She was always very attentive and invited me up for a cool drink several times, but I found myself too busy to accept.

About halfway through my junior year, I had my bicycle accident, breaking a couple of ribs and injuring my chest, so I did not pass my physical examination to continue ROTC. As a result, I dropped my study hall and took two more required subjects. I thought at first that by taking these additional required subjects, I would have sufficient points to graduate after completing my junior year; but later on, that was not approved.

Shortly after school started in my junior year, I met a girl who was in a couple of my classes, and we dated quite frequently during the school year. Tammy Woods was a very attractive girl, who had been adopted five years previously by an older couple who had no other children. Up until the time Tammy was adopted, she had been in an orphanage since she was a small child. She knew she had an older sister but did not know her name or where she lived.

Tammy's adoptive parents were very strict, and at one time, her mother told her that the only reason she adopted her was so she would have someone to do the washing, ironing, and housework. Tammy's father was a large man, well over six feet tall, and, as I recall, worked as a manager for a construction firm.

Over time, I developed more of a brotherly feeling for Tammy, rather than romantic, and we had some good times together. However, as her parents were so strict, she could only go out one or two nights each week and was required to be home by 9:00 p.m.

I had met Tammy's parents a number of times, and they had a very nice home with a large open front porch that was well furnished for entertaining. As the front of the house was set high, there were eight or ten steps from the sidewalk up to the porch level. Several times, when I would come by to pick Tammy up, her parents would be sitting on the porch, and they would invite me to sit and talk with them for a little while. Tammy and I had been friends for some time, and one Sunday evening, we had a date to go to a movie. I came by to pick Tammy up, and she was not quite ready, so I sat and talked with her parents for a short time, and they were most friendly.

When Tammy came out and we were leaving, her mother said, "Be sure to be home on time."

I do not recall what Tammy said, but she did answer her mother in a polite way. The movie was considerably longer than usual, and when we were leaving the theater, Tammy looked at her watch, and I remember her saying, "Bob, it is nine fifteen. My folks will kill me when we get home."

I tried to comfort her and said I would talk to her dad and it would all be OK. I remember her saying, "Bob, it won't be OK. You don't know my father."

We arrived at her house, and her dad was on the front porch waiting. As we went up the front steps, he said, "Where in the hell have you been? Get in the house." He then turned to me and said, "Well, what do you have to say?"

I explained to him that the movie was longer than anticipated, and if he didn't believe me, he could telephone the theater, and that I was sorry for being fifteen minutes late.

He said, "Boy, I don't know what you have been up to, but you need a lesson."

He then grabbed my right wrist, swung me completely around him, then let me go. I sailed off the porch, landing on the grass eight or ten steps below. I got up, and as I ran toward my car, I looked around and saw Tammy standing on the porch. I remember her calling out, "I am sorry, Bob."

The following day at school, we met in the hall, and she apologized for her father's action and advised me that she had been put on restriction for six months. Her father told her the only time she could leave the house was for school and church. This would certainly end our dating.

Several months before this incident, Tammy had talked to one of her teachers, who I will call Ms. Blackstone. Tammy had told Ms. Blackstone about her family problems.

A few days after my run-in with her father, Ms. Blackstone called Tammy into her office and said, "Tammy, about your problems at home, I do not want to become involved, but I may have been able to help you to some degree. Here is an envelope, which contains an out-of-town telephone number and name. I suggest you make the call, tell them your name, and you will have to take it from there."

Tammy showed me the envelope and told me the story. I asked her what was in the envelope, and she replied, "I don't know. I am afraid to open it."

She then opened the envelope, and saw that it contained a Denver, Colorado, telephone number and a name that I do not recall, but will say Jean Middleton. Tammy then told me that she did not have enough money with her to make a long-distance call. I reminded her that if she was going to get home on time, she did not have adequate time to make the call today anyway. However, I would bring enough money the following day, whereby we could make the call at lunch break. She said she had some savings hidden at home, so she could bring some money tomorrow. She then looked at me and said, "Bob, I don't know what I would do if I didn't have you to support me."

The following day, we met before school started, and the first thing she said was, "Bob, I was so excited I didn't sleep a wink last night."

We agreed where to meet at noon when classes would dismiss for a one-hour lunch break. I had spotted an enclosed pay telephone booth at the Old National Hotel, which was located in the downtown area, not too far from the school. At noon, we met as agreed and headed for the hotel. Between the two of us, we had ample change to make the call. Tammy entered the telephone booth and left the door open so I could hear the conversation. I was holding the change, ready to give her the money as needed. I remember her telling me that she was so excited and nervous that she did not know if she could talk. She dropped a nickel in the telephone slot, and the operator answered and told her it would be $1.75 to call Denver, Colorado. Tammy dropped seven quarters in the slot. I could hear the phone ringing on the other end of the line. It rang several times. No answer.

Suddenly someone answered. Tammy said, "This is Tammy Woods in Leavenworth, Kansas. I have been given this number to call. Are you Jean Middleton?"

There was a pause, then a gasp, then a shout. "Tammy, this is your older sister, Jean!"

They were talking so loudly that I could clearly hear the conversation, and both girls began to cry, which made me start to cry as well. Shortly, the operator came back on the line and told them it would be a dollar for another three minutes, and I handed Tammy four quarters.

She knew her sister could not contact her at her home, as the Woods' would never discuss anything concerning her previous life. I had previously advised Tammy that she could use my home address anytime she so desired. Jean gave Tammy her full name and address, and Tammy gave my name and address. They both agreed to write immediately.

During the next month, I would receive a letter weekly addressed to Tammy from her sister. Tammy told me that her sister was ten years older than her, and that when she was three years old, her parents were both killed in an automobile accident. As they did not have any relatives who could care for them, both girls were sent to a children's home. Due to their age difference, the two sisters lived in different dormitories, but they did meet and visit several times each week. One day, when Tammy was about five years old, she was called to the manager's office, and her sister was there sitting in a chair, crying. The manager told Tammy that she had ten minutes to tell her sister good-bye, as her sister was being adopted, and they would probably never see each other again. The manager then left the room. Tammy and her sister grabbed each other and began crying, as they did not want to be separated, but the family who was adopting Jean wanted only one girl. Shortly, the manager returned, pulled them apart, and Tammy was taken to her dormitory. She said she probably cried for a week, thinking she would never see her sister again.

Through their correspondence, Tammy learned that Jean had graduated from nursing school, had become a surgical nurse, and had married a young physician. Jean and her husband, Jack, wanted Tammy to come to Denver to live with them, and they had agreed to send Tammy to nursing school, where they had some contacts.

Tammy was ready to go, but she knew the Woods would never agree to release her. Therefore, Tammy decided the only thing for her to do was to run away, and she asked me to help. Jean had agreed to send her money for a bus ticket if she could make all the other arrangements. School would be out in about three weeks, so Tammy decided to stay until she could complete her junior year. This would give us planning time.

We met frequently at school to discuss her plan, and she decided she would catch the bus for Denver the afternoon of the last day of school. The Woods were scheduled to leave sometime that day for an out-of-town meeting. Therefore, Tammy would not be missed until they returned a few days later. We went together to the bus station to purchase her ticket and found she was about ten dollars short, so I was glad to make up the difference.

During the next three weeks, Tammy and I frequently discussed her plan to join her sister in Denver, and we finally decided we had it fine-tuned.

On a Sunday afternoon, a few days before the end of the school year, Tammy telephoned me and asked if I could come to the side entrance of her house, as it was rather secluded, to pick up two suitcases she had packed. The Woods were away from home for a few hours, and this would be the only time she would be able to slip the suitcases out without their knowledge.

I borrowed my buddy's car, drove to Tammy's house, picked up her two suitcases, and put them in the trunk of his car. I immediately left, as I knew if her father should come home early and find me there, he would probably beat the tar out of me.

Driving home, I asked myself, *now what do I do with these two suitcases?* I did not want to involve my buddy in this caper, so I decided to store the suitcases in the garage with some other luggage. This accomplished, I thanked my buddy for the use of his car and went home to dress for the Epworth League meeting, which was a young people's church meeting. This group met at the church at six o'clock every Sunday evening for one hour, and I expect it was made up of twenty or twenty-five young people, including my two sisters, Bessie and Hazel, who were both older than I. After our meeting, many of us would take in a movie, go to someone's house for a little party, or in the winter, go sleigh riding.

The last day of school arrived, and I knew we had a busy schedule, including getting Tammy to the bus station to catch the 4:30 p.m. bus to Kansas City, then on to Denver. Jean had told her that she would be at the Denver bus terminal at any time during the day or night, so we were not too concerned about the bus schedule to Denver. I asked my buddy if I could use his car for a little while after school. He agreed and said, "Anytime you need it, you will be most welcome."

I met Tammy before school at our meeting spot, and she had several paper grocery bags in her pocketbook. When we got to her locker, she took them out, and I asked her what she was going to do with the paper bags.

She said, "Bob, after giving you the two suitcases, I found two more dresses that I just can't part with, so I brought them along and will put them in my suitcase this afternoon."

I said, "If you brought them with you, where are they?"

She replied, "I have three dresses on, and I have to get to the ladies' room and get two of them off, as I am perspiring."

We had lunch together at a small fast-food shop near the school and double-checked our schedule. We had not told anyone about our plan, as we were afraid the information would get back to her folks. School was dismissed early, about 2:30 p.m., and as planned, I walked directly to where my buddy had his car parked, picked up the car, and drove back to our meeting place at the school. Tammy was there, talking to some of her girlfriends. As she walked to the car, she turned, waved to the girls, and I heard her say, "See you all next year." I could see she was concealing her scheduled departure and playing the game to the fullest degree.

Tammy jumped into the front seat and indicated that she was ready, and then she turned and looked at her friends and the school building, which she had attended for two years. I could see tears in her eyes and streaming down her cheeks. She turned to me and said, "Bob, in many respects, I loved that school. The teachers and my classmates made me forget, for a short time anyway, the hell I was living in at home. Now I am leaving it all and probably will never return, thanks to one of my teachers, my sister Jean, and your support and assistance."

We arrived at my house, and my mother was sitting on the front porch, sewing. Tammy had met my mother several times previously, so they were not strangers. My mother greeted us and mentioned that school must have let out a little early.

I said, "Yes, as it was the last day this year. I am sure all the teachers were anxious for their summer vacation to arrive. I know we are ready for a little time off."

My mother said to us, "I just baked some cookies. How about a cookie and a cold drink?"

We both agreed, and Mother headed for the kitchen and returned with a dish of cookies and three cold soft drinks. I finished with my refreshments quite quickly as I was anxious to move on with my mission. I excused myself and jumped into the car.

I drove up the street and back down the side street to my dad's garage. Removing the two suitcases from their safe hiding spot, I loaded them into the truck of the car, closed the garage door, and drove back to the front of my house. As I entered the porch, my mother asked me where I had been, and I responded by saying, "I had an errand to run for a friend."

I looked at Tammy, and there was a smile on her face; she knew where I had been and what I had been doing. I checked my watch and noticed it was getting late, so we told my mother that we should be on our way and thanked her for the refreshments.

As we were departing, my mother said, "Tammy, you are a very attractive and sweet girl. I hope you will come again."

I knew what Tammy was thinking. She looked my mother in the eye and said, "Thank you so very much, Mrs. Day. I do hope to see you again."

As we got into the car, Tammy turned and waved to my mother. Then she said, "Bob, I don't remember my mother. You are so lucky to have such a sweet mother."

I thanked her, and we headed for the bus station. We still had plenty of time, but I did not want to miss the bus, as that would have created quite a problem. As we drove into the parking lot, we did not see anyone we knew, and the bus was sitting at the terminal marked "Denver."

As we unloaded her two suitcases from the car, she slipped her two extra dresses into one of the cases. I said, "Tammy, please be careful on the trip to Denver, and let me know soon that you arrived safely. I hope everything works out living with your sister, and that the Woods do not go looking for you and try and make you return."

"Bob, after what I went through and the way you were treated," she said, "I will never return to live with the Woods—you can count on that."

We went into the bus station, and she gave the station manager her ticket. He checked her bags, mentioned that the bus would be leaving shortly, and told her she could board the bus anytime. Tammy and I walked to the bus, and the driver loaded her cases with a few others into the bus storage area. There were only a few passengers, as most would be boarding at Union Station in Kansas City.

Tammy said, "I had better board the bus so I can get a seat forward near the driver as I hear that is safer." Then she turned to me and said,

"Bob, I don't know how I can ever thank you for all your help and kindness. I will write you soon."

We gave each other a big hug, and she boarded and slid into one of the front seats. I stood near the door, and soon the bus driver came out of the station and asked me if I was also going.

I said, "Not this time. Maybe one day."

The driver closed the door. Tammy and I waved good-bye, and I could see she was crying. As the bus departed from the station, she was still waving. When I returned to my friend's car, I sat there for a little while just thinking. She was so young to have to deal with this monumental problem, and I shed a few tears and said a little prayer for her, a great friend.

After returning my friend's car, I met my dad at his store on time, and we drove home in his car. That evening at dinner, my mother commented on what a very nice girl Tammy seemed to be, but I did not mention that she was on her way to Denver to live with her sister. For several weeks, I was a little apprehensive, as I expected Mr. or Mrs. Woods to call me or come by my house and accuse me of having something to do with Tammy's disappearance, but I never heard anything from the Woods, for which I was thankful.

About a week later, I received a letter from Tammy saying that she had arrived safely in Denver and that her sister and her brother-in-law had met her at the station. She mentioned that they had a beautiful large house, and she had a large bedroom and her own bath. In one of her letters, Tammy mentioned she had corresponded in confidence with Ms. Blackstone, her former teacher, and thanked her for her assistance. Ms. Blackstone told Tammy in one of her letters that she had a friend who was an investigator. He had worked on her case for nearly three months before he located her sister in Denver. Tammy told me that she did not know who the investigator was, but she was most grateful to him and Ms. Blackstone for what they had done to reunite her with her sister. We corresponded for about a year, but we both developed other interests and drifted apart, and never met again.

Approximately five years later, I was married, and we were home on a short visit. My mother told me that she was holding a letter for me that had arrived a few weeks earlier. She handed me the letter, but it did not have a return address. I thanked my mother and put it in my pocket.

When I was alone, I opened the letter, and it was signed, "Love, Tammy." I thought for a moment, *who is Tammy?* Then it all came back. It was from Tammy Woods. She had changed her name to that of her biological parents' and was now Tammy Livingston. She explained that it had taken somewhat longer to graduate from nursing college as she had taken a number of other specialized courses. She mentioned that she recalled my interest in the US Air Force, so after graduating and becoming a surgical nurse, she had applied for a commission in the military service. Subsequent to some waiting time, she was granted a commission as a second lieutenant in the US Air Force and had recently been promoted to first lieutenant. She was now First Lieutenant Tammy Livingston. I knew she must have been very proud. She brought me up to date on her life since that day we parted at the bus station, mentioning that she had never heard anything from the Woods, so she assumed they had obtained another housemaid.

Tammy ended her letter by saying,

> Bob, this is a terrible war, but we must win, and I just hope that I am able to do my small part. I have just received notice that I will be leaving this air base within a few days. I do not know my next assignment, but I have been told that I will be doing a great deal of flying, which I love. Thank you again for all your support in my earlier years and for being such a great friend. Take care of yourself and possibly, one day, we will meet again."
>
> Love,
> Tammy

I responded to Tammy's letter, congratulating her on her great accomplishments and for receiving a commission in the US Air Force, but I never heard from her again. It was quite evident Tammy had adjusted and made some major accomplishments in her life since the day she boarded the bus for Denver. I do not know if she survived WWII. To my understanding, there were many casualties of the nurses who flew on the medical evacuation planes, if that was her assignment.

Several times since Tammy left her home in Leavenworth, I have wondered why the Woods made no effort to contact me when they arrived home and found her gone. Tammy and I had been good friends, and I thought they would have suspected me of knowing something about how to locate her. *Did they fear prosecution as a result of their treatment of Tammy while she was in their home? Or did they consider that Tammy was no longer needed to do the housework and this was a good time to discontinue their relationship?*

During my sophomore and junior years, students were encouraged to take some form of music, so I selected the glee club, as I was considered to have a fair baritone voice. Near the end of each school year, our music instructor, Ms. Minnie Taylor, in conjunction with Mr. John Trollman, band director, would present a musical program. As I recall, this annual program would be performed for two or three nights during the week, as it was usually quite a production.

During my junior year, a very attractive girl by the name of Janet Goodjohn and I were selected for the part of world travelers for the annual musical. As we were both tall and slender, Ms. Taylor considered that we qualified for the part quite well. The name of the musical was *They Went to Baghdad*. All the costumes, except our American dresses, were of the Middle Eastern dress. As I recall, it was about a two-hour program. The performance was well received and a great success due to the costumes and the music that were patterned around the culture of the Middle East. Ms. Taylor and Mr. Trollman were commended on their outstanding achievement. Prior to this production, I had seldom heard of Baghdad, never realizing that later in my career, I would be living in Baghdad for over two years.

During early February of my junior year, I received a telephone call from Jim Simons, manager of a Chevrolet dealership, and a friend of my father's. Jim and I had talked a number of times. He had just sold a new Chevrolet sedan to a lady whose name was Mrs. Betty Rogers, and she did not know how to drive. He had given Mrs. Rogers my name, a good recommendation, and mentioned that I should call her if I were interested in teaching her how to drive and earning a little money.

I called Mrs. Rogers, and she asked me to come by the following day after school. When we met, she appeared to be very well educated, well dressed, had a nice home, and was widowed. She mentioned that she had wanted to learn to drive for a number of years, but her late husband did all the driving, so he contended there was no need for her to learn to drive. After talking with her and looking at her new car, I decided to accept the offer. She had asked Jim Simons the going rate for a driving instructor, and he had suggested seventy-five cents an hour. Mrs. Rogers and I agreed on this rate, and we decided we would try driving lessons twice a week for two hours each time during my after-school hours.

Following her driving lessons, we would frequently sit on her front porch, discuss her driving of the day, and go over some of the state driving rules and laws. Many times during this period, we had a cool drink or a hot chocolate. One afternoon, in confidence, she told me about her personal life. She had been widowed three times, and, as I recall, it had been three years since her last husband passed. Possibly two times during the driving instructions period, we visited her husbands' graves, and she would always place flowers at their headstones.

After approximately two and a half months, we decided she had sufficient instruction and experience to take her driving test for the state driver's license. I had obtained a copy of the state driving laws and regulations, and she had memorized most of the requirements.

We drove to the State Drivers License Bureau, and she filled out the necessary papers and paid the license fees. The clerk told us there would be a short wait until the testing officer returned from a driving test. We sat and waited fifteen minutes, and then thirty minutes. Mrs. Rogers was talking about the driving laws and regulations and becoming impatient and a little nervous. I suggested that we change the subject, and she agreed and asked me what my plans were for the summer. I told her that I would be looking for a summer job, as I was trying to save some money in order to attend college after I graduated from high school. In addition, I told her about our football team, and that there was a game that evening. She then started telling me about her desire to go to college, but that she got married instead. By then, she had relaxed somewhat, and the clerk advised us that the testing officer had returned and was waiting for her in the drive-way.

I was hopeful that she might have the same testing officer who had given my driving test, but there was a new officer. He introduced himself as Officer John Stanley, and, looking at her driver's license application, he then turned to Mrs. Rogers and said, "You are Mrs. Betty Rogers?"

Mrs. Rogers said, "Yes, and he is Robert Day. He has been my driving teacher."

The officer looked at me and said, "Robert, I am going to take Mrs. Rogers for a drive and test her driving skills. We will see how good of a teacher you have been. You stay here at the office while we go for the driving test."

They got in Mrs. Rogers's car and drove out of the drive and down the street. I thought, *good luck, Mrs. Rogers. I hope we covered all the driving subjects you need to know.*

I sat in the office for at least forty-five minutes, possibly an hour before they returned. As they entered the office, they were talking, and I wondered what he was saying to her. I decided it was best for me to stay seated. They walked up to the desk and talked for a short time. Then Officer Stanley motioned for me to come to the counter. As I joined them, Officer Stanley said, "Robert, Mrs. Rogers passed with flying colors. I tried to confuse her a little, but she remained cool. You did a good job teaching her how to drive."

As I recall, I said, "Officer, it was not difficult teaching Mrs. Rogers as she is a very intelligent lady."

Mrs. Rogers looked at us and smiled; she was a very happy lady.

Mrs. Rogers and I drove to her house, and she said, "Bob, let's sit here in the living room and celebrate by having a cold drink and a piece of chocolate cake that I baked this morning."

As I recall, I said something like, "I think that is a great idea, and I do want to congratulate you on passing the test, Mrs. Rogers."

Soon she returned with two glasses of a cool drink and two small dishes with large pieces of double chocolate cake. She then said, "Bob, we have gotten to know each other quite well during the last few months, so after this, why don't you be less formal and just call me Betty."

I said, "Mrs. Rogers, if you would rather that I call you Betty, I will do so, but you seem like Mrs. Rogers to me."

After we had talked for a short time and finished our refreshments, I said, "Betty, I expect I had better go shortly. As I previously mentioned, there is a big football game this evening."

Mrs. Rogers said, "Bob, let me get my pocketbook from the other room so I can pay you for today." And she left the room. Shortly, she called from one of the other rooms and said, "Bob, I have been trying to get a picture hung for some time. Would you help me before you go?"

I said, "Sure, Betty. Where are you?"

She replied, "In the family room."

As I entered the family room, I noticed Mrs. Rogers was standing near a small stepladder holding a fair-sized picture and a hammer. To my surprise, she had changed into a skirt and a loose blouse with a very low neckline. She handed me the hammer and the picture hook, and showed me on the wall where to place the hook. Then she handed me the picture, and I placed the hanging wire on the hook. As I stood on the ladder, she stepped back, looked at the picture, and indicated her approval.

When I was coming down the stepladder, Mrs. Rogers had moved forward, and when I turned around, she was directly in front of me and we collided. I felt her nearly bare breasts against my chest, and a tingle went through my entire body. She whispered in my ear, "Bob, I know you have plans for this evening, but when you have time, I would like to teach you a few new tricks. Please call me."

Before I could say anything, she opened her purse to pay me the usual two-hour driving lesson fee and handed me an extra twenty-dollar bill. I thanked her very much and told her that I hoped to see her again, and she walked to the door with me.

As I walked home, I felt a little confused. Within a two-month period or so, I had been propositioned by two ladies twice my age. Was this my fault, was I saying something to lead them on, or was this their great desire to have male companionship? I thought about it for some time and decided, at this time, I did not have an answer.

My junior year would be ending in another month, so I was checking the newspaper each day to see if there were any summer jobs being advertised, and I was making inquiries in the business community. In mid-May, there appeared an advertisement in the paper whereby Raymond Electric Service needed an electrician's helper for the summer months.

Due to the Depression, my dad had closed his business, Day's Battery and Electric Service, and had taken a position as an electrical engineer with the Leavenworth County Water Department. I showed my dad the advertisement, and he told me that he knew Jack Raymond quite well. If I was interested, I should give Mr. Raymond a call, as he was a good man. I had gained considerable experience in the electrical field from working for my dad, so I felt comfortable in applying for the job. After contacting Jack Raymond, he asked me to come into his office the following day for an interview. We talked for some time, and he explained that I would be assisting him in various types of electrical installations, including wiring houses. The hours were 8:00 a.m. to 6:00 p.m. six days a week, and the salary was fifty cents per hour. I accepted the position and was scheduled to report to his office the first Monday after school was dismissed for the summer.

Near the end of the month, I got a call from Mrs. Rogers. She asked me how I was doing and mentioned that she had not heard from me and that she missed our little talks. She then went on to say, "Bob, as I probably mentioned to you somewhere along the line, I own half-interest in an exclusive gift shop in Colorado Springs, and I spend the summers in Colorado operating the gift shop with my partner. My former husband purchased a beautiful chalet up in the mountains some years ago, where I live during the summer months. My partner and I have just been talking, and we expect business to be quite good this summer. Therefore, we will need some assistance in the gift shop. I would like to offer you a job as our assistant. The salary will be about seventy-five dollars a month, plus room and board. I have plenty of space in my chalet, so you will have your own private room and bath. We will drive out together the first week in June. Are you interested?"

In order not to hurt her feelings, I replied, "Betty, your offer sounds most interesting, but I have just accepted a job with the Raymond Electric Service for the summer, so I am committed. But I want to thank you for the offer, and I do hope you have a great summer."

She said, "Bob, I am very disappointed, as I thought you might enjoy spending the summer with me in beautiful Colorado in the mountains."

As my dad had been quite busy, I had not told him about my summer job with Raymond's Electric Service. As a joke, that evening at the dinner table, I mentioned to him that I had a summer job all lined up, and that I would be going to Colorado Springs with Mrs. Rogers for the summer to work in her exclusive gift shop.

He said, "Bob that sounds rather interesting. Where will you be staying, as I understand housing in Colorado Springs is rather limited during the summer months?"

I replied, "Mrs. Rogers has taken care of that, as I will be staying with her in the chalet."

My dad said, "I don't think that is a very good idea, and I suggest you call Mrs. Rogers and call off your Colorado trip, as you will not be going."

I then told my dad that I was just kidding, as I wanted to get his reaction. Then I mentioned that I had a job lined up with Raymond Electric Service for the summer. He then laughed and appeared rather relieved and said, "Bob, I'm pleased to hear that you have a job with Jack Raymond. I thought you had better sense than to go off for the summer with a lady more than twice your age."

Some years later, we were back in Leavenworth with my daughter Betsey, who was then three years old. I decided to take her out west of town to visit some old friends. On the way, we passed Mrs. Rogers' home, and she was sitting on the front porch. I stopped and introduced Betsey to her, and we sat and talked for a little while. She was very happy to see us and to meet my daughter.

As we were leaving, she said, "Bob, I want to thank you again for those driving lessons, and sorry you were unable to go to Colorado with me that summer. I sold my chalet and half interest in the gift shop a few years ago, so I do not travel to Colorado anymore. I am still driving and I bought a new Chevrolet last year, and thanks to you I know how to drive it."

We said good-bye, and that was the last time I saw Mrs. Rogers. I am sure she is long gone by now.

The Monday after school was out for the summer, I reported to Jack Raymond's office as scheduled, and he explained to me what our projects were for the week. We would frequently take two trucks, as many times he would be called to another project and leave me to work by myself.

The second week I worked for Jack, he said, "Bob, I have another job for you, if you're interested. My father, who operates the Raymond Dairy, is going to Europe for the summer, and I am going to have to help at the dairy. You will be on your own part of the time on our work projects. In addition, we need another milk truck driver to make early-morning deliveries to food stores. If you want to earn some extra money, you can have that job. If you accept, this will mean that you must be at the dairy every morning, except Sunday, at 4:00 a.m. You will make deliveries to food stores and be back at the dairy by 8:00 a.m. to pick up the electric truck and meet me at the work site. You will then be working thirteen hours daily except Sundays, and the pay is fifty cents per hour."

I agreed with this arrangement and worked this schedule all summer. The second week I drove the milk truck, one of the loading men at the dairy asked me if I liked chocolate milk, and I told him I drank it frequently. After that, I found on my inventory list two extra pint bottles of chocolate milk.

Frequently, I would meet the pie deliveryman on the route, and I would trade him a bottle of chocolate milk for an apple pie. One morning, the pie man was out of apple pies, and all he had was lemon pies, but we still traded. I wanted to gain a little weight, so that morning, when I stopped for a quick rest and a snack, I ate the small lemon pie and drank a half pint of double whipping cream. My snack tasted very good, but about fifteen minutes down the road, I had to make a quick stop and lost everything. I have not cared too much for lemon pies since that day.

One morning, Jack told me that a third man would be working with us for two days, installing a very large exhaust blower fan in the top attic of the Presbyterian Church. Jack and the other man, who I will call Ken, took the fan apart, making smaller sections in order to move it through the small openings in the ceiling. There was a long walkway about five feet above the rafters from the back to the front of the church where the fan was to be installed. Therefore, it became necessary to move the smaller parts of the fan down the walkway to the point of installation.

My assignment was to run the 220-volt electric line from the meter and cutoff switches in the basement to where the fan was being installed in the attic. It was decided to attach the electric line to the walkway posts, where it would be very secure. By noon of the second day, we had completed the project and it was ready to be tested. It tested perfectly, but Jack decided we should replace a connecting box about halfway along the line. Jack told me to open all switches, pull all fuses in the basement to cut off power in the attic, and watched me as I followed his instructions. Jack and Ken went out to load the trucks, and I headed to the attic with the additional parts he wanted installed at the midway location.

Knowing the power was turned off, I removed the cover of the old connecting box and placed my screwdriver into one of the connecting screws. There was a loud bang, a flash of fire, and the 220 volts hit me like a truck.

Fortunately, it threw me, rather than grabbing and holding on to me. I did a flip-flop off the walkway, falling six feet down to the rafters of the ceiling of the sanctuary. For a second or two, I thought I would stop when my feet hit the lath and plaster, but my legs went through, and my arms caught the rafters as my body passed through the plaster and lath. Here I was, hanging by my arms from the ceiling of the sanctuary. My hands were slowly slipping from the rafters. I looked down and saw it was at least fifty to seventy-five feet to the seats below. I thought, *if I live through this, I will sure catch hell from someone.*

I did not know how long I would be able to hold on to the rafters, so I began to call for help. No response. I knew if I fell into the seats below, I would not survive. So I called repeatedly as loud as I could.

Suddenly, I heard Jack call out from somewhere below, "Hold on, Bob. We are coming to help you!"

It was probably only a very short time before Jack and Ken arrived above me, but it seemed like an hour as I was slipping through the hole. I knew I could hold on for only a few more minutes, and then they arrived and slowly pulled me back through the hole in the ceiling. Jack and Ken took me down to the basement, and I took off my shirt and pants. Fortunately, I did not have any major cuts, but quite a number of rather deep scratches. Jack went to his truck and brought in his first-aid kit. First, they washed me down with alcohol, and then they covered my scratches with iodine. I recall how that did burn!

Just then, the plumber came in and said, "Who cut the power off on me?" And then we knew what had happened. The plumber saw all the switches were pulled, and he needed some power to operate his equipment, so he connected the power lines.

Ken called the plumber a name and said, "Don't you realize you nearly killed this boy by turning the power back on?"

For a short time, I thought there was going to be a fight between Ken and the plumber. Then Jack explained to the plumber what had happened, and showed him the big hole in the ceiling of the sanctuary. As I recall, the plumber apologized to the three of us and agreed to pay for the damage to the ceiling of the sanctuary. I sat down in a chair with a glass of water and waited until Jack and Ken returned from the attic after replacing the new connecting box.

Upon returning, Jack asked me how I was feeling, and I remember telling him that I was OK.

Jack looked at his watch and said, "Fellows, we have a couple of hours before quitting time. Let's go back to work."

Before quitting that evening, Jack told me to meet him back at the church at eight o'clock the next morning, as there was an item he wanted to check.

I followed his instructions, and when I arrived at the church, I parked directly behind Jack's truck. I noticed that Tom Davis, owner of the Davis Electric Service, and his assistant were working on the outside of the building next to the church. Even though Tom and Jack were competitors, they were very good friends.

As I got out of the truck, Tom called to me and we exchanged good-morning greetings. After entering the church, Jack wanted to show me how he had replaced the fuses in the switch box. The job was now completely finished, and as we went out the church door, we heard a very loud shout for help coming from the building next to the church.

We saw that Tom Davis was on a long ladder, above the second floor of the building, working on an electric line. His assistant had been holding the base of the ladder but had gone to the electric truck to obtain a tool that was needed. The ladder was slipping and falling backward with Tom at the top. We did not know what we could do, but we ran toward the ladder; however, we were too late. Tom had fallen backward landing on his back on a small concrete wall.

As we approached, we saw that he was not moving and his eyes were closed, but he was still breathing. Jack called to Tom's assistant, telling him to call an ambulance immediately. As it was rather chilly that morning, he told me to get some canvas from the truck so we could cover Tom to keep him warm.

After Jack had covered Tom, he took his hand and said, "Tom, can you hear me?"

Tom did not move, but he opened his eyes, and softly mumbled, "Jack, tell Mary I am sorry to leave her and that I love her."

He then closed his eyes for the last time, and Jack just sat there holding his hand with tears running down his face until the ambulance arrived. I remember thinking, *how can this be? This is not happening. I was just talking to Tom fifteen minutes ago.*

The ambulance arrived, and the medics very carefully slid Tom onto a backboard and rushed him to the hospital, but it was too late.

As we walked back toward our truck, Jack put his arm around my shoulders and said, "Bob, in this business, we have to be so very careful. Accidents happen when you least expect them. No doubt he broke his back when he hit the small cement wall. Yesterday, when you were thrown through that ceiling over the sanctuary, you sure scared hell out of me. I don't know if you realized it or not, but you were slipping fast through those rafters, and I was afraid we were not going to get you out before you fell to the floor below."

I worked for Jack Raymond the rest of the summer, driving the milk truck and working as an electrician's helper, and I saved some money.

A number of years later, when I was home on a visit, I went to see Jack, as he still had his business. He mentioned that he would offer me a job, but he was getting ready to retire. I told him that I was not interested, and that I had a different career path now, and told him a couple of stories of events in the Foreign Service.

During our conversation, I do remember Jack saying, "Bob, I certainly recall the day you fell through that church ceiling, and I was afraid we would not get to you before you went through to those seats below."

I told Jack my angel was on my shoulder that day and had been with me a number of times since. That was the last time I saw Jack, but I will always remember him as a very fair and honest man. I learned a lot that summer working with him as an electrician's helper.

Approximately twenty-five years later, when I was back in Leavenworth to visit relatives, I was passing the First Presbyterian Church where I had worked helping to install that large fan in the attic. A thought suddenly occurred to me; *I wonder if they ever completed repairing the hole in the ceiling where I fell through.* I drove into the parking lot, and found that the front door of the church was unlocked. I entered the sanctuary and looked up at least seventy-five feet or more. There was the patch, which had been repaired but still visible to some degree, covering the hole in the ceiling where I fell through. I thought, *those are the seats I would have fallen into creating my demise if it had not been for Jack and his friend who rescued me.*

I walked around behind the church into the alley where our good friend Tom died suddenly when the ladder fell and Tom landed on the small concrete wall. The concrete wall was still there, and it was difficult for me to look back to the accident that happened many years ago that caused Tom's death. I stood there observing the area again and said a prayer for Tom, who had left a wife and daughter behind; I had attended school with his daughter.

The incident in the church was not my first encounter with the Leavenworth Electric Company. I recall my mother told the story a number of times about an incident that occurred when I was about ten years old. She said it was a Friday morning, and I was home, as the school was closed for the day due to a teachers' meeting. She had just finished washing on the back porch, which was quite wet from the laundry water. She asked me to unplug the electric extension cord from the washing machine and roll it up. I replied in the affirmative and pulled on the extension cord and the washing machine cord to separate them.

One of the cords had a small bare spot exposing the wire, so when I grabbed it, it shocked me, and I was unable to let go of the cords. I stood there frozen with my mouth open, being electrocuted. My mother ran into the kitchen and pulled the other end of the extension cord out of the wall, cutting off the power to the cords. I fell onto the wet floor, unable to move. Crying, she tried to wake me, but was unsuccessful. She ran to the phone and called Dr. Skaggs, our family doctor, who said he was just leaving the office for lunch, but would come immediately. According to my mother, he arrived shortly and tried to stimulate me, but it was not working.

He said, "Mrs. Day, I'm afraid we have lost him but let me try one more thing." He quickly gave me a couple of injections. Shortly, I opened my eyes and tried to talk. Dr. Skaggs and my mother then rubbed my arms vigorously, and I came around more fully. She said that he stayed with me then for a couple of hours and I seemed to get back to normal. He told my mother to let me rest the remainder of the day, and I would probably be OK. Later, he told my mother that when he was giving me the injections he did not know if that would have helped, but fortunately, I did come through it.

The summer passed very rapidly, and now we were going back to school. This was my senior year. As I would have enough credits to graduate in the spring, I decided to take just four subjects during the morning and have the afternoons free. Looking back, it was probably not the wisest decision I ever made, but I was interested in working afternoons and earning additional money for my college fund.

Sunday evenings, as usual, I attended the young people's church service, which was known as Epworth League, at the Methodist church. Usually, after the service, a group of us would take in a movie, have a little party at someone's home, or take in some type of activity. That evening, a friend of mine, Francis Moore, who was a couple of years older, told me that his employer, the Noon Funeral Home, was looking for a young man to work part-time and suggested that I call Mr. Charlie Noon if I was interested.

The following afternoon, I called Mr. Noon and asked him if he was still recruiting for a part-time person as mentioned by my friend, Francis Moore. He indicated that he was still looking for a young man, and if I were a friend of Francis, he would like to talk with me. We arranged to meet the following day in early afternoon.

After our discussion, we agreed on a one-week trial period, working afternoons only, and the salary would be thirty-five cents per hour. My job would be working with several men who maintain all the vehicles, the chapel, and driving the cars for funeral services.

Prior to ending my interview, Mr. Noon said, "Bob, let me brief you on a subject; there are two other funeral homes in town—the Davis Funeral Home and the Sumpter Funeral Home. The hospitals in town do not provide ambulance service. All three funeral homes operate ambulance service and even though we are good friends, we are competitors. We are all in a deep depression, and we need all the business available. I want you to know that all of my personnel must provide ethical, courteous, and respectful service." He ended by saying, "By the way, everyone calls me Charlie, and so I expect you to do the same."

I told him that I understood the requirements and that I would adhere to them. I said, "If it is your desire, I will call you Charlie." And that was the way we operated during our relationship.

During the week, Charlie asked me several times to drive one of the vehicles during a funeral, and he rode with me. Charlie had red lights and sirens installed on the hearses in addition to the two ambulances.

One of the funeral services that week was in Leavenworth, but the internment was in Topeka, Kansas, which was about seventy miles away. On the return trip to Leavenworth, I was driving the hearse with

Charlie riding as passenger. Suddenly, Charlie said, "Bob, I want to see how you handle this buggy at a little faster speed. Turn on the lights and siren, and let's go."

I remember saying, "Charlie, we are doing sixty-five now, and we are not on an emergency."

Charlie replied, "Bob, if you can't drive this buggy per my instructions, I will get someone who can. Now let's go."

My reply consisted of only two words: "Yes sir."

I turned on the red lights and siren; and in a matter of seconds, the speedometer registered seventy, then eighty, and then eighty-five, and I was passing everything on the road. I glanced at Charlie, and he was sitting back, smiling and relaxed. As we approached the Leavenworth city limits, I slowed down to the speed limit, and Charlie nodded his approval.

The following day, my trial period week was completed; and so far, Charlie had not indicated whether I had met his expectations or failed. I reported for work at 1:00 p.m. as scheduled, wondering if I would still have a job, and was assigned with one of the other men to arrange the chapel for a large funeral scheduled for the following morning.

Late in the afternoon, the assistant funeral director came in, inspected the chapel, and said, "Charlie wants to see you in his office right away."

I thought, *here it comes. Do I stay, or do I get fired?*

Charlie said, "Come on in, Bob, and have a chair."

I recall thinking, *he appears to be in a fairly good mood, and I thought, maybe I will get to stay.*

Charlie said, "Bob, how do you like this kind of work?"

I told him that I liked working for him, and that it gave me an opportunity to learn something about the funeral business, and a chance to meet people and, in some small way, assist them by being kind and courteous when they have lost a loved one.

Charlie then said, "Francis did both of us a favor when he suggested that you give me a call. I like your work, and it will give you a chance to gain some additional experience and earn a few dollars. I have a couple of questions for you, how old are you, Bob?"

I told him I was eighteen, and he said, "You look and act a few years older than eighteen, but that is good. My second question is, how much do you know about administering first aid?"

I told him I was a Boy Scout for over three years and attained the rank of Star Scout. During my scouting years, I earned several merit badges on first aid and related subjects and taught first aid to some of the younger Scouts. A number of times during hiking or camping trips, I had the opportunity to use my first-aid experience to assist other Scouts who were injured during our scouting activities.

He then asked me why I had left scouting after reaching the rank of Star Scout, and mentioned that at one time he also had been a Scout. I briefly explained the tragedy that our troop had experienced involving our Assistant Scoutmaster. I recall his comment: "Bob, the disappointment of not continuing in scouting must have been great, but you seem to have accepted and recovered from that tragedy."

Charlie then said he was going to make me an offer to see if I was interested. I would work from 1:00 p.m. to 9:00 p.m., Monday through Friday. During this eight-hour stretch, my main assignment would be to ride in one of the ambulances as a medic (Francis would be the driver-medic). Any afternoon that I was not on an ambulance run, I would be doing other duties assigned by Charlie's assistant. Francis and I would be served our evening meal about 6:00 p.m., and then I would sit in the office and take any telephone calls until 9:00 p.m. During the evening hours, I would be free to read or do my homework.

Francis had a room at the funeral home, so when I received an ambulance call, I was to hit a red button, which was connected to an alarm in Francis's room. We would meet each other in the garage and head for the accident, where we would work as a team. Francis had already worked there a couple of years and had his instructions, which were to get to the scene of the accident as fast, but as safely, as possible, and render first aid to anyone injured. My job was also to render first aid to the best of my ability. In an emergency, the ambulance could fit two injured or two deceased people in it, though it would be a little crowded. If the injured person did not have a preference, we would take them to the nearest hospital.

"From experience, I can tell you at times it will get rather stressful, but keep your cool, and you will be OK," Charlie said. "Your new salary will be forty-five cents per hour, and you will be paid weekly. Are you interested?"

I said that I was, but wondered if I had enough experience to provide first aid to a seriously injured individual.

Charlie reminded me that a medic was not a doctor, and all I was required to do was provide first aid to accident victims, stop the flow of blood if possible, comfort the victim, and make them as comfortable as possible during the trip to the hospital. It was the driver-medic's responsibility to assist the medic in treating the accident victim, and get them to the hospital as safely and as fast as possible.

Charlie also mentioned that the following week, I would be attending two four-hour courses in advanced first aid, which were being given by a medical group in town. He said most of his men had taken the course and found it very useful.

Feeling better about the job, I responded, "Charlie, I would like to accept your offer and I will do my best to meet your requirements."

I completed the advanced first-aid course and responded to a number of ambulance calls using my first-aid training. Fortunately, we were able to save many of the accident victims we treated or transported, but there were some who were killed in the accidents—we couldn't do anything for them before we transported them to the hospital.

I had worked for Charlie for about a month when one morning, he called Francis and me to his office. When we arrived, he asked us to sit down, and we talked about a couple of new cars that had just been delivered, one new ambulance and one limousine. Then he said, "Francis, you are doing a good job as medic-driver, and Bob, you are doing fine as the medic, but I am going to make a change in your assignments. As of now, Bob, you will be the medic-driver, and Francis will be the medic. Francis, you have had more experience as a medic, and I like the way Bob handles the ambulance. Do either of you have any problem with this proposed change?"

Francis said, "It's certainly OK with me. How about you, Bob?"

I replied that it was OK with me. We shook hands, and from then on that was the way we worked.

One cool fall evening, Francis and I had just finished dinner, so we sat and talked a little while about sports before he retired to his room to do a little reading. That suited me fine because I had homework to complete, and I needed to study for several tests coming up in the next few days. I had just settled in, concentrating on some problems, when the red phone rang. It was the local telephone operator advising that there had been a bad automobile accident about twenty miles south of town on Highway 73, and an ambulance was needed immediately.

I pushed the red button to Francis' room and put on my long white coat as I ran toward the garage. Upon returning from a run, I always backed the ambulance into the garage in front of the other vehicles to avoid any problem getting out quickly the next time we were needed. As I was getting into the ambulance, I saw Francis entering the garage, putting on his white coat as he ran toward the passenger side of the vehicle.

Just as I started the engine, Charlie came running out and asked, "Where are you headed?"

"Accident," I replied. "Twenty miles south of town, Highway 73. Should be back in less than an hour and I suggest that you alert the hospital."

As we started down the drive, I turned on our red lights and hit the siren easy, as there was little traffic in the residential area. It was just one-quarter of a mile to Highway 73, and then I turned on the siren full blast. During the two-mile run through the city limits, I maintained a speed of around sixty miles per hour, and then increased the speed to seventy-five or eighty as we crossed the city limits. This stretch of highway was a two-lane paved road, so we were constantly passing and meeting traffic, which was rather hazardous driving. As we approached the scene of the accident, we could see the sheriff's red lights blinking, and saw the sheriff himself attempting to control the traffic.

We immediately realized that a large truck had stopped on the highway and a passenger vehicle had run into the back of the truck.

I stopped the ambulance, leaving sufficient space in the event a fire developed within the wreckage.

The driver of the truck had not been injured, but Francis and I immediately discovered there was one person in the wrecked vehicle—a female, possibly in her mid-thirties. At the time of impact, her head had passed through the glass windshield. At the time we did not have shatter-proof glass as we do today. She was semiconscious, seriously bleeding, and her head was stuck in the windshield.

Francis and I placed towels around her head and neck to prevent additional damage, and I used a small hammer to break away sharp pieces of glass in the windshield that were preventing us from taking her head out of the windshield.

When this was accomplished, Francis and I, with the sheriff's assistance, carefully lifted the lady's body and pulled her head back through the broken windshield and placed her on the stretcher. As we placed the stretcher in the ambulance, where the lighting was bright, we realized she had a sliver of glass stuck in her neck like a spear, which appeared to be the cause of the hemorrhaging. We knew only a surgeon should remove this, as removing it now would only create additional hemorrhaging and she could easily bleed to death before we could get her to the hospital.

We carefully placed additional bandaging around the area of her head and neck as Francis was comforting her. I heard her whisper to him, "Am I going to make it?" He said, "Lady, you will be OK."

As I closed the back doors of the ambulance, Francis looked at me and softly said, "Bob, hit it, and hit it hard." I knew exactly what he was saying.

Our red lights were still blinking, and the sheriff had cleared the way for us to turn around. I turned on the siren to constant, and we headed to Leavenworth, knowing that at this point, speed and the nearest hospital, which was Cushing Memorial Hospital on the south side of town, were the only way to save this lady.

Traffic was not too heavy, and I hit the accelerator. Soon we were doing seventy, then eighty, then ninety. I knew this vehicle would do well over a hundred miles per hour, but I wanted to be careful and not wreck us on the way to the hospital. Arriving at the city limits, I slowed down somewhat, but it did not take us long to arrive at the hospital. Fortunately, the emergency room attendants were waiting for us at the door, and the doctors were immediately available. As we wheeled the stretcher into the emergency room, we noticed our patient was not responding; she was unconscious. One of the doctors advised us that, pending immediate examination, they did not want to transfer the patient to one of their surgical tables. He asked us to return the next morning to pick up our stretcher.

Francis and I returned to the funeral home, cleaned up, restocked the ambulance for the next emergency, and then wrote our brief report, which was kept on file for further reference. By now, it was well past my quitting time, and Francis indicated he was bushed and ready for bed. I rang Charlie's doorbell, handed him a copy of our report, and told him it was well after 9:00 p.m. and that I was headed for home. He would now take over as driver in the event they had any emergency calls during the night.

When I arrived home, which was just a very short distance from Highway 73, my dad was sitting in his chair reading one of his many mystery stories that he thoroughly enjoyed. He said, "Bob, earlier this evening, I heard an ambulance going north on the highway, probably headed for the hospital—was that you on a call?"

I said, "Yes, Dad, that was Francis and me answering an accident call."

My dad responded, "Bob, I heard the ambulance when you were still out a ways. I went out on the porch to see if you were going to come by our intersection. When you did, you were sure traveling fast."

I said, "I will tell you a little about it in the morning as I still have some studying to do tonight."

As I turned to leave the room, I saw my dad sitting there, with his book on his lap, looking into space, smiling. I have since wondered, *was my dad wishing that he was riding with me, or just happy that he was sitting home reading one of his many mystery stories?*

As I moved into the other room to do some studying, I picked up my history book and started to read, but I was having difficulty concentrating on my lesson. I kept thinking about the lady with her head stuck in the windshield, bleeding profusely, and could see her lying on the stretcher at the hospital. Then suddenly, I realized something was telling me, *Bob, turn the page on this incident and move on.* Even though it has been difficult, many times since then, I have attempted to follow this perception in moderating my emotions over events I have experienced in my lifetime.

The next afternoon, Francis and I were working in the chapel when Charlie sent for us to report to his office. As we entered Charlie's office, he said, "Fellows, I just received a most unusual telephone call from the chief of surgery at Cushing Memorial Hospital."

Francis looked at me and twisted his face, and I said, "gee, did we do something good, or are we in deep trouble?"

Charlie went on to say, "Francis, tell me in detail what happened regarding the accident run last evening. Did you add anything to it, Bob?" Again, I thought, *this doesn't sound good. Maybe, unknowingly, we did make a mistake last evening.*

Francis responded by saying, "Charlie, I believe it is all in our report, which Bob and I prepared upon our return. We did everything we could to remove the lady safely out of the broken windshield, curtailed the hemorrhaging as much as possible, then we transported her safely to the hospital within minutes. I was busy taking care of the patient, so I do not know how fast we were traveling. But I will tell you one thing: I know we were really moving."

"Bob, do you have anything you want to add to Francis's statement?"

"No, Charlie. I believe our report covers everything, but I do want to say, Francis did a commendable job administrating first aid to the lady and trying to stop the hemorrhaging in her neck to save her life. If she didn't make it, I am certainly very sorry, but I believe we did everything possible to save her life."

At that point, Francis interrupted and emphatically stated, "Charlie, we certainly did everything we could, but as you know, I am not a doctor. Bob certainly gave me great assistance in getting her out of that windshield, administering first aid, and I am sure Bob pushed our vehicle to the limit getting her to the hospital."

Charlie chuckled and said, "OK, fellows, back off. I just said that I had received a most unusual telephone call from the Chief of Surgery at Cushing Memorial Hospital, and I say, most unusual, because it was unusual. I have never received any similar call from a hospital concerning a patient we transported. The doctor was calling to commend the medic and the driver of the ambulance that administered first aid and transported Mrs. Joan Lambert from the accident scene to the hospital last evening. He went on to say that Mrs. Lambert will survive, but only because of the professional emergency treatment provided and the rapid transport to the hospital by the ambulance crew, as there was only a matter of minutes between life and death in her case. Therefore, both of you are being commended for the professional service you performed last evening. I am very proud of both of you. Francis, you and Bob make a great team, and I would hate to lose either of you."

At that time, we did not know that fate had other plans for us.

One Sunday afternoon in late spring, my dad and I were sitting on the front porch reading the daily newspaper when one of my buddies, Lyle Wilkins, drove up in his car and joined us. My dad liked Lyle, as he was a hard worker, had a great personality, and always dressed very neatly. We sat there talking for a short time, and then my dad mentioned he had a business appointment and would see us later. He left Lyle and me discussing the Friday evening football game.

Suddenly we heard a siren approaching our intersection. When it came into sight, it was an ambulance from the Noon Funeral Home. It was headed south on Highway 73, moving very fast. Then we heard a second ambulance, which was following close behind, also from the Noon Funeral Home.

Lyle looked at me and said, "Come on, Bob. Let's go."

Within seconds, we were on our way to an accident that was just a short distance from the highway.

The track for our city's interurban or streetcar, was constructed in the middle of the highway and served as the third lane for traffic. In order to pass a vehicle traveling in the same direction, it became necessary to drive on the interurban tracks. That day, a black sedan traveling south got caught on the interurban tracks and crashed into a northbound interurban, causing the accident.

The two ambulances were the only emergency vehicles at the scene when we arrived minutes later. The impact of the two vehicles had ruptured the gasoline lines of the black sedan, and the fronts of both vehicles were on fire. All passengers on the interurban had escaped through the rear exit and were standing on the grass strip away from the wreckage. There were two adults and four or five children in the black sedan, and flames were moving under the vehicle and into the front seating compartment.

The ambulance attendants rushed forward. Lyle and I were right behind them. We tried to open the doors of the sedan, but they were jammed shut from the impact of the collision. One of the attendants ran back to the ambulance and got the small hammer I had used in a previous accident, but unfortunately, it was not heavy enough to break the thick glass.

By this time, the flames and smoke had entered the vehicle, and all the passengers were at the doors and windows trying to get out. They were pleading for someone to open the doors, break the glass or do something to get them out of the inferno; but their cries and screams were in vain. There was no way to open those heavy doors or break the windows with the equipment that we had available. Flames were engulfing the interior of the vehicle.

Suddenly, there was the sound of more sirens; it was the fire trucks approaching. The firefighters motioned for everyone to get back as it was possible the gasoline tank of the vehicle would explode. The firefighters quickly broke the windows and broke open the heavy doors with their fire axes.

Other ambulances arrived at the accident scene, and the victims were all rushed to the hospital. Only one child survived with severe burns; the others were pronounced dead on arrival at the hospital. They had all suffered a most painful and tragic death. The Noon Funeral Home took care of the funeral arrangements for all members of the family. I worked the day of the funeral, and it was a very sad occasion. Even though this incident took place many years ago, I can still see those children, faces pressed against the window glass, screaming, as their bodies were engulfed in flames. To my understanding, the fire trucks were delayed due to another fire in progress.

For the next few months, Francis and I worked together as a team at the funeral home, driving vehicles for funerals and making a number of ambulance responses. I am confident we both respected each other's capabilities. On many ambulance runs, we made our way to the hospital at rather high speeds, though some patients were not seriously injured and did not require a rush to the hospital - others died at the scene of the accident. I do not recall losing any accident victim while we were transporting them to a hospital.

In early May 1938, Charlie called me into his office one afternoon and advised that business was very slow. Due to the Great Depression, more individuals were arranging for less expensive funerals, and changes in the economy were creating a financial problem. Therefore, he was going to have to reduce operating expenses, which required eliminating two members of his workforce. As I was the last person hired and had the least seniority, he considered my position should be eliminated. He mentioned that he certainly did not want to lose me, and that I would be missed, especially by himself and Francis, but unfortunately, he had to reduce operating costs.

Then he said, "Bob, to meet employment requirements, here is a letter giving you two weeks' written notice. I will have a favorable letter of recommendation for you on your last day, and there will be a bonus in your last paycheck."

I remember telling Charlie that I understood the situation and that I had enjoyed working for him and I appreciated the two weeks' notice, which would give me a time to look around for another job. As I left his office, Charlie called to me and said, "Bob, I have a question for you, and your answer will be treated confidential, but there is something I want to ask you. This question may seem a little strange, but how fast will that new Studebaker ambulance go?"

I replied by saying, "Charlie, that sounds like a loaded question. I will give you a straight answer, but I would appreciate it if you ask Francis to come in to verify what I am telling you."

Without saying a word, Charlie picked up the paging phone and called for Francis to report to his office immediately. When Francis arrived, I explained to him the conversation we were having, and I wanted him to sit in on my response as we were together at the time.

Francis said, "Go ahead, Bob. I think Charlie will enjoy this as he likes a good, fast ride."

I remember saying, "Charlie, to give you an honest answer, I do not know how fast the Studebaker ambulance will travel because I have never had it wide open, and I don't think Francis has either."

Francis interrupted, "Correct."

I continued, "One afternoon, about a month ago, we received a call from the local telephone operator. She said, 'Another funeral home is on the line also. There is a very bad accident on Highway 73 about twenty-five miles south of town, and they need two ambulances immediately. Francis and I were in the ambulance within two or three minutes and on our way. As soon as we turned onto the highway, I turned our siren on constant.

"After reaching the city limits, we traveled about seventy-five to eighty miles per hour. When we arrived at the straight stretch about ten miles out, I saw the other ambulance coming up behind us. Following your instructions to be the first at an accident scene, I gave it more acceleration. We hit ninety, then a hundred. As there was no traffic to speak of, the other ambulance pulled alongside of us, and I applied more pressure on the accelerator. That was the last time I glanced at the speedometer, so I know we were doing over a hundred. I could see approaching traffic about a mile down the road, so I let the other ambulance pass us. I did not like giving up the lead to the other ambulance, but I did not intend to wreck your new vehicle.

"Nevertheless, Charlie, it all worked out in your favor. When we arrived at the accident, the other medics were just starting to check out a victim in the first car and were administering first aid. They called to us to check the other vehicle. By the condition of the victims, we immediately knew both men in the second vehicle were deceased. They had been killed on impact. However, we checked their heart, breathing, and pulse, and all were flat. We then checked with the other medics, and they did not need any assistance with their injured victims, so we removed the deceased victims from the wreckage, placed them on the stretchers with the assistance of a highway patrolman, and placed both stretchers in the ambulance. Francis got in the back with them, and we headed for the hospital. The doctors in the emergency room examined both victims and declared them deceased. Francis and I returned here, but shortly thereafter, you were notified by the hospital to come and pick up the two bodies as their families had selected your funeral home for all funeral arrangements."

Charlie said, "Yes, I remember the case very well, and I want to thank you fellows as to how you handled the situation, but I did not know the details concerning your run for the accident. I would certainly have enjoyed being on that run with you, as you know how I enjoy a fast ride, but I don't have the nerve to drive that way anymore."

Then I said, "So to answer your question, Charlie, I cannot give you a straight answer as to what the top speed of the Studebaker is, but I do know it has plenty of power."

At the end of the two weeks, I said good-bye to Charlie, Francis, and the others, and received my letter of recommendation and my final paycheck, which included a very nice bonus. During the next two or three years, I would stop in to visit with Charlie and the others now and then. To my understanding, the Noon Funeral Home has been consolidated with another firm, and it now has a new name. Francis died of a serious illness during the war years. He was a great friend, and I think we made a good team.

One Sunday evening in May 1938, I was attending the Epworth League meeting at the Methodist church. I expect we had a group of thirty-five or forty young people present that evening. We had a good out-of-town speaker scheduled, so we were all looking forward to his talk.

Several of our members were still coming into the chapel, and I was sitting next to one of my buddies, Stanley Wade. Two very attractive new girls came into the room and sat down several rows in front of us. Stanley nudged me and said, "Bob, I will take the shorter one."

I replied, "OK, the taller one is fine for me."

After the evening service, our group always greeted any newcomers and invited them to return for future meetings. As we had all decided to take in a movie later that evening, Stanley and I approached the two new girls, introduced ourselves, and asked them if they would care to take in a movie with us. I expect there were possibly eighteen or twenty in our group who attended the movie that evening.

After the movie, we all stopped at a hamburger shop and had refreshments. The two girls were sisters. The one I was with was Charlotte, and Stanley had selected Betty. Their last name was Russell and they lived in a smaller town about ten miles south of Leavenworth. They were both seniors at Lansing High School and would be graduating this year. Stanley and I invited them back to Epworth League, but they mentioned they were involved in some end-of-year school affairs for the next few weeks, but would like to join us again at a later date. That evening, we did not have any idea what the future had in store for us.

Bob's mother, Bob, sister Hazel, sister Frances, Bob's father, and sister Bessie
Leavenworth, Kansas 1941

CHAPTER 6

Moving On

My senior year was ending at Leavenworth Senior High School, and I would be graduating in another couple of weeks. I had not seriously considered attending the senior prom, but decided if I was going to attend, it would certainly be more fun and appropriate if I had a date. Students of Leavenworth High were the only ones permitted to attend the senior prom. I had been dating a girl by the name of Claudia Kennedy, but she was a senior at the Catholic high school, so she would not be eligible to attend. There was the new girl, Charlotte, whom I had just met, but she was a student at Lansing High, so she was off the list. I had not been dating any of my classmates, but there was quite an attractive girl by the name of Jean McCorkle, who had always been very friendly, but for some reason, we had never dated.

Jean and I had gone to school together since the first grade, and I heard she was a very good dancer. I was not the greatest dancer, but I decided to call Jean and invite her as my partner, and she accepted my invitation. When I arrived at her house with my dad's car, I presented her with a white gardenia corsage that she thought was great. She immediately called her mother and dad into the living room and introduced me to them. Her mother pinned her white corsage onto her sky-blue formal dress. She was very beautiful.

There was an excellent band at the prom, and we enjoyed the program very much, dancing with our various classmates and having refreshments. After prom, we went to a restaurant with a small group for dessert, a coke, and more dancing. We were all celebrating our graduation and thought we had the world by the tail. We had no idea that within a few years, our country would be at war with other nations, many of us would be in the military service, and a number of our classmates would not return from the tragic war.

Later in the evening, we decided it was time to say good night, and I took Jean home. It was late, and Jean thanked me for the evening and said she had a wonderful time. We exchanged kisses on the front porch, said good night, and that concluded the evening. As I drove home, I thought, *gee, she is certainly a nice girl and a lot of fun.*

Jean and I dated a couple of times after that, but for some reason, a real relationship did not materialize. We did not see each other again until our fiftieth class reunion.

Earlier in the month, I had told my dad my job with Noon Funeral Home would be ending before long and I would be looking for a job to keep me busy for the summer. As previously mentioned, my dad worked as an electrical engineer with the Leavenworth County Water Department, and had recently been transferred to a construction site called Pilot Knob. There had been a large open water reservoir at this location for many years, but it had deteriorated and needed major repairs. The city and county had decided they would not only repair the interior of the reservoir, but they would also construct a large cement cover. Even though this large reservoir was being drained for the construction work, to my understanding, it became necessary to keep an engineer at this location around the clock to monitor the flow of water at various locations within the city and county, and my dad was assigned the twelve-hour night shift of 6:00 p.m. to 6:00 a.m. Pilot Knob was in a remote section of the county at that time, so my dad was deputized and required to carry a firearm when on duty.

One evening in late May, my dad advised me that he had talked to Bill Jackson, chief construction engineer for Greeley Construction Company, and he would like to consider me for a job beginning in early June, if I was interested. As I was no longer working at the Noon Funeral Home, the following day, I went to talk to Bill Jackson. After we talked, he hired me as a laborer at forty cents per hour, and I started work on June 1.

As I turned to leave, he said, "Bob, if you have any buddies who are interested in doing some hard work during the summer, bring them with you next Monday. If they pass my inspection, I may be able to use them."

I replied, "Fine, Mr. Jackson. I will see what I can do for you."

Monday when I reported for work, I took four of my buddies with me: Stanley Wade, his older brother Rolland, Kenneth Hardman, and Floyd Davis. They had all planned on going to South America to work for the summer, but at the last minute, the political situation became so uncertain they decided to cancel their trip. I introduced them to Bill Jackson, and he was pleased to see them, as he was still short of people on his workforce. After a short discussion, he hired all four of them at forty cents per hour. They were assigned to the cement crew, and I was assigned to the carpenter crew. My buddies were most grateful for setting them up with a job for the summer, during the Great Depression, as jobs were very scarce and many men who had families were out of work.

After about two weeks on the job, Bill Jackson called me into the construction office one morning. He said, "Bob, we have now reached a total of about hundred employees on this project, including supervisors and laborers. I need some help in keeping track of how much time these guys work. Your dad tells me you know something about accounting and you are a good typist. How would you like to join me here in the office? It will be your responsibility to keep track of these guys by recording their time, checking them in each morning and out at night, and handing out their paychecks each Friday evening."

"Mr. Jackson, it certainly sounds good to me, and I will be glad to assist you in any way possible. When do I start?"

"Bob, you start right now, and I am giving you a raise to sixty cents per hour. I am also giving you a whistle to carry with you at all times. When you have finished your work in the office, you are to be out with the workers. If there is an emergency, blow three long blasts on the whistle, and I will come running. One other thing, some of these guys have a habit of going into the woods after lunch and taking a nap. It is your job to check the wooded area. If you see any of them out there, do not blow your whistle or say anything to them—just come and get me. I will take care of the situation and fire them right on the spot. I do not like goof-offs, and hereafter, Bob, you can call me Bill."

I told Bill I would follow his instructions and thanked him for the new job.

The following Sunday evening, Stanley and his brother Rolland came by and picked me up to go to the Epworth League church meeting together. As I recall, Rolland had the program that evening. As we sat talking and waiting for the meeting to start, two sisters, Charlotte and Betty, came in and sat down across the aisle from us. We greeted them, and they smiled. After the meeting, the two sisters joined a group of us that were going to the movies. During the remainder of the summer, Stan and I dated Betty and Charlotte rather frequently, either on a Friday or Saturday evening. We were not too serious, as Stan and I were also dating some other girls. In addition, Charlotte and Betty had told us they would be going to teachers' college in September, and we knew Stanley would be going back to college. Therefore, our relationship was on a good-friends basis, for now anyway.

I worked for Bill full-time during the summer months, and by late October the job was winding down, so I worked part-time until mid-December when the project was finished. Stanley, Rolland, and Kenneth, who were approximately two years older than me, went back for their second or third year of college. As I recall, Floyd stayed on with the construction company until the project was finished, then joined the military service. My dad remained assigned to the project as electrical engineer until the project was completed, and then he was transferred to the Division of Electric Engineering in Fort Leavenworth.

There were two most unusual and exciting events that took place during those summer months, which I will relate.

Some evenings, I would drive to Pilot Knob and visit my dad, as he was there alone at the construction site, and I was sure he got rather lonesome at times. One evening in mid-July, I had been out on a date with Charlotte, and she mentioned that her folks were leaving early the next morning on an out-of-town business trip. She was going with them and had to be home early, so I took her home about 9:00 p.m. and decided to go visit my dad at the project.

To get to the construction project, all vehicles had to go up a very steep, unpaved one-way road about a quarter of a mile long, which ended on a flat area where the reservoir was located. There was a high wire fence completely around the project, which consisted of a number of acres. At the main gate all vehicles would have to wait until the electric lock, which was controlled at the construction office, opened the gate. That evening when I arrived at the gate, I honked my horn four times, which was our signal. My dad opened the gate and I drove up to the construction office. He appeared to be pleased that I had come by to see him and had brought a container of hot coffee. My dad had some time to visit after he had finished checking all the pressure gauges, making his rounds, and writing his hourly report.

As we sat in the office with the door open, drinking our coffee, we heard another vehicle coming up the steep hill to the project. As it came up the road toward the gate, there were two fast honks. My dad said, "That is Bill Jackson and he sure must be in a hurry."

My dad opened the gate, Bill drove in, and the gate was immediately closed. Bill jumped out of his car and ran up to my dad and said, "Minor, is everything OK?" Then turning to me he added, "Hi, Bob."

We both acknowledged his presence, and my dad said, "Sure, Bill, everything is fine. Have some coffee with us."

Bill then told us that he had just received a call from the main out-of-town office, and someone advised them that the project was going to be knocked off that evening because we did not hire union employees. However, they believed it could be a hoax so maybe we should not be too worried.

Then Bill said, "However, if those guys do come around here, I am ready for them." Nothing more was said, but my dad looked at me and nodded his head. "Bob, let's have some more of that coffee."

We shared the remaining coffee with Bill and sat talking for fifteen or twenty minutes. I was getting ready to leave for home when we heard the roar of engines starting up the long incline. Bill jumped up, ran to his car, opened the trunk, and called for me to assist him.

He said, "Bob, do you know how to use this?" He handed me a 12-gauge semiautomatic shotgun with a box of 00 shells. "If you do, load it up."

I replied, "Yes, Bill, I had training in ROTC and have done a lot of rabbit hunting."

Bill said, "Good, maybe you will have to shoot some two-legged rabbits if they try to destroy this project."

Turning to my dad, he advised him to have his .45 ready with plenty of ammunition. Bill then turned to me again and said, "Bob, your dad is a deputy sheriff, so he is authorized to protect this property, but you are not. Raise your right hand."

I raised my right hand, and Bill said two or three sentences, something about defending the laws of the State of Kansas. I replied, "Yes, I will. I do."

Bill then said, "Bob, you are now a deputy sheriff and authorized to protect this property based on my instructions." He then gave us orders. "Minor and Bob, you are not to shoot unless I give the order. If I give the order, do not shoot to scare them. Shoot to stop them. Now get behind some protection."

By then, two large sedans came over the ridge and stopped just in front of the main gate. I recall that eight or ten men got out of the two cars, each carrying some object. I could not tell if they had guns, ball bats, or something else.

Bill then turned on the floodlights in that area, and we could see they were quite rough-looking men. Bill called to them, "What do you want? This is private property!"

One of them shouted, "We are from out of town and here to bust up this place. Now open the gate."

Then they ran toward the gate and started pounding on the locking device. Bill called out to them again.

"Men, this is private property. You have no right to be here. Move now! This is your last warning."

Bill then turned to us and said, "Minor and Bob, remember, do not shoot unless I give the order."

At that point, Bill raised his rifle and fired two shots over their heads. For a few seconds, which seemed like an hour, everything was very quiet; there was not a sound. Then suddenly, their leader called out, "Men, they have guns. We need to get the hell out of here," and they were in their cars and down the hill in short order.

Bill turned to us and said, "Thanks, fellows. You did great. I am sure glad we did not have to shoot because it would have been a mess with our firepower." I noticed Bill was carrying a rifle with a large clip and realized the significance of what he had just said. That was the last of any disruption to our work project. A number of times since then I have asked myself the question, *what would have happened if those men had used guns or broken through the gate? How many of them, or us, would have survived?*

It was late September, and most of the construction on the interior of the reservoir had been completed, but there was still considerable work to be done on the exterior, such as finishing the piping system, control valves, and landscaping.

As I made my rounds one afternoon, checking on the workers, I decided it was time to go down inside the large underground tank and see what was taking place. This tank would eventually hold millions of gallons of water and serve as one of the major sources of water for the city and county. The only entrance to this underground reservoir was through one of two large six-foot square holes in the roof of the reservoir. Eventually, two large steel doors would cover these entrances. There were two long ladders at least forty to forty-five feet long, which extended from the entrances to the floor of the reservoir.

These were the only entrances or exits to the interior and all workers had to use these ladders. At times, it became quite thrilling to travel up and down on these ladders. As I climbed down, there appeared to be a large cloud of smoke hanging in the air just above the heads of the workers. By the time I reached the bottom of the ladder, I had counted twelve workers, all very busy. They were putting the final touches to the walls by blasting them with liquid cement or something similar, using several machines operated with gasoline engines. The men were all concentrating on their work and did not pay much attention to me.

About halfway back up the ladder, I stopped, as the fumes were getting stronger. I said to myself, *this is not smoke. It is carbon monoxide gas.*

I rushed to the top of the ladder, jumped out onto the ground, and started blowing my whistle, three long blasts, and then three more long blasts. Suddenly Bill came running, and I told him the reservoir was filling up with carbon monoxide gas due to the operations of the gasoline engines. Bill looked down the long ladders into the tank, then turned to me and said, "Bob, get those men out of there immediately!"

I climbed about halfway down the ladder and started blowing my whistle. The men shouted, "What is the problem?"

I told them to shut the equipment off and get to the surface immediately. They first acted as if they were not going to follow my instructions, but then several of them began coughing, and they dropped their tools and cut off the equipment before starting up the ladders. Some of them appeared to be rather dazed and had trouble climbing the ladder. I reached the surface first, and Bill was waiting for us. The first man reached the surface and fresh air, and he began coughing, gasping for air, grabbed his throat, then fell to the ground and started flopping around. Even though I had responded to many accidents while driving an ambulance, I had never seen a person act like that before. The next man climbing out of the reservoir acted the same way, and shortly, there were six or more of the twelve men on the ground not able to breathe and flopping around like an animal that had been shot.

Bill knew immediately what had happened, and he shouted to us, "Grab them and hold them down on their backs. They have swallowed their tongues."

We followed Bill's instructions, but they were fighting like wild animals. It took several of us to hold each man down. Bill ran to the first man and fell to his knees. He pried the man's mouth open, then, reaching in with his forefinger, he pulled the man's tongue out of his throat so the man could breathe. He then jumped up and ran to the second man doing the same thing, then to the third man until he had taken care of all of them. Bill told the men to stay on the ground for a little while and get their wind, and he told me to run and get the big water jug and a number of cups from the office.

Soon they were able to sit up and I gave each of them a large cup of water, which I am sure soothed their throats. In a short time, their breathing returned to normal, and Bill told the men it would be quitting time in the next three hours or so, and they could go on home for the day. He told them their throats would be a little sore, so they should have a light dinner—soup or something like that—and be back to work the next day.

As Bill and I walked to the office, he said, "Bob, by being alert and recognizing that was carbon monoxide gas, you probably saved the lives of those twelve men. You are to be commended. I am going to relate this incident to your dad when I see him this evening. By the way, mark these guys down for a full day's pay. They have earned it."

I turned to him and said, "Thanks, Bill. I was only doing my job, but I am sure glad we got them out of the tank before they passed out. Otherwise, we would never have saved them. I will take care of marking them down for a full day's pay. But how did you know what was wrong and what to do?"

Bill looked at me and said, "I did not spend ten years in the Marines for nothing. Someday I will tell you more about it."

Bill never did relate any of his marine stories to me, but I did have a better understanding of why he was so self-confident the night the gang was going to break up the project and had been ready to stand his ground.

By mid-December, the Pilot Knob project was completed. Bill thanked me for my assistance, and I told him that I certainly enjoyed working for him and appreciated being given the job of timekeeper. He laughed, we shook hands, and I never did see Bill again. Later I was told he had been assigned to another project out west.

During the months of October and November, some of us were working part-time on the Pilot Knob project, so I had some free time. Stanley was home from college part of the time, and we saw each other quite frequently. One afternoon, he asked me if I would care to help him with a project he was working on.

A man by the name of Mr. Walter Biddle, a well-known attorney, was running for office—county attorney, as I recall. Stan and Mr. Biddle had been friends for several years, and Mr. Biddle had asked Stan if he would help him with his campaign assignments. I did not know Mr. Biddle, but my dad knew him quite well and told me he was a good, honest man, so I told Stan I would be glad to help Mr. Biddle with his campaign.

Stan took me up to Mr. Biddle's office and introduced me to him. I recall Mr. Biddle telling us he would not be able to pay much for our services, but would certainly appreciate our assistance. During the next few weeks, while I was not working, Stan and I did what we could to help Mr. Biddle with his campaign, including driving individuals to the polls for voting on Election Day.

As it worked out, Mr. Biddle won the election, and the following day, we all celebrated in his office. Before leaving his office that day, I remember Mr. Biddle telling Stan and me that if we ever needed his assistance, we should come see him. During the next few years, several times I needed an attorney for consultation purposes. I would contact Mr. Biddle, and he was always very accommodating and helped me with my small legal problems in a very satisfactory manner.

During the Christmas holidays and on into late January, I worked at a men's clothing store in town and learned a lot about men's clothing, such as how it was priced, how to identify good materials, and how to decorate the show windows.

In early February 1939, jobs were still difficult to find, as the economy was very slow and the country was still in a deep depression. My savings were insufficient to allow me to start college, and there was no such thing as a student loan. I heard the Kansas State Highway Department was hiring men for a construction project, so I sent an application for the timekeeper position, which was similar to my summer job with the construction company.

A few days later, I was notified to report the next Monday morning to the courthouse for transportation to the construction site. Upon arriving at the construction project, I was advised that the timekeeper slot had been filled, but they offered me a job at forty cents per hour with the rock mining crew, which was very strenuous work. I did not want to be a construction worker, but it would have to do for now. My work partner was an intelligent boy named Paul. He and I had attended school together.

After about two weeks on the job, our boss, Jim Burke, advised us that he was giving us a raise to sixty cents per hour, and we were now dynamite helpers. Both of us thought that was great and asked what we would be doing. Jim told us that I was assigned to carry sticks of dynamite in each of my two hip pockets, and Paul was to carry the dynamite caps in a wooden box. We were to follow Jim around and assist him in loading the dynamite and dynamite caps into holes in the rock that had been prepared by other workers. Paul and I were told to stay at least forty feet apart at all times to prevent an unscheduled explosion. I remember Paul saying, "Jim, isn't this rather dangerous work?"

Jim replied, "Paul, I have been doing this for a long time and I am still here, but that is why you will be getting sixty cents per hour."

Paul and I went to work as dynamite helpers, but we noticed many of the other workers on the project kept their distance. Paul and I had been on our new assignment for about two months, and we were very careful to follow the safety instructions. This job was much easier than the previous assignment, but we realized it carried a certain amount of danger. However, at that age, we believed nothing would ever happen to us.

One evening, my dad asked me how things were going at the construction site. I told him that everything was going fine. I mentioned that Paul and I had a different assignment. I proudly told my dad I was now a dynamite helper, earning sixty cents per hour.

He looked at me and, in a very stern voice, said, "Bob, do you realize what would happen to you if those ten sticks of dynamite you are carrying should explode? Nothing would be left of you but small pieces. You mentioned when you needed to resupply yourself you go to the dynamite shed and refill your pockets. As I recall, you said there was usually twelve or fifteen boxes of dynamite in the shed. Do you realize that much dynamite could level a city block? When I was a young man, I worked on the line crew for the Bell Telephone Company for several years before I became wire chief. When we were working out in the country, we used just half of a stick of dynamite to blow postholes through solid rock. Can you imagine what would happen to you and Paul, plus anyone else nearby, if those ten sticks of dynamite you are carrying were to explode? Bob, you are my only son, and I would like to keep you around for a while. When you go in Monday morning for work, I want you to resign immediately and leave the area. You never know when something will blow." After that, I resigned, and that was the end of my explosive dynamite career.

Six months later, a friend of mine told me there had been an explosion at the rock mining project approximately fifteen to twenty miles from Leavenworth the previous day. He said the explosion could be heard at his farm west of the city. Unfortunately, I never did learn what had happened, but I certainly hope no one was injured, especially Paul, my dynamite partner.

CHAPTER 7

The Beginning Of A New Career

A week or so later, I received notice from the Civil Service Commission that I was being considered for a temporary position, which was based on a civil service test that I had taken several months previously. In those days, I was taking all the civil service tests that were posted for available positions for which I was qualified. This notice was generated from one of the tests I had previously taken. The notice stated that if I was interested, I should report to Mr. L. W. Looker, US Treasury Department, at the new federal building in Kansas City, Missouri, for an interview at 9:00 a.m. on the following Tuesday.

Tuesday morning, I took the early bus to Kansas City, arrived at the federal building, and reported to Mr. Looker's office. The receptionist greeted me, and I gave her the letter from the Civil Service Commission. She escorted me to a waiting room and advised me that someone would be with me soon. I was the only one in the waiting room and wondered if I was the only one applying for the new position.

Shortly, the receptionist ushered in two more young men, and soon there were two young women, leaving five of us waiting for an interview. We exchanged small talk for a short time, and then a rather well-dressed young man arrived and introduced himself as George Staley, the office manager. He shook hands with each of us and took us into another room, where there were a number of office machines in operation. He demonstrated a check-writing machine.

Mr. Staley interviewed all five of us separately. One of the ladies and one of the men, along with myself, were selected for a ninety-day temporary appointment. He advised us to report to work the following Monday. I thanked Mr. Staley for the opportunity to work for the department. As I left the office, I was delighted to have the opportunity to be working in a large office with approximately seventy-five other employees and management personnel.

I arrived home that evening and told my family that the department had chosen me for one of the check-writing positions. They congratulated me, and my father laughed and said, "I am glad you will not be carrying dynamite around in your hip pockets like you were doing in your previous job."

On April 14, 1939, I reported for work at 8:00 a.m., along with the other two applicants who had been hired. We joined the present staff of four machine operators. Within a short time, I mastered the operation of the check-writing machine and established a new record of writing over 2,500 checks a day for ten straight days without an error. This record had not been broken in over twenty years using this check-writing machine model.

It was approximately thirty-five miles from my home in Leavenworth to Kansas City. A lady who worked in the office offered me a daily ride for a small fee. After approximately six months, I purchased a car of my own, which allowed me to drive to Kansas City daily for about two years. Five other individuals rode with me for the period of time I was with the US Treasury Department. One of the passengers who rode with me was a man by the name of James Voorhees, an attorney. I had met Mr. Voorhees several years previous when I worked at the drugstore in Leavenworth.

After a little over two years with the treasury department, I was given an opportunity to transfer to the regional office of the Department of Agriculture in Lincoln, Nebraska, as an accountant. I was hesitant to accept this position as I enjoyed working for the US Treasury Department, but the offer for advancement enticed me to accept and move on.

I had been dating Charlotte since we were both seniors in high school. She had been teaching at a country school in western Kansas for the last couple of years, so we had only been seeing each other every four to six weeks. I knew that if I took this position in Lincoln, it would certainly not bring us closer together, and I didn't want to lose her. I was confident that the two of us loved each other very much, and we had many common interests, so I believed that now was the time I should propose. I was scheduled to report for the new position in about ninety days, and I would be visiting Charlotte the coming weekend. I figured that this would be the right time to pop the question and, if she accepted, report to Lincoln with a new wife. I proposed to Charlotte, she said yes, and we were married in the early summer of 1941 at the Methodist church in Raymond, Kansas, and her father, who was a minister, officiated the wedding. In attendance was a large group of our friends and church members.

Following our one-week honeymoon at a lake resort, Charlotte and I drove to Lincoln, Nebraska, to rent a furnished apartment. I reported to work for my new position in the summer of 1941 and enrolled in night courses for finance and business law at the University of Nebraska. Life was great for us until December 7, 1941, when the Japanese attacked Pearl Harbor and the United States declared war on Japan. Within a short time, the Lincoln office closed, all the employees were transferred to other federal positions, and I was transferred to the National Housing Agency-War Housing Division in Wichita, Kansas, with a promotion.

Bob's first wife Charlotte - 1939

CHAPTER 8

Military and World War II Service

In September 1942, I was transferred to a position as an accountant and deputy housing manager of an 800-unit federal housing development with the National Housing Agency in Wichita, Kansas. The Department of National Housing provided housing for war workers in various cities throughout the United States, which were located near defense plants or airports where housing was otherwise not available. People moved from all areas of the Midwest to work in the war-related facilities, and they took their families with them. The men and women worked shifts around the clock, seven days a week, building aircraft that would soon be in combat in the war zones over the South Pacific and Europe.

After about six months working as an accountant and deputy housing manager, I was transferred to a position as Finance Officer of the Plane View Housing Project in Wichita, Kansas, which was a 4,400-unit housing development for defense workers. Plane View was a small community in the Wichita suburbs and federally operated with a population of approximately 20,000–25,000 residents. This promotion was a major change in responsibility and came with a favorable advancement in salary. The Plane View housing manager, in effect, was the mayor and I was the Finance Officer. Americans were united and were doing their duty to assist in the war effort. The US Air Force Procurement Office employed my wife, Charlotte, as secretary to the Commanding General during my assignment to Wichita.

While in Wichita, I took my written test to become a pilot in the Air Force. I had always admired one of my high school friends, Stanley Wade, who was a captain in the Air Force flying the B-25 over Germany. In July 1943, I received notice to report to the training station in Texas for my final physical examination and entrance into pilot training in the US Army Air Force. I was ecstatic, but my dreams were short lived. During an exercise session, we were playing baseball and a man up to bat just ahead of me threw his bat after hitting a home run. The bat hit me in the face, and I suffered a broken nose and facial wounds. Because the accident occurred prior to the swearing in ceremony, my flight training was discontinued. They said they would mail me an authorization to join another class for flight training after six months when my injuries had healed. I was extremely disappointed and returned home to Wichita. Naturally, Charlotte was very surprised to see me back in Wichita, as was my former supervisor. The office had not filled my previous position at Plane View and I was welcomed back to the position as Finance Officer. All 4,400 housing units became occupied and my staff and I were very busy at the office and frequently worked overtime. This did not bother me or other members of the office because we were all trying to do our small part to help win the war.

One evening in early October 1943, when I returned home quite late, Charlotte met me at the door and told me I had a letter postmarked from Uncle Sam and she did not want to guess what it contained. When I opened the letter, I found greetings from the draft board and instructions to report for induction into the armed service in early November 1943. The following day, I advised my supervisor, and a person from within the organization was found to fill my position which allowed me to start training him immediately. As mentioned previously, Charlotte had been working as a secretary to the commanding general, Mid-Western Procurement Division, US Army Air Force, so she decided to stay in Wichita during my military service.

In early November, I said good-bye to my supervisor and staff members. Charlotte took me to the train station, as I would be reporting to the draft board at Leavenworth. Following processing, I joined thirty to forty other men and left for induction at Fort Leavenworth. I ran into Frank McClure, a high school friend on the bus, and we were assigned to the same five-hundred-man company for processing.

Within the first week, Frank was processed and assigned to a communication company and shipped to the West Coast for training. I was assigned to a processing team at Fort Leavenworth. Within a week, all the other original men in this company were processed and shipped out. I began to wonder what had happened to my shipping orders. I continued to work on the processing team, testing hundreds of new recruits arriving daily.

At the end of the fourth week, I was notified to be at headquarters at 1300 hours with my personal baggage. When I arrived at headquarters, the captain handed me a large brown envelope and advised me that I was the only one on his shipping order and a truck would take me to the train station, where I would take the troop train headed north at 1400 hours.

After boarding the troop train, I found the transport captain, who had a small office in a private compartment, and handed him the sealed envelope. As he slowly opened the envelope, he told me to sit down across the desk from him. He read the papers to himself, then looked at them again and reread some of the information. Then he said, "You lucky dog—you have been assigned to the US Air Force Officer Candidate School for finance and will start training at the air base in Lincoln, Nebraska. Assuming you will not have any trouble taking this course, or passing the final exams, you'll be commissioned as a second lieutenant in the US Air Force and assigned to your duty station."

As instructed by the captain, when I arrived in Omaha, I transferred to another troop train headed west and in a couple of hours arrived in Lincoln, Nebraska. An air force bus met my train and delivered a number of young recruits including myself to the receiving station. It was in the afternoon, so the processing procedure was short. We marched to the mess hall for our evening meal after being assigned to a sixty-man barracks.

Prior to beginning specialized training, we were assigned a special field-training course. During the next few days, there was more processing and testing, then basic training started. It was very difficult for most of us because the temperature was zero or below most of the time, and the majority of the men, including me, had previously been working in an office and were not used to exertion in such a cold climate. Weeks rolled by, and we eventually adjusted to our new way of life.

One cold winter night around midnight, someone in the barracks called out, "Fire, fire, fire!" We jumped out of bed and discovered that our end of the barracks was filled with smoke and we were having difficulty breathing due to the heavy smoke and fumes. It was well below zero, and the men took time to slip on their shoes and overcoats. However, my friend Joe was in the upper bunk still asleep. Apparently, he had been inhaling more of the fumes and had been overcome by the smoke. I called to him but could not rouse him, so one of the other men and I pulled him out of bed, put his shoes and overcoat on him, and carried him into the cold air where finally he woke up.

Fortunately, the red exit light showed dimly in the smoke-filled room, and all sixty men quickly vacated the barracks. Someone had pulled the fire alarm switch, and the fire trucks, along with the ambulance, soon arrived. The firefighters found that the chimney of the large coal stove used to heat the barracks was blocked, causing the smoke and fumes to fill the barracks.

Five of us, myself included, had serious breathing problems, and the medics took us to the base hospital, where we were administered treatment and held overnight for observation. The following day, the physicians found that we had developed double pneumonia, and all five of us were running a very high fever. At that time, the medication "sulfa" was used to treat serious open wounds and was being prescribed on a trial basis for the treatment of internal infections. We were administered various doses of sulfa during our medical treatment of pneumonia.

After a few days, one of the men, who I will refer to as John, became very allergic to sulfa. Because John and I had become good friends during training, the hospital allowed me to visit him. I was very concerned because John developed large blisters over most of his body. The physician told John that the blisters were the result of his allergic reaction to the sulfa. A few days later, when I went to visit John again, his mother and his father were sitting at his bedside, as they had been called due to John's serious condition. The following day, the nurse told me that John had passed on during the night. This was a tragic blow to the four surviving friends as well as others.

My three friends and I remained hospitalized for a total of thirty days and then were referred to the medical review board for consultation. The medical review board determined that all four of us were given an honorable medical discharge effective immediately. We would be called back to duty in six to twelve months, and in the meantime returned to our hometowns. I now had two mandates, one to be recalled to the US Air Force for pilot training sometime in the next few months and a second to be recalled to the US Air Force Officers Candidate School for finance within the year. Within a couple of days we completed our discharge debriefing, were provided our discharge papers including our final pay, and were given a voucher to pay for our transportation back home. In addition, we were told to report to our local draft boards and to remain in contact with them.

I returned to my barracks and packed my bags, told my buddies good-bye, and caught the next train back to Leavenworth, which was my parents' home and my point of draft registration. It took four or five hours to make the rail trip because it was necessary to transfer in Omaha. During the trip, I wondered, *what my parents would say when I arrived home and whether Charlotte would be surprised.* I knew my previous position was probably filled by now, and I wondered what my future would be. When I was being discharged in Lincoln, the debriefing officer told me that my agency was required to offer me a position similar to my old position with similar pay. I decided not to worry about the job, figuring I would cross that bridge later. However, I did want to continue doing some meaningful work for the war effort until I was called back into the military service.

When I arrived at the train station in Leavenworth, I called my parents. As it was about 7:00 p.m., they had just finished supper. Naturally, they were surprised to hear that I was in Leavenworth and would be coming to their house in a little while. I caught a taxi, and when I arrived home, even though it was quite cold, my mother and my father were waiting for me on the front porch. I was greeted by each with a big hug. As we entered the house, my mother headed for the kitchen to fix me some dinner.

After dinner I had a good visit with my parents, and then called Charlotte in Wichita to give her the news. She could hardly believe that I was out of the military service, for now anyway, and would soon be returning to Wichita. I explained to Charlotte that I had to check in with my draft board before returning to Wichita. I advised her that it might be difficult to obtain a train ticket, but I should be home in a couple of days. She said, "Bob, I am ecstatic. Call me every evening and give me the news. I will meet you at the train station when I know your schedule."

When I hung up the phone, my mother said, "Bob, the guest room is all ready for you. As it is quite late, I know you are ready to hit the sack."

As I turned in, I said to myself, *gee, it sure feels good to be in a normal bed again.*

As the next day was Sunday, I tried calling some of my close friends, but found they were either in the service or working in other cities, so I spent the day visiting with my mother and dad. Monday morning, I was up early and visited the draft board. I explained the situation to the clerk and signed some papers, letting them know where I could be reached, when, and if necessary. They advised me that I would probably be called back into the service within the next three to four months. My next stop was the train depot to make my reservation. I would be arriving in Wichita at 7:00 p.m., when Charlotte would be off work and could pick me up.

The following morning, I told my parents good-bye for now, and as usual, the tears flowed. At that time, the future was so uncertain that one never knew when they would meet again. My dad took me to the train station and then I was on my way to Wichita.

Charlotte was at the station waiting impatiently as the train drew near. She later said it was difficult to find me at first, as so many service personnel were getting off the train, and I was still in uniform. We greeted each other with a big hug and a kiss, and stopped on the way home for a cocktail and dinner to celebrate my homecoming. We sat in a small booth for a couple of hours to bring each other up to date on events that had taken place during the last few months, then decided it was time to leave and head for home. We left the restaurant hand in hand and Charlotte told me, "I can't believe you are here with me in Wichita. It seems like a beautiful dream."

In order to save money during my military service, Charlotte had moved into a small apartment, which she had exquisitely decorated;

and it was very adequate for a single person, but was really small for a couple. However, we did not know when I would be called back into the US Air Force, so we decided it would be more economical to remain at this location for the present time, as life was so uncertain during the war years. Charlotte had arranged to take a couple of days' leave, and I was still recovering from my double pneumonia problem, but I wanted to go back to work as soon as possible.

CHAPTER 9

A New Assignment: Traveling Auditor

A few days later, I called my former boss in Wichita and made an appointment to discuss my employment status. During our meeting the following day, I was advised that the officials were pleased with the individual who had replaced me as Finance Director. The regional office in Kansas City was contacted, and I was given travel orders to report to the regional director in Kansas City for consultation. During this consultation, I was asked to take an assignment as Management Auditor for a few months, traveling to new defense housing projects in Kansas, Missouri, and Nebraska to set up the finances and other records, as well as organizing the new offices. Consequently, I was home only approximately every other weekend, but I enjoyed the travel and my assignment.

After two months on this assignment, I received an unexpected call from the regional director asking me to take a special assignment in Wendover, Utah, 125 miles west of Salt Lake City, on the Utah-Nevada border. As this was a new housing development, consisting of approximately nine hundred permanent residences and a small seventy-five-room hotel for air force officers and noncommissioned officers, I was to serve as Deputy Housing Manager and Finance Officer of this development.

According to the offer, this was a temporary assignment of ninety days. After the development had been well established, I would be transferred to the Kansas City regional office as Budget Director. After discussing this subject with Charlotte, I called the regional director back and accepted the assignment. I was advised that I would be getting travel and transfer orders soon, and I was to arrange my current workload in order to report for duty in Wendover in three weeks.

Since I had authorization to drive, this would be a great opportunity for Charlotte and me to see the country between Kansas and Western Utah. Charlotte gave her supervisor with the Air Force Procurement

Division two weeks' notice of her departure, and I had two weeks to wind up my present assignments and sufficient time to pack and drive from Wichita to Wendover.

During the second week, I had a most unusual experience. I was driving my vehicle into town to obtain additional gasoline coupons for the trip west, as gasoline was rationed during the war years. I noticed there was a flooding on the main road going into the city, but it did not appear to be too serious. I proceeded on to the rationing board, obtained additional gasoline coupons for the trip west, and then returned to my car to drive back home.

On the way back, I found the area completely flooded with more than a foot of water on the road. I decided it would be wise not to drive through the water, not knowing how deep it was. Returning to a downtown area on high ground, I parked my car in a parking lot and decided to walk the two or so miles home. As I approached the flooded area again, this time on foot, there was a very large aircraft truck with a high flatbed taking on passengers to ride through approximately two city blocks of high water. I climbed on the truck with about twenty other men and women. The truck started through the water, which was about four feet deep. Soon, the water was nearly up to the flatbed of the truck, which was now about five feet above the roadway.

Without warning, the truck engine stopped, and there the truck sat in at least five feet of swiftly running water. Suddenly, a police boat came alongside, and the officer on the boat told us he could not help as he had orders to rescue a number of children in an emergency up the street. He did advise us that a dam had just broken upstream, and within the next half hour, an additional three to five feet of water was expected in the area.

As the police boat pulled away from the truck, we looked for someone else who could offer assistance, but there was none available. Shortly, the truck driver said, "Sorry, friends, but it looks like the only thing we can do is swim."

Without a word, everyone tucked their billfolds or small purses within their clothing to keep them safe. I noticed a young woman, probably in her mid-twenties, who had a small handbag with a long strap. She slipped the strap over her head and under one arm, and then tightened the strap to keep it safe. After securing our valuables, all members of the group slid off the truck bed into the cold, muddy water. Fortunately, everyone could swim sufficiently to reach the side of the road where the sidewalk was higher than the roadway, and the water was only about three to four feet deep. It was a different story when we reached the next cross street, which had become a small river with very swift running water, possibly six or seven feet deep. All of us stood in shock, not knowing what to do next.

Soon, another small police boat pulled up to a telephone pole near us at the edge of the cross street. The police officer tied a long rope tightly around the pole about two feet above the water, then maneuvered the boat through the swiftly flowing water to the other side of the street and tied the other end of the rope tightly to another telephone pole. When he was finished, he called to our group, "If you go hand over hand across the rope, there is higher ground up the street a short distance. That is the best I can do for you now. Good luck."

As the police boat moved on up the flooded street, we all stood there looking at each other. Suddenly the truck driver said, "Well, friends, I got you into this mess. I will go first. If the rope breaks and I go downstream, tell Boeing Aircraft what happened to old Joe."

Joe grabbed the rope and made it, hand over hand, through the water to the other side of the street and higher ground. He then called out, "The water is very deep and swift, so hold on tight, work fast, and you will make it."

All of us lined up to take our turn. Being the last in line, I watched as each group member reached the other side to higher ground. They did not wait for the others but went their own way.

The young woman with long blonde hair was just ahead of me. As each took their turn, with several on the rope at a time, they were making their way through the high, fast-moving water to safety. Before long, it became the young lady's turn to cross the rope. Suddenly, she turned to me and, with tears running down her face, said, "Mister, my name is Jeannie. I had surgery recently, and I do not want to die, but I do not have the strength to make the crossing."

I told her my name, that the water was rising, and that this was the only way to save ourselves, as there was no one around to help otherwise, so I would assist if possible. After looking at the rope again, Jeannie turned to me, drying her eyes with her sleeve, and said, "Let's go."

We grabbed the rope and started across. By then, all the others had crossed to the other side of the street and were walking through shallow water to higher ground. Jeannie turned to me and called out, "Bob, they did not wait for us, and I am getting tired."

I was getting tired as well, but I told Jeannie to keep going and hold on to the rope. We had nearly reached the pole where the rope was tied, and with only four or five feet to go, I could see her hands slipping from the rope.

Suddenly, Jeannie turned, calling out again, "Bob, I can't make it! Tell my mother I tried, and I love her."

With those last few words, Jeannie's hands slipped off the rope, and she fell into the cold water. I was not a great swimmer, but I had told Jeannie I would assist her if possible, so I let go of the rope and fell into the water several feet behind her. I tried swimming faster, but to no avail.

By this time, we were at least a city block farther downstream, and Jeannie had disappeared below the surface of the water. Suddenly, either I was swimming faster or she was slowing down, because I could see a large part of Jeannie's hair coming to the surface of the water. Reaching out as far as possible, I grabbed a section of her hair and pulled her head above the water. We were moving very quickly, but at the same time, I saw a large metal signpost just ahead of us. As we reached the metal post, I grabbed it with my left arm, with my right hand holding tight to Jeannie's hair. Wrapping my body around the post, I was able to get a much better hold of Jeannie's clothing, and I slowly dragged her and myself out of the water.

Jeannie was semiconscious, coughing and spitting out a lot of water. We were out of the water now, but the ground was very wet, so I carried her to a nearby park bench. Laying her on the bench on her stomach with her head to the side, I called out for help and started artificial respiration that I had learned years before when I was a Boy Scout.

This was an unusual method of administering CPR, as under normal treatment conditions, a person sits astride the patient and pushes with their hands pressing the patient's rib cage, pushing the water out of their lungs. However, this was the only method I could use because she was on a park bench. My calls for help went unanswered, but Jeannie was responding to my efforts. She was spitting up a lot of water, but she opened her eyes and did not say anything. I called out again for help; there appeared to be no one around, but I kept pumping her lungs, and she continued expelling water. Now Jeannie had opened her eyes wider and seemed to know what was taking place.

Suddenly, a voice said, "What is the problem? Can I help?"

I turned, still administering CPR, and there was a lady, possibly in her mid-thirties. I briefly explained what had happened.

The lady said, "My name is Judy. I am a nurse working at a nearby hospital. I was on my way home and heard you calling for assistance. You look like you're exhausted. Please let me see what I can do to help this young lady."

About that time, Jeannie opened her eyes again and tried to sit up. Judy advised her to lie there for a little while longer. We asked Jeannie her name and where she lived. She pointed to her purse, which was still strapped to her shoulder, and inside, we found her driver's license, which indicated her name and address. Fortunately, she lived just a couple of blocks up the street.

Jeannie was still spitting out water, but we eased her off the park bench and put her arms around our necks and half walked, half carried her home. We rang the bell, and her mother answered the door. She was shocked to see her daughter in such dreadful condition. We explained to Jeannie's mother what had happened and suggested that Jeannie get medical attention immediately.

By this time, Jeannie was able to assist us in getting her into her mother's car, but she was very weak. Judy told me they would be able to handle the situation and I did not need to go to the hospital with them. Thanking me for rescuing Jeannie, they took me to my home, which was on the way to the hospital. As I got out of the car, they said they would give me a call later.

When I arrived home, I found that Charlotte was still at her office, so I showered, changed into dry clothes, and rested the rest of the afternoon. That evening, Judy called me and mentioned that Jeannie's mother was still at the hospital, but Jeannie was doing quite well and was scheduled to go home the following day. A couple of days later, I called Jeannie to see how she was doing, and she invited Charlotte and me to come by. As we were leaving for the west in a couple of days, we went by to see Jeannie and her mother that evening. We found Jeannie to be very cheerful and greatly improved. She and her mother thanked me again for saving Jeannie from the floodwaters.

After Charlotte and I arrived in Wendover, I received several letters from Jeannie thanking me again and telling me about her life in Wichita. She had now completed her nursing training and had an offer from the US Air Force to become a nurse with a commission, which she had decided to accept. A couple months later, I had one last letter from her relating to her assignment with the US Air Force. She was now on active duty. I never heard from Jeannie after that. I hope that she had a very active and successful career in the service.

CHAPTER 10

Assignment: Wendover, Utah

A few days later, Charlotte and I packed our car and started for Salt Lake City and Wendover, Utah.

After two days of driving, we reached Salt Lake City and stayed at a nice motel. We got up early the following morning and headed west on Highway 50 for Wendover. About thirty miles west of Salt Lake City, we started crossing the salt flats, which at that time was a rather desolate trip as all we could see on each side of the road was just salt, salt, salt.

Upon arriving in Wendover, we found it was a small town of approximately two hundred civilian residents, but the air base was very large, and we did not have any difficulty locating the National Housing Office where I would be working. The office was closed as it was Sunday morning but my new supervisor, the housing manager John Nelson, was waiting for us. He was very happy to see us, and we sat and talked for a little while, and then he said, "Bob and Charlotte, it is past lunchtime, let's go up to the hotel restaurant and have a quick lunch and then I will show you to your new residence."

After lunch at the State Line Hotel, we drove around the project and then went to our new residence. It was a furnished one-bedroom unit with one bathroom, a living room, a dining area, and a kitchen. John helped us unload the car and suggested that we go back to the office to discuss the operations. Charlotte stayed at our new home to unpack some of our personal belongings.

John and I proceeded to the office, driving throughout the housing project, which was approximately a 40-acre development. After John and I completed our short tour, we entered the office building. John had a large office, and my office was next to his. There was plenty of space for our staff, a good-sized meeting room, and other offices, which were smaller. We went back to his office, where he gave me a briefing of the project. When we were discussing the development, he told me that we had the office staff, which consisted of about fifteen employees, and had filled every position except for three. Therefore, it would be my responsibility beginning Monday, to reorganize the office and to fill any vacant positions. After talking for an hour, John suggested that he and his wife pick us up from our residence at about 6:00 p.m. to have dinner at the State Line Hotel to discuss things further.

During dinner, John explained more about the project. Highway 50 split the development into two sections, with a large portion south of the highway and about one-third above the highway, behind the office. We could see out the window that we were considerably higher than the air base, due to the mountainous area behind us. This allowed a clear view of the base and some of the runways. The base was very large and highly classified and with the desolate area on the western edge of the salt flats, it was very secluded. He went on to explain that Wendover was divided between Utah and Nevada. Wendover, Utah, had a private residential area, along with a small shopping area. Our office was located next to the business area, and contained management, accounting, engineering, leasing, maintenance, and personnel sections all in one building. I would be serving as John's deputy for all sections but would be directly responsible for the accounting section. Wendover, Nevada, had the State Line Hotel, where we had lunch earlier in the day, and also had six casinos where gambling was permitted.

He finished up by telling us that the current commander of the 509th Composite Group was Colonel Paul Tibbets. He also said he would set up an appointment for me next week, so I could meet Colonel Tibbets. John explained that the colonel was a strict commander, but a really nice fellow. There was another commander, but his name was unreleased for the time being.

John said he figured we must be tired, so we would discuss the project further the next day. That was when he also planned to introduce me to the people I would be working alongside and also start the process of reorganizing the staff. John had just arrived at the project a couple months prior and he had been recruiting new staff for the operation of the project. He said he also planned to take Charlotte and me down to the base during the first part of the following week and introduce us to the chief administrative officer, so we could obtain passes that would give us access to the officers' dining room, and another pass for our car to enter through the gates of the base.

The following day, John told me that I would not only be Budget and Finance Officer for the project, but also Deputy Housing Manager. He introduced me to our staff, which consisted of approximately fifteen employees, with a few more still to come on board. Most of the staff were wives of military personnel who had recently arrived at the post. John told me that we would be attending a luncheon briefing on the base in about a week, which would be conducted by the commanding officer of the base.

After introductions were made, he then took the opportunity to explain more items concerning the development. The project consisted of approximately 800 residences. The construction of the project was still under way, so it would be several months before all residences were finished and turned over to us. However, they had started renting the homes to qualified personnel, so the project was nearly full of occupants. There were a few larger two-bedroom units assigned only to special guests. These were standard housing for military and civilian usage. The project also included approximately seventy-five housing trailers, each of which would accommodate families of two or three individuals, plus a dormitory hotel of approximately fifty rooms. In addition, I understand there was a large number of military living on the base.

When we were in Wichita during my time in the service, Charlotte was secretary to the general, who was commanding officer of the Midwestern Procurement Division for the US Air Force. Therefore, during the first week in Wendover, Charlotte filed her application with the personnel office of the air base. After her application checked out, she was immediately employed as secretary to the general at the air base.

The following week was a luncheon that Charlotte and I were invited to attend, and John and his wife were also invited, and we all accepted. When we arrived we were introduced to the officers conducting the briefing, as well as to the other attendants that included Colonel Paul Tibbets. The commanding general advised those attending that Wendover was a highly classified air base specifically for training the 509th Composite Group commanded by Colonel Tibbets, and the material discussed at this luncheon was classified. Each of us had been cleared to attend the officers' club, the theater, and some other activities of the post. We would be advised, in writing, of the areas that we were allowed to attend and those that were restricted. The commanding general went on to say that the base was mainly designed and built for training purposes of the B-26 and B-29 airplanes.

I did not know until twenty-five years later that this was a base connected to the super-secret Manhattan Project. Looking back, I know that my wife was acquainted with a great deal of this classified information coming into the general's office regarding the Manhattan Project. However, at that time, and for the remainder of her life, she never did discuss this subject with me. I never had any idea that we were doing anything regarding the Manhattan Project, and I am proud of her for being able to keep this subject a secret.

As we all know now, the war officially ended on September 2, 1945, as an aftermath of dropping the A-bombs. Colonel Tibbets, who we had known quite well during the later years of the war, dropped the first A-bomb on the city of Hiroshima. During the final stages of the war, the United States dropped an A-bomb on Nagasaki as well, which ended the war with Japan by their announced surrender on August 15, 1945.

Several interesting events took place while we were in Wendover. One had to do with the fact that Wendover was 126 miles west of Salt Lake City.

About every other month, Charlotte and I would go to Salt Lake City for two or three days, usually including a weekend, to conduct business or pick up equipment needed at our project. It was always an exciting event to spend a little time in the city, eating out and attending a movie or two, or other events, as Wendover was quite a desolate area.

One time in Wendover, I became good friends with one of the pilots, who was a captain. One evening during a social event he said, "Bob, as you know, Sir Malcolm Campbell used to race his racing vehicles on the salt flats in the 1930s. I flew over that area recently and could still see the markers on the flat salt beds where he used to race, and as I recall, he could get up to over two hundred miles per hour on his Bluebird. I think it would be interesting if you and I took our cars out to that location some Sunday soon and see how we can match his speed."

I said, "Well, I agree, and if you don't have anything special going on this coming weekend, let's do it. Let's bring our wives along; otherwise, they may not believe what we tell them."

He thought that was a great idea, so the following weekend, we took a couple extra cans of gasoline, and the four of us drove our vehicles out to the spot, which was not too great a distance from Wendover. He drove his car first after he put some gasoline in his tank, mixing a little high-test aviation fuel with his. The strip was approximately ten miles long, so we drew straws to see who would race first, and he won. He had a Buick Straight-8, as I recall. He got in his vehicle, and I had a stopwatch. He started his engine, and when his wife said, "Go!" he sped off. He said he eased it up to about 100 mph for the first few miles and then floored it for the remaining five or so. He said his top speed was 126 miles per hour. He ran it twice, and on the second run, he made 128 miles per hour.

When he came back, he said, "Bob, that is almost like flying."

Then it was my turn. On the first run, with my Ford Mercury, I hit 130 miles per hour. On the second run, I hit 136. We decided that was enough for the day, as our tires were certainly not built for that kind of speed.

A couple weeks later, he called me one evening, and we talked for a little while. He then said, "Hey, Bob, I just wanted to pass along to you that I was very lucky the day we raced our vehicles on the salt flats."

He told me a few days earlier they had driven into Salt Lake City. They had been driving sixty to sixty-five miles an hour, and one of his rear tires blew. He said that if that tire had blown a couple Sundays before, he did not know where he would be today. I think both of us were foolish for testing our vehicles that did not have high-grade tires for racing, but I guess young men have pulled foolish stunts since the beginning of time.

Another event happened one day when I was coming back from lunch. As I drove into the parking lot near our office building, I heard a woman screaming. I drove down the street a short distance and saw her standing in the roadway behind the building calling for help. I quickly drove down to see if I could assist her. She said her house was on fire and that her baby was in the bedroom. I cautiously rushed into the house and saw where the smoke and fire had originated at the foot of the baby's bed; The baby was screaming!

It seemed that an electric fan had shorted out and set the curtains, as well as some boxes, on fire near the foot of the bed. I grabbed a towel, rushed to the plug in the wall, wrapped the towel around the hot wire, and jerked the wire out of the outlet. The flames died down just as they were beginning to ignite the bed.

Rushing to the head of the bed I pulled it nearer the front door, then I slipped the baby out from between the covers and noticed some of her toes on one foot were burned. I rushed her out to the front room where the mother was waiting with a blanket, and she wrapped the baby in the blanket. We then rushed outside, and I saw the fire alarm button at the end of the building. I pushed it, and the base fire department arrived shortly.

The baby's mother was Jean Cox, a resident of our project. Jean and a neighbor of hers took the baby to the base hospital, where the small burn on the baby's foot was treated. Jean was most grateful for me rescuing her baby, whose name was Joan.

A few nights later, as we finished dinner, Charlotte and I heard a knock at the front door. It was Jean and her husband, who was a pilot and had just returned from a mission. We invited them in, and they both thanked me very graciously for saving the baby, who was their only child. The apartment only had smoke damage, which could easily be repaired.

After that, Charlotte and I saw them frequently on the base. One evening, the couple came by with baby Joan. They wanted to say their thanks again and to say good-bye, as they would be leaving the base for another post. They were good friends, and we wished them well. A few weeks later, I did receive a short letter from them saying they arrived at their new base, were settling in, and they wanted to thank me again for the wonderful gift I had given them by saving their little baby. The baby's foot healed up quickly, and she was doing quite well.

Another incident that occurred, which was rather exciting, happened one afternoon after I had been home for lunch. I drove into the office parking lot, where I usually parked, and as I was getting out of the car, I heard gunshots fired on the base. They grew louder as I heard engines roaring, coming up the strip from the base to the main highway. I also heard sirens blaring. I stood by the car as the vehicles approached.

There were two armored vehicles; the first vehicle was firing at the second vehicle with what appeared to be automatic weapons. As they came closer, I decided it was time for me to take cover. All I had time to do was kneel down behind the front wheel on the opposite side of my car to shelter myself from the gunfire. The vehicles arrived at the intersection of the highway and turned west toward the mountains. The automatic fire from the first vehicle sprayed the parking lot.

By this time, I had laid down near the front wheel that would give me the best protection. As the weapon fire sprayed the parking lot one of the bullets hit my rear tire and it blew instantly. Another bullet hit the pavement and ricocheted hitting my upper pants leg and ripped the cloth about six to eight inches, but it did not penetrate the leg itself. I felt very lucky that the bullet did not hit me in a more vital location.

About that time, the second vehicle opened fire on the first vehicle and they continued down the highway firing at each other. Not knowing why the two vehicles were shooting at each other, I got up and dusted myself off, then reported the incident to the marshal's office. I called I called the local garage and they came and fitted my vehicle with a new tire, which took care of at least one problem.

About an hour later, we received the report that the first vehicle contained three escaped prisoners from the military brig, who had stolen a car near the main gate. They opened fire and shot one or more MPs at the gate. The other MPs had taken off after the escapees, but they did not open fire along the main road as they were afraid they would hit some bystanders. However, as the vehicles headed west, they turned off onto a mountain road. After two tires were shot out on the MP vehicle, they had to give up the chase. Within an hour, spotter planes from the base located the escapees several miles into the mountains with their vehicle broken down. Later that day, the escapees were apprehended and returned to base. I did not learn how seriously the MPs at the front gate were injured, or the penalties the escapees received after capture; but there is no doubt the penalties were severe.

One other incident was a very sad one. I had been called to the office of the Union Pacific Railroad about a business problem. I knew the manager of the freight section very well, and after our meeting concluded, he said, "Bob, I know you hear certain brief information concerning crashes involving base personnel from time to time, which are currently classified. I want to briefly show you something."

He led me out of his office and to the main warehouse for outgoing shipments. As we entered, he said, "I want you to see what has happened in the last ten days at the base."

He opened the second door and we entered a large room with flag-draped coffins.

"Last week was a bad week," he said, "because these are some of the men we lost during air plane crashes."

I was amazed at the number of flag-draped coffins. As they were in rows of ten, I quickly counted off sixty coffins and there were still more rows to come.

The manager said, "Yes, this was a very bad week for this base. There will be an eastbound special train coming in late tonight to pick up most of these poor chaps."

I stood there thinking of the wives, and mothers and fathers, who had received notice that their loved one would be coming home, but not in the condition for which they had prayed or hoped. We should not forget the number of men and women who lost their lives in training accidents before they were ever able to go into combat. I paused as I began to weep, and then said a prayer for these men and their families, coming to attention and giving them my farewell salute. The manager and I left the large warehouse without saying a word.

After arriving back in my office, I realized that this railroad warehouse was only one of many warehouses throughout the nation that held bodies of men and women who had been killed in accidents.

We must be grateful for all men and women who served our nation, regardless of how they gave their lives during wartime. They should be remembered for giving their lives so we could live in peace, for the time being anyway.

My assignment in Wendover was only supposed to be ninety days, but was extended indefinitely; my main headquarters was transferred to San Francisco. However, my duty station remained in Wendover, Utah, for approximately a year and a half and is where my wife and I resided for longer than anticipated. After Japan surrendered, John Jacobs called to tell me that he knew I was disappointed when I was not transferred back to the Kansas City office after my first assignment of 90 days in Wendover. He wanted me to know that he had transferred from National Housing Office to a new agency known as War Assets Administration as the Personnel Director. If I was still interested in returning to Kansas City, he had a position available for me as Deputy Budget Officer for the new agency. He said I should let him know as soon as possible if I wanted to transfer back into this position, which would come with an increase in pay grade.

After discussing the subject with Charlotte, we decided we would like to return to the Kansas City area, so I told John that I was definitely interested and to let me know at an early date when I was needed in Kansas City, so I could give my boss and the San Francisco office a thirty-day notice on my proposed transfer. Within a week, I received notice from John that he was processing the papers and would let me know of the plans for my transfer soon. I sincerely thanked John for remembering that I was interested in a position in the Kansas area.

The following week, my boss received an unexpected call from the San Francisco office saying that he and I should come into the office for a consultation, as most of their projects would be downsizing due to the end of the war. During the meeting, it was revealed that the department did not intend to close down all the housing projects, but some would be downsized. It was announced that Wendover would be downsized and our office staff would be reduced accordingly.

By early October, we had received information regarding our program reduction, and my transfer orders to Kansas City were authorized, with my departure planned for late November. Soon, we were notified that our departure date had been set for November 25, 1945. When the day came, after saying good-bye to all the friends we had made over the years, both military and civilian, we departed Wendover for the next assignment in Kansas City. This departure ended four years of military and war-related civilian service for Charlotte and me.

CHAPTER 11

Government Assignments

WAR ASSETS KANSAS CITY, MISSOURI

As we drove toward Kansas City, Missouri, we stopped in several places along the way to visit friends, some of whom we had not seen for several years. We spent a few days with Charlotte's parents in Western Kansas, and then visited my parents in Leavenworth, Kansas. We called and made reservations at a motel in the suburbs of Kansas City, Kansas; this would be our home until more suitable quarters were located.

After arriving and checking into our motel, we decided to relax for a few days. I called John, the Personnel Director of War Assets, and we arranged to meet after three or four days to discuss my transfer to the new agency. When we did meet, we decided that the start date of my new job with War Assets would be on the first of the following month. This allowed us two weeks to find a new apartment and get settled. He said I would be placed on leave with pay during this vacation period, which I thought was a great idea, as I had not taken any vacation leave for several years during the war.

During this two-week leave, Charlotte and I moved into our new apartment, which was in Kansas City, Kansas. My workstation would be in Kansas City, Missouri, so I would have about a four or five-mile drive to work every morning.

After meeting with John, I had several meetings with other officials, and it was determined that my best assignment would be as Deputy Budget Officer. I would be assigned to reimbursements to military operations for the maintenance of declared surplus property until the property was sold. This reimbursement by War Assets to the military operations amounted to millions of dollars, as the military would be required to maintain the declared surplus property for several months until it could be sold. This was a very interesting assignment dealing with high-ranking military and civilian officials, but it did require considerable travel within our region, which included Missouri, Kansas, Oklahoma, and Nebraska. Often, I would be in a travel status for two to three weeks at a time.

This assignment lasted five years. In 1948, Charlotte and I were blessed with a daughter, who we named Betsey. By the time this position with War Assets ended, Betsey was a year and a half old.

In the spring of 1950, a number of us at War Assets received our reduction-in-force notice that our jobs were being terminated as most of the property, which had been declared surplus by the military and other civilian agencies, had been disposed of or sold.

US PUBLIC HEALTH SERVICE
BALTIMORE, MARYLAND

After searching the recruitment listings thoroughly, I was unable to find any suitable transfers in Kansas City, but I did find some in Washington DC, so I went to Washington to see what was available. After ten days of visiting various offices and taking certain tests, I found three available positions and accepted a position with the US Public Health Service in Baltimore, Maryland, as Budget and Finance Officer with a promotion. This position was still in the government service and was considered a transfer from one agency to another.

I returned home, and the following week, Charlotte and I packed our car and drove to Washington. I enjoyed this tour of duty, as I was stationed at the US Marine Hospital, a 500-bed teaching hospital. My supervisor was a Mr. Paul Burke, and the director of the hospital was Dr. D. W. Patrick, Medical Officer in Charge. Dr. Patrick had a unique way of thinking concerning training, so we were required to spend a certain amount of time in each of the different services, such as surgery, nursing, registration, purchasing, and maintenance. It was Dr. Patrick's philosophy that at our level of responsibility, we should all be familiar with all departments of the hospital. We came to know many positions in the medical field with this philosophy.

I had been working on a request from headquarters in Washington to develop a new form of federal budgeting. Instead of budgeting by item such as personnel, travel, and so on down the line, I was to develop a budget by programs. This type of budgeting, called program budgeting, permitted a much quicker review of a program, and a hospital could have many programs in operation at one time. If it were desirable to increase the operations of a hospital, or any department, a program would be established that would include personnel, travel, and all the other expenses depending on the type of program. After a year of preparing a test operation for budgeting and spending purposes, in addition to my regular duties, I had it well lined up, and our agency was considering submitting such a budget to Congress for approval.

One day, Dr. Patrick received a request from the budget director in Washington for me to present my new program at a budget officers meeting, which was being held in Washington and would consist of about forty or fifty budget officers from various agencies.

After discussing this program with Dr. Patrick, I created a program budget for presentation and attended a two-day meeting in Washington to present it. After presenting my program to the budget officers, two men from one of the agencies approached me at lunchtime and asked me if I would join them. I agreed, and we had lunch in the department cafeteria. When we had finished eating, they asked me if I would be interested in accepting a position with the Department of State, and I said I would be, under certain conditions.

They gave me a number of documents to read about their employment, and, to make a long story short, after discussing the subject thoroughly with my wife and attending several seminars, we accepted an appointment for overseas duty. I was assigned to the American Embassy in Baghdad, Iraq, as Budget Management Officer at a comparable grade and a higher salary than my Baltimore assignment. This assignment was not only as a Budget Management Officer for the American Embassy, but also for the Joint Administrative Services. This required providing financial services to eight other US agencies who drew most of their administrative services from the American Embassy staff.

After a month of orientations in Washington DC, about living and working in the Middle East, I received travel orders for myself, my wife, and our four-year-old daughter, Betsey. We knew we would be going to a hardship post, which would include some difficult duties at the embassy, as well as different health conditions. There were a certain number of risks involved in accepting this post, but we believed we were prepared for the future.

CHAPTER 12

Arriving In Baghdad, Iraq

We left for Baghdad, Iraq, in October of 1952, traveling via London, England; Paris, France; Rome, Italy; and Beirut, Lebanon, and arriving in Baghdad around noon on a Thursday.

We were greeted at the airport by Tom Linthicum, administrative officer, and his wife, Jenny, along with a couple of other embassy officers and their wives, and then taken to our quarters at the Zia Hotel. The hotel was located on Rasheed Street in the downtown area, and it backed up to the Tigris River with a beautiful lawn and garden overlooking the river. It was a three-story building, with approximately fifty or sixty rooms, and was surrounded by about a ten-foot heavy metal fence, with a heavy gate across the driveway at the front. Our room was quite large, overlooking the lawn in front of the hotel, and had a separate, smaller room attached with one bed, giving Betsey her own bedroom. There were also eight other embassy officers or employees who were waiting for housing assignments, as quality housing was most difficult to locate. Tom and Jenny took us to lunch, and afterward, they invited us to dinner at their house that evening with a small group of friends.

The following day was Friday, and as the embassy respected the Muslim Holy Day on Fridays, the embassy was closed. The embassy was also closed on Sunday, our day of rest, so the embassy's days of operation were Monday through Thursday, and Saturday.

On Saturday morning, Tom introduced us to the Ambassador and the Deputy Chief of Mission (DCM), and then we made the rounds to meet the other embassy officers. Later, I was taken to my office and introduced to the Budget Management staff. I was the first Budget Management Officer for the embassy and for Joint Administrative Services. As I was appointed to a new position and not replacing anyone, I would have to set up a staffing plan for the two sections.

To explain Joint Administrative Services, or JAS, some embassies, such as in Baghdad, had been authorized by the Department of State to perform their administrative duties. Therefore, any US agency that wished to do business with the American Embassy was required to purchase their administrative services from the JAS. In Baghdad, there were eight other US agencies besides the embassy operating under JAS. The agency being serviced was required to reimburse JAS for the services they received, which were calculated by the Administrative Officer and the Budget Management Officer of the embassy.

During these first few days, Betsey was invited to stay at Tom and Jenny's house during the day, as they had a full-time nursemaid for their daughter, who was the same age as Betsey. This gave Charlotte free time so she could attend meetings during the day with the ladies of the embassy and others in the community with whom she would be associating. During the first week, Charlotte and I were invited to several welcome dinners given by officers of other agencies, who were being serviced by JAS, so we could become acquainted.

As there were no schools in Baghdad for American children to attend, this presented a real problem. However, there was an officer with the Foreign Aid Program assigned to Baghdad whose wife had taught school in the United States for several years. Therefore, the embassy was able to get a permit from the local government for this officer's wife to establish a class of twelve American children for kindergarten, first grade, and second grade. This instructional program had just been established, and fortunately for us, the officer's wife, Mrs. Janice Bailey, had one slot available so Betsey was permitted to attend this class each morning for a combination of kindergarten and first grade and receive US educational credit for this course. The second year, she would be able to attend a new American school, which was going to be created if authorized by the local government. This subject will be discussed in more depth shortly.

The embassy did have a very small commissary, which was stocked with wine, beer, cigarettes, and a few basic food items. Other food items for consumption could be purchased, to a limited degree, from the local shops, but these items were very expensive, so the embassy's administrative staff originated a monthly group order system, which required bringing food products in, under the embassy's diplomatic status, from wholesale food houses in the United States. Therefore, each month, American employees would send a grocery list with a check to cover these items to the embassy Administrative Officer for delivery to an American wholesale food supplier. These shipments could include staple canned foods, various frozen meats, ice cream, or most any product that could be frozen. This required a family to have a ninety-day order of food in the pipeline all the time and could become quite expensive, but this was our source of supply.

Regarding our housing, there were only a few government-owned apartments on the compound for American personnel that needed to be on frequent duty. In addition, the Ambassador and the DCM had residences on the compound. Therefore, under General Services, there was a housing office that assisted newcomers to locate housing. There was a normal waiting period of one to three months of living in a hotel awaiting completion of the house desired, as most of the housing available was new housing still under construction. This housing rented for fair market value and was expensive, but approximately 80 percent of the housing cost could be covered by our rent allowance.

After two months, we were able to move into our home in a nice residential area. On the first floor were two bedrooms, two bathrooms, a living room, a dining room, a nice-sized kitchen, and a laundry room with a nice rear porch. On the second floor, we had one large bedroom with a bath and one large storage room with closets. In addition, there was an open flat roof accessible on the second floor, where we set up our lounging equipment so we could sit during the evening and avoid the small insects that flew near the ground.

We had been in Baghdad approximately six months when the Ambassador sent out a notice to all American employees stating that he and the DCM had been working with the local government to obtain authority to establish and operate a school for American children. The local government was now ready to approve such a school for up to five hundred American children, covering grades one through nine. Those authorized to attend must be children of the American community such as the embassy, foreign aid programs, or any other American program authorized by the US Embassy.

The Ambassador called a meeting and an announcement was made that a new school would be established, which was greeted with much enthusiasm. He added that shortly, we would have another meeting to elect a nine-person school board. The nine persons should be qualified to help set up a new school. To establish this new school, urgency was one of the main issues, as it had to be done quickly so the new school could be in operation within three to four months. This would place a terrific burden on the new board to take care of all the necessary details.

In three days, the next meeting was held. A few more individuals joined the large group, and a new board of nine individuals was elected. I was elected as Finance and Budget Officer and was delegated to set up the accounting system that the school office was required to follow. I was also required to determine the estimated cost of school operations and to develop a rate of tuition. It would be necessary for the Department to approve this fee as they would be providing the necessary funds. The other board members also had challenging assignments, such as securing a location for the school, obtaining furniture, books, and supplies, finding qualified teachers with stateside licenses and a superintendent to manage the new school, and so on. Each of the school board member's experienced a terrific increase to their workload in addition to their regular office responsibilities. But it was accomplished with a lot of smiling faces, and the school was opened on schedule.

My daughter, Betsey, attended this school for over one year prior to our being transferred to our next post. I believe she received a very good education by the new school system during this period.

Bob's house - Baghdad 1953

CHAPTER 13

Baptism Under Fire

While we were still in the hotel, we were invited to attend a local parade, which was being organized by the local university, among others. The Deputy Chief of Mission (DCM) suggested he would pick us up with some other officers, as a number of us would be sitting on the balcony of one of the embassy buildings overlooking the parade.

There were about twenty of us watching from the balcony, enjoying the parade, when a disturbance broke out. Some of the bystanders started attacking the parade participants. At first, this attack consisted of individuals throwing objects at the police on horseback and the parade participants. Several individuals then began to jerk a policeman off his horse, and his boot was caught in the stirrups, dragging him down the street. The DCM said it was time to leave, as things were getting rough, and we left the building by the rear exit. His driver took us back to our residences by a safe route, and he advised us to stay inside and off the street, as there was indication that more disturbances were yet to come.

The next morning, I was awakened at sunup by machine-gun fire. The gun-fire became louder as the revolutionary group had overtaken and captured a police station using an 88mm weapon against the military or police who were trying to protect the area. Suddenly, I received a telephone call through the hotel switchboard from my supervisor, Tom. He said, "Bob, we have a serious problem at the hotel and will have to evacuate all of our embassy members currently staying there."

As I had had military training, the Ambassador named me as evacuation leader of the embassy employees and their families residing at the hotel. There were eight other Americans temporarily housed at the hotel. One of the young couples had a two-year-old baby, and we had four-year-old Betsey. I was tasked with getting the Americans and their families onto an embassy launch, which was being sent five miles down the Tigris River, to take all of us back up the river to a safe location at the embassy.

I called the group together, and we met within ten minutes in a room on the first floor at the hotel, ready to go. I briefed the group and told them that everything would be all right. As this was the first overseas assignment for some employees, including myself, I didn't want anybody to be too nervous.

Shortly, the hotel manager said that I had another call from the embassy. It was Tom again, letting us know that they had been unable to get the launch started; it seemed someone had damaged the engine. All the streets were blocked, so they couldn't reach us by automobile, leaving us on our own to walk through bush country to the embassy five miles up the Tigris River. Two men from the embassy would meet us on the way, and the hotel manager was sending two of his trusted employees with us to guide us and to carry bolo knives to kill any snakes we encountered on our trip through bush country. Tom ended the call by wishing us luck and saying he would see us later that day.

I went back into the room where the others were waiting and advised them that the launch would not be coming down the river to rescue us. We would need to leave immediately and walk along the west bank of the river with the two hotel employees a little ways ahead, watching out for cobras alongside the river.

At that point, a large revolutionary group had gathered at the gate, shouting and saying they had orders to kill all Americans. They started to climb the big gate in front of the hotel. The hotel employees were trying to beat them off, but one could see it was a failing mission. Suddenly, we heard a roar, and three military tanks came down the street at full speed. They stopped in front of the hotel and the soldiers shouted to the people on the gate to get off and go home.

Meanwhile, we remained inside the hotel. It appeared that the people attacking would succeed, so I ordered our group out of the hotel, down the embankment behind the hotel, and approximately a block up the river, where they could hide out and not be seen. I told them that I did not want them carrying the little ones through bush country if there was any way to avoid this problem. I would remain behind the hotel building where I could not be seen. If the tanks were successful in fighting off the crowd, I would give them a signal, and we could abort our departure up the river. However, if the military did not succeed in defending the hotel, I would quickly join the group and lead them up the river toward the embassy.

The group went down the embankment as instructed and waited for my signal. By this time, there were a number of rioters on the gate, rocking it. Suddenly, the leader of the tank group opened his tank hatch and, with a bullhorn, ordered the attackers to get off the gate and go home, or he would open fire in two minutes.

Two minutes passed, and more offenders climbed the gate, which was beginning to bend at the hinges. The tank commander closed his hatch, and two of the tanks opened fire on the crowd with short bursts. After the firing stopped, more rioters attacked the gate, and then we heard sirens, and two more tanks sped down the street. The leaders of these tanks came down and positioned themselves to open fire on the crowd. Several of the individuals at the top of the gate caught the burst of fire and dropped, fatally injured. The following burst caught the next attackers climbing the gate, and they went down. The tank commander then ordered the crowd to go home, or he would open fire again. Stampeding and knocking others to the ground, they ran up the street as fast as they could. I waited anxiously in my hiding spot to see if any other offenders were going to attack, but they seemed to be on the run now. The tank commander ordered two of the five tanks to follow the attackers down the street to keep them moving, and then ordered the other two tanks with him to cover the entire city block.

Prince Abdullah, the regent for Faisal II, came on the radio and announced that Baghdad was now under martial law. Curfew would be from 6:00 p.m. to 6:00 a.m., and any offenders would be shot without question. As I remember, the city remained under martial law for the next two weeks.

Meanwhile, I gave the signal, and my team of eight, plus the two embassy employees, returned safely to the hotel without having to make the difficult trip through bush country. I then called Tom to relate what had happened and asked if he agreed that we should stay at the hotel as it appeared to be a safe location, for the time being anyway. He agreed and mentioned that he did not want us traveling through that bush country if it could be avoided.

We were ordered to remain at the hotel for a couple of days until the embassy could send two embassy cars to ensure we had a safe ride to our workstations. Each evening the commander would sound a whistle at 6:00 p.m. The men operating the tanks would close their hatches and anyone roaming the streets would be shot. Our room was on the third floor of the hotel and I could see the action that was taking place on the street after the commander blew his whistle. It was always necessary to stand back from the window because a couple of times we received a bullet through one of our windows. However, I did see several individuals shot on the street after they violated the curfew.

By morning, the streets were very quiet. The embassy cars picked up all of us working at the embassy and took us to our workstations. During nonworking hours, we remained inside the hotel to avoid contact with the local population as we did not know who might be offended by our presence. After two weeks, it was okay again to get back on the street, and we went shopping and did a little socializing.

CHAPTER 14

A Serious Accident

About three o'clock one afternoon, I was sitting at my desk in the office. An embassy security officer brought in Charlotte and Betsey, saying, "Mr. Day, your wife and daughter had a serious accident. A large truck ran into them."

Poor Charlotte and Betsey were both bleeding from the head and needed medical attention immediately. I rushed both girls to the embassy nursing station, which was next door to my office, for assistance. The nurse cleaned them up and called the European physician we used for emergencies. The doctor and the nurse took care of their injuries and gave them some medication to quiet their nerves. They did not seem to be seriously injured. This was true for Betsey, even though she was bounced around some in the vehicle, but it soon became clear that it was a different story for Charlotte.

After a week or so, our physician said we must get Charlotte out of Baghdad to a hospital in Beirut, Lebanon, which was 700 air miles west of Baghdad, as her condition was becoming more serious. Therefore, arrangements were made to transport Charlotte by air attaché to Beirut. The embassy nurse, Betsey, and I accompanied her, as we knew Charlotte would be admitted to the hospital. When we arrived at the airport in Beirut, there was an embassy vehicle and an ambulance waiting for the trip to the hospital. At the hospital, we were met by a couple of nurses who had arranged for her admittance, and she was thoroughly examined.

Within a day or two, special treatment was started, and they found that she'd had a serious concussion. During the next three months, Betsey and I made a number of trips to meet with the doctors and Charlotte concerning her condition. We usually traveled to Beirut on these additional trips by air attaché, but at times, the plane was on other assignments, and it was necessary to make other travel arrangements.

One trip, I decided to take another means of transportation, which was a public bus company that had special buses built for this type of travel over the desert. It consisted of a well-built bus carriage similar to an 18-wheeler truck pulled by a truck cab. The truck cab held four men, two drivers, and two security guards who could operate a machine gun through a turret opening through the top of the cab. When I talked to the manager of the bus company, he said that this type of protection was seldom needed. I decided this travel would be interesting and purchased two tickets for Betsey and me for the twelve-hour trip from Baghdad to Beirut.

A few days later, we boarded the bus with our one suitcase each and took our reserved seats in the middle of the bus. As we sat there, other passengers, who were mostly Middle Easterners, boarded, and it was not long before the bus reached the full capacity of thirty travelers. The attendant closed and locked the door, and then gave us a short briefing of our trip's agenda. He stated that the door would remain locked until we arrived in Damascus, Syria, where two passengers would get off and two more would board, which would be around ten o'clock the next morning. According to the company rules, the door would not be unlocked for any reason. The trip into Beirut should be safe, and our arrival time was estimated to be around noon to one o'clock the next afternoon. They had been having safe, undisturbed trips for the last six or eight months, but in the event of a disturbance or shooting, everyone was to kneel down with their head below the windowsill, as the windows and the lower sides of the bus were bulletproof to provide safety for travelers. He went on to say there was a lavatory at the back of the bus, and that dinner would be served shortly, which would include cold drinks or coffee.

We would be going west out of Baghdad on the main highway and would be traveling this route for approximately a hundred miles, then, instead of continuing on the highway, we would enter the desert, using the stars for navigation, and take a shorter route of four hundred to five hundred miles across the desert to Damascus, then from there on to Beirut for approximately a hundred miles.

We started out on our journey, and we were riding very comfortably because the bus had springy seats, which absorbed the roughness of the road. Shortly after we left, our dinner was served—which consisted of lamb shish kebab and curried rice, as well as pastries for dessert. After several hours, we pulled off the main highway and started our desert crossing as scheduled. Approximately an hour passed, while over the intercom, the assistant driver was summarizing information about where we were and what was going on.

Suddenly, we heard shooting, and the driver said, "Everyone, put your head down. The lights are going out. It looks like we are being ambushed."

Betsey and I heard machine gun fire and a considerable amount of shouting in the background. Betsey whispered, "Daddy, what is going on? Are they going to shoot us?"

I replied, "No, Betsey, the windows are solid, and I do not think we will be shot."

The shooting stopped, but there was still a lot of shouting. The driver said, confidently, "It appears that they are moving on."

Everything was quiet for a short time, and then the shooting picked up again. In the background, I could hear one of the security men say, "Well, I got two of them. They are trying to hold us up. Well, we got two more now, and it looks like they are leaving the area. So, hopefully, this will be the end of it for a while."

Suddenly, the bus stopped, and we heard it choke out. The driver said it seemed as though they had punctured one of the gas tanks, but it wasn't a problem, as he could switch to the reserve tank. Soon, the engine started again, and we headed off through the desert at full speed.

After a little while, one of the drivers said, "Now that things have quieted down, I will brief you on what took place."

He explained that there had been nine bandits on camels making the attempt to hold us up. Apparently, we had surprised them with our gunfire, which left four of them lying in the desert, presumably seriously or fatally injured. It looked as though the others had abandoned their companions and headed west toward Syria.

About five or ten minutes later, one of the drivers or security men shouted, "The five men are back! This time with a wide-tired truck."

It appeared they were determined this time, and we could hear a considerable amount of shooting as they came closer. At that point, there was a terrific noise as our men apparently started shooting with both guns. Suddenly one of the men said that the bandits were leaving. Our men stopped shooting, and things were quiet. The lights came back on, and everyone sat back and relaxed, feeling much safer after the shooting had stopped. Over the PA system, to my surprise, our waiter said, "I will be serving hot coffee and cake, and I hope you will all enjoy. Sit back and relax."

After that, it was a very quiet journey, for which we were all very thankful. Our memorable travel was worth it because Betsey and I were able to visit Charlotte several times. Charlotte's health had shown improvement, making for a good visit for us.

Monday morning Betsey and I took the air attaché plane back to Baghdad, and I must say it was a much smoother ride. For several weeks, we did not have the opportunity to visit Beirut again. Dr. Younger, Charlotte's physician, called me and said that it would be wise to visit Charlotte again soon and to please stop and see him at his office during our visit. I called the air attaché office, and he said that he would have a plane going to Beirut on that Friday afternoon and would have plenty of space if Betsey and I also wanted to ride. I obtained a short leave from the Ambassador, and we left on schedule.

Upon arriving in Beirut, we checked into a hotel. We then headed to the hospital to visit Charlotte. We found that her health had deteriorated, and she was quite unhappy that she was in a hospital for treatment. She said that she was dissatisfied with the service and wanted to go back to Baghdad.

This attitude did not appear to be the Charlotte that I knew, and I made an appointment to see Dr. Younger the following Monday. When Betsey and I visited his office, he explained to me that Charlotte's treatment was going as well as could be expected, but she was not responding favorably to the treatment. He was very concerned about her condition and was doing everything possible to correct her problem.

Dr. Younger said, "I may need to change the current treatment. If she does not respond more favorably, it would be wise to transfer her back to the States. I will call you in a few days to let you know what results we are getting concerning her treatment."

Monday morning, we got up early. We had breakfast and caught a cab to visit Charlotte for a little while, as we were scheduled to return to Baghdad on the 1:00 p.m. flight. We entered the room at the same time Charlotte's nurse came in with a tray of food. Unfortunately, Charlotte was not in a very good mood and made several unfavorable remarks to Betsey and me.

The nurse said, "Mr. Day, I think it would be good to keep your visit short today. Charlotte will most likely be in this mood all day."

After thirty minutes or so, we told Charlotte good-bye and left her room. We went back to see Dr. Younger and he advised us that Charlotte's condition was declining, and that I should contact him later in the week. We went back to the hotel, checked out, and headed for the airport.

The following week, I called Dr. Younger. He said that he and a team of several physicians had reviewed Charlotte's case and had been unable to successfully treat her, and had reached a decision that it would be wise for her to be discharged from their hospital and transferred back to the States. Charlotte's mother and father had been keeping in contact with Dr. Younger, so they were aware of her condition and had made arrangements for her to be transferred to a hospital not far from their home in Kansas City.

Once they contacted me to let me know of their plans, I arranged passage and talked to the Ambassador to get ten days' leave. The following week, Charlotte was transferred to the hospital her parents had selected, and Betsey and I stayed in the Kansas City area visiting Charlotte daily. Even though Betsey was just five years old at this time, she seemed to have the mind of a much older person. Charlotte's parents, and Betsey and I sat down with the doctors and discussed Charlotte's condition. We discussed the subject thoroughly and decided that there was nothing more that Betsey and I could do for Charlotte by staying in Kansas City. It was decided that I should finish my contract and tour of duty in Baghdad and make the best of the situation. A week later, Betsey and I returned to Baghdad, and Charlotte remained under the care of the Kansas City physicians and her parents.

Most of our visits to Charlotte in Beirut had been uneventful, but I recall one Sunday morning when Betsey and I were invited by some very good friends of ours to attend a church service with them, followed by lunch. After lunch, they mentioned they had a previous engagement for the afternoon, so Betsey and I decided to attend a movie.

After checking the newspaper movie ads, we found one that Betsey said she would like to see and that sounded interesting to me. We took a cab to the movie, which was in the downtown area of Beirut, and purchased a couple of tickets and some popcorn. When the movie was over, at about 4:30 p.m., we came out of the theater and saw there were no vehicles or pedestrians on the street. I thought this was most unusual and concerning.

There was a bookstore next to the movie theater, and Betsey said she could use a couple of new books to read in English. We entered the bookstore, and she found some books she was interested in. As we were leaving the store, the manager said, "Mister, be careful. There are some riots taking place not too far from here. They are burning the buildings. I am closing up!"

I did not want us to be caught in a burning building, so I decided to get out and head on down the street. As we came out of the bookstore, a very large group of rioters came around the corner carrying torches. Betsey and I were the only ones on the street. When they saw us, they shouted, "They are the ones that started this problem. Let's kill them!"

We started running for our lives down the empty street away from the rioters. After about a block, Betsey said, "Daddy, I can't run anymore!"

As I already had hold of her hand, I just knelt down, still running, and picked her up to carry her on my shoulders. There was no one on the first side street, so I kept running. They were beginning to close in. By this time, I was getting very worried that the rioters would catch us.

I continued running to the next cross street. There were still no visible people or traffic. The crowd was now about two hundred feet behind us.

As I looked both ways on the cross street, I saw a large black sedan coming at full speed toward us. It sped through the intersection, slammed on its brakes, slid to a stop, and the back door was thrown open.

They called out, "Friends! We are students at the American University. Those rioters are right behind you! Please get in here for safety."

We ducked and went into the back seat even though there were already four people back there, and the driver said, "We will take you to your hotel. Where are you staying?"

I told them the name of the hotel, and they sped off.

We were headed toward the hotel, but we had to cross one of the main streets where there were two street-cars burning. As we started down the slight incline of the street, several rioters ran out and tried to flag us down.

The driver said, "Duck down, friends, and hold on! We are going through!" And then he hit the gas. As I had my head slightly above the door, watching the rioters in front of the vehicle, I saw two of them jump aside, but three of them kept running toward the vehicle. Suddenly, there was a *bump, bump, bump* as we hit all three of them, and we sped on. We continued down the street, another six blocks or so, and finally arrived safely at our hotel.

As we exited the black sedan, I reached into my jacket pocket and pulled out two twenty-dollar bills. I handed these to the driver, but he did not want to take them. I insisted, and he said, "You are an American, and I am an American. We all must stick together."

Suddenly, his friend said, "Joseph, I hear a siren. We better get out of here!"

Joseph said, "Thank you very much!" and sped off.

We started to enter the hotel, but there were some very comfortable-looking chairs on the patio. I said, "Betsey, even though it's getting a little late, let's sit down here and relax for a few minutes and be thankful for our rescue."

After a short time, we got up from our chairs, and Betsey said, "Daddy, I'm kind of hungry. Can we go to the dining room and have a dish of ice cream?"

I replied, "Betsey that is the best idea I've heard all day!"

At that point, Betsey pulled her jacket open and pulled out a package and said, "Look, Daddy, I still have the three books from the bookstore."

"That's great, Betsey," I said. "I thought you had dropped those when we were running."

She said, "Daddy, I couldn't do that. You bought those books so I would have some reading material when we got home."

I was surprised that she held on to those books during our desperate run down the street when the mob was after us.

After returning to Baghdad from our trip taking Charlotte to the States for the medical care she required, I needed to hire a second governess for Betsey. I hired a Swiss woman named Thelma. I wanted to spend as much time with Betsey as possible. During the summertime, the weather was so hot in Baghdad that the embassy closed at 1:00 p.m. and opened again at 4:00 p.m., so each afternoon, Betsey and I would go swimming at the British American club, where there was a beautiful pool. I spent a great deal of time there and then would return to work to finish off the day. I taught Betsey how to swim, and she became a very good swimmer, attending many swimming and birthday parties; and she and I became very attached.

Betsey and Thelma became good friends, and Thelma did a very good job of caring for her. School was still in recess for the summer, but Thelma took over caring for Betsey when I was not home, and she saw to it that Betsey was properly dressed each day and her hair was done in a braided ponytail. They spent considerable time reading and preparing for the next school year.

CHAPTER 15

Mistaken Identity

During the summer of 1953, my workload was very heavy, mainly due to additional projects under JAS. A number of evenings, I would go back to the office around 8:00 p.m. after I'd had dinner and spent some time with Betsey and had seen that she was safely in bed with Thelma present.

One evening, I was sitting at my desk in the office, engrossed in some work that needed to be completed within a few days. My office was in a building on the corner just across the street from the main embassy. We had just moved to this building due to the increased workload generated by JAS, and the window blinds had not yet been installed, so outsiders had a clear view of my office at the front of the building by looking through the large iron gate. The ten-foot brick wall surrounding the building had a heavy lock on the gate, which was used constantly after six in the evening.

As I sat at my desk reviewing some documents, I heard a rifle being fired twice somewhere near my gate. Having been through the riots a few months earlier, I was always aware of the need for tight security, and I slid out of my chair to the floor and hit the light switch. As I peered out of the dark window to the front of the building, I saw two or three policemen standing at the gate looking down toward the ground. As I did not see any offensive action, I went to my door and opened it.

One of the officers motioned that it was all right for me to come out. I asked the officer what was going on, and he said that a man had been shot outside of my gate. I could see that the man on the ground had a bullet hole through his head. The policeman asked me if I knew who he was, and I told him I did not know, but I thought he was a neighbor who lived down the street, as several times I had seen him pass this way in the evening.

About that time, two policemen came walking toward us holding on to a man, and one of the policemen was carrying a rifle. He said, "Sergeant, this is the man who shot him."

The sergeant said to the suspect, "Why did you shoot him?"

The man said, "It was an accident. I was shooting at the man in the window. It was accidental."

The sergeant looked at him and then turned to me and said, "He was trying to shoot you!"

After a few more questions, the sergeant said, "This man was trying to shoot you, but the man lying here accidentally walked into the line of his fire as he shot. If you will allow me, I want to come in. I want to look at the window."

As he entered the gate, he said, "Look here—this is where the bullets grazed the bars on the gate, which slightly threw them off target. I see now where they hit the metal windowsill just above your head. Mr. Day, that was very close for you!"

Feeling shaken, I agreed that it certainly was; and they took the man and put him in their van and took him to the police station.

As I went home later that evening, I thought about Betsey's mother being critically ill in the hospital. If that gunman had been a little more accurate, I would not be coming home to kiss my daughter good night; but by the grace of God, this did not happen.

The following day, two detectives came out and checked the bars on my gate and where the bullets hit the metal frame just slightly above my head. I also reported the incident to my supervisor, Tom, and the embassy security office checked it out.

Several days later, our consular officer came in and told me that the man would go to trial the following week, but he didn't think I would be called to testify. However, I did ask him if he would go to the trial with me as I intended to go as an observer, and he said no, but he would have one of his local security men go with me if I wanted to go.

The trial date was set, and the American security officer came to me and said, "Bob, I don't believe it would be wise for you to go to the trial, as you have not been called to testify. One of the other officers will go to record proceedings and will let you know exactly what was said."

I said, "That suits me. I would just like to know what takes place at the trial."

A few days later, one of the other embassy officers came to my office and related what took place. The man was tried for murder and the attempted murder of a diplomat. He pled innocent and called it an accidental death but was overruled by the judge. He was sentenced to be hung at a public hanging the first of the following month.

A few days before the first, I asked the administrative officer if he had any objection to my attending the hanging, which was on a Friday, a non-work day, and he replied that he would check with the deputy chief of mission (DCM). The DCM replied that he was not anxious for me to go, but it was OK if I would give him a report, and he would have an Arabic-speaking man go with me.

As the hanging was at ten o'clock on a Friday morning, the local security man, who I will call Alex, picked me up early. We did not dress in a jacket, but in older clothing, so we would not stand out in the crowd. We arrived at the public square, where two scaffolds had been constructed, and, as I recall, there were ten men on the list to be hung that day. We picked a spot close to the gallows but near a small building where there were a number of other people. Alex had told me that we should not speak English at the hangings, but as I knew some Arabic, this worked out fine.

There was a large number of people at the hanging, and merchants had set up several shish kebab stands for those who wished for refreshments. Others had set up drink stands, so it was like a carnival. They had all ten men sitting on the gallows waiting their turn. Shortly before the hanging, Alex said, "I think I know the man up on the gallows who will be placing the rope on their necks. Please stay here. Don't talk to anyone."

Alex slowly slipped through the crowd to the man in question. Then he returned to me and said, "I will tell you later what he said." Then he added, "Watch the third man. He is going to dance. Your man is number 2."

Ten o'clock arrived, and the first man climbed up the ladder of the first gallows. Then the second man climbed up the ladder of the second gallows. They were both blindfolded, and the ropes were put around their necks with the knot just below their left ears. Their feet were tied, and their hands were tied behind their backs.

The trap on first gallows opened, and as the gallows were open at the bottom, you could see the condemned hanging by his neck, dead. The same happened to the man who had tried to shoot me. The third man was required to climb up the ladder. The noose was put over his head, the rope around his neck, with the knot to the back of the head. He did not have his hands or feet tied. This was the man who, according to the gallows man, would be made to dance. Then the fourth man climbed the ladder, but he was treated as the first two had been treated—rope at his left ear, hands and feet tied. As the third man went through the chute and hit the end of the rope, it did not break his neck, and he hanged there choking to death, his arms and feet flailing; and I saw what was meant by "dancing." According to Alex, the hangman did this on his own initiative by placing the knot at the back of the head. I have no doubt that this was not authorized by local officials.

By this time, the crowd was cheering loudly, and Alex looked at me and whispered, "It is time to leave now." We slowly slipped through the crowd and left the area.

This was the only public hanging I attended while I was in the Middle East, and I did not sleep well that night.

The consular officer did a background check to find information about the man who wanted to shoot me. It was discovered that he had applied for a visa to the United States, but the consular officer found that he had a criminal record and denied his visa. This man was angry with the consular officer, and since the officer and I were approximately the same height and build and were very similar in appearance, the man had mistaken me for the consular officer. Mistaken identity.

CHAPTER 16

Accident On The Babylon Highway

One Sunday in August of 1953, I had just finished lunch and was considering what would be the best way to spend my afternoon. I decided a relaxing way to spend the afternoon would be to take Betsey to the British American club to swim. We had spent a considerable amount of time there in the last few months.

Sadly, the phone rang, and it was the marine at the embassy. He said, "Mr. Day, I have a distress call from a man that just came into the embassy saying there has been a bad traffic accident about seventy-five miles down the road on the Babylon Highway. They need immediate assistance, as there are several Americans that were killed or seriously injured. I have been unable to reach the duty officer team captain for this month, and as you are the duty team captain next in line, I'm calling you to handle the situation."

I instructed him to call the other six members of my team and have them to report to the embassy in ten minutes.

I explained to Thelma that I was leaving on an emergency and that I hoped to be back sometime before dark. I left my house immediately for the embassy, and upon arriving, I found the embassy nurse, three other members of my team, and three local drivers. They had already pulled out in a column with the five vehicles: three black sedans, a one-ton military truck, and a three-ton military truck with a hoist. The smaller and larger trucks were equipped with all kinds of emergency equipment. We should have had two more team members and two more drivers and trucks on an emergency such as this, but this was all that responded to my call, so we had to make do with what we had.

I got in the first black sedan with the driver and the nurse was already in the back with her medical kit. The local drivers had their engines running and were ready to roll.

We rolled down the Babylon Highway as fast as we could, but as it was a Sunday afternoon, the traffic was rather heavy, so it took us a little longer than usual to locate the accident. When we found it, we saw it was partially blocking the highway, and traffic was going off the road around it.

As we pulled up near the accident site, we saw six Americans sitting on a blanket, holding their heads. The accident was caused by a local truck that had broken down in the middle of the highway. The truck driver who had been working underneath the truck attempting to repair it was still lying underneath the rear wheel, which had pinned one of his legs to the ground, and he had not been able to free his leg even though this accident had happened nearly two hours before our arrival.

The truck had a sharp tailgate extended out, and a station wagon with nine passengers aboard had come up over a slight ridge in the road. The driver had not been able to swerve soon enough and had caught the sharp edge of the truck's tailgate in the windshield. The windshield hit the tailgate about two feet from the side of the vehicle, penetrating the vehicle from the front clear to the rear. This entry of the tailgate through the vehicle instantly decapitated the three Americans riding on the right side of the station wagon. Their bodies were still in the station wagon. The six people sitting at the side of the desert road were the driver and the five other passengers. None of these passengers were seriously injured, but most of them were in shock and hysterical.

One of the large trucks of our convoy pulled up alongside the six Americans sitting on the ground, and they were helped into the back of the covered truck out of the scorching sun. We passed out bottles of water to everyone and the nurse started administering a sedative to calm them down.

Meanwhile, I was checking the station wagon with one of my team members and saw the three Americans who had been decapitated - one lady and two men. I later found out that they were friends of some of the others and were visiting them from the States. There was nothing to be done for these individuals at the moment, so we closed the doors of the station wagon. We then checked the driver of the truck and found he was unconscious. We backed up one of our trucks that had a hoist on the back of it, and our local drivers lifted the wheel of the other truck off the legs of the driver and slipped him out from underneath the truck. The local drivers flagged down a taxi, and we sent the injured driver to a hospital back in Baghdad with a friend who was passing by. The truck was then pushed off the highway onto the side of the road where it would no longer interfere with traffic.

Two of my team members and I pushed the station wagon off to the side of the road so the traffic could move freely. I then opened the rear doors of the station wagon while the other team members removed three of the gurneys with sheets from one of our trucks and set them down behind the station wagon. I raised my hand for silence, and two of the team members and I said a short prayer for the three poor souls who had been killed. Then we lifted the first body, and its parts, onto the gurney and covered it with a sheet. It was then moved into one of the trucks.

At this point, one of the team members who had been assisting turned very white and collapsed on the side of the road. The nurse immediately administered first aid to him and put him in an air-conditioned vehicle. We then turned our attention to the second and third bodies. As we were getting ready to place the second body on a gurney, someone placed a hand on my shoulder. I turned and saw it was Jim Staley, general service officer (GSO). He had been on another emergency and had been delayed.

He said, "Bob, it looks like you and your team have done a superb job. My team will now take over. Why don't you and your team take one or two of the vehicles and head back to Baghdad? I will finish up here."

We followed his suggestion and headed back to Baghdad. Later, I called my team members together and thanked them for their services. One of the men said, "Fellows, I hope we never have to do this again." We all agreed.

This was a terrible experience for our team members, most of whom had no emergency training. But that was life of an emergency team member back in 1953, when we did not have emergency ambulance service at the post. I was personally thankful for my experience driving an ambulance for the Noon Funeral Home many years prior.

The following day, Jim arranged to have the embassy carpenters build three pine box coffins and, per local law, bury them in the local cemetery for a period of ninety days. After ninety days, the local government approved the bodies' exhumation. The bodies were placed in transfer cases and shipped back to the United States.

CHAPTER 17

A Family In Distress

One Sunday afternoon in mid-September of 1954, when I was duty officer, I received a call from the marine on duty at the embassy saying that he had an American man in distress. His wife was quite ill at the hotel where they were staying and needed a doctor right away, but he did not know whom to call.

I immediately drove to the embassy and found that the man's name was Donald Stafford. He worked for one of the oil companies; and his wife, who had terminal cancer, had unexpectedly arrived in Baghdad a week before with their seventeen-year-old son. She knew she did not have long to live but wanted to be with her husband when she passed.

In order to find a physician, I called our embassy nurse and found there was a well-known British physician whom the embassy used in emergency cases. The nurse gave me his telephone number and I immediately called him. I explained the situation, and he agreed to come to the hotel where the Staffords were living at the time.

I went to the hotel with Mr. Stafford, and we joined his son, who had stayed with his mother to comfort her. The doctor arrived shortly after I called him and said he would try to provide medication to ease her pain. I returned home, and later that day, Mr. Stafford called to thank me very profusely for helping him get medical attention for his wife. He mentioned that he was unaware that his wife's cancer had progressed so rapidly and that her health was quickly failing, or he would have returned to the States to assist her.

A few days later, I received notice that Mrs. Stafford had been admitted to a small Christian hospital and had died. They had placed her body in the hospital morgue pending arrangements for Mr. Stafford and his son to take her body back to the States.

The following day, after my normal working hours, I received notice from the marine at the embassy that the local police had received notice that there had been an accident involving an American on a country road about twenty-five miles north of Baghdad. They said that there were two policemen standing by at the scene of the accident, as there appeared to be only one vehicle involved, and they were there to protect the injured man and his vehicle until someone from the embassy could arrive.

I was aware of where this accident had taken place and knew it was a rather desolate area. I was not anxious to head to this location alone at night with just a local embassy driver for company, so I called Consular Officer John Johnson, explaining the situation. He said, "Bob, I certainly understand. I will go with you, but let me call and see if our embassy nurse would be able to go with us."

He soon called back, saying that she was not available. As this was late afternoon and I had not had lunch, I went by my house, picked up some sandwiches for us to eat on the way, and then picked up John.

With the embassy driver, the three of us drove north to the country road where the accident supposedly occurred. It was very dark, and no other vehicles or pedestrians were on the road. John and I were in the back seat together, and he tapped me on the arm and said, "Bob, I have my .38 just in case."

I said, "That's good, John! I am dressed the same."

John said, "Very good! You never know when you may need it."

The driver slowed down and said, "I see a dim light up the road. Maybe that is it."

Suddenly, there were three gunshots somewhere behind our vehicle. The driver hit the accelerator, and soon we were doing about sixty miles per hour. The light ahead became more visible, and as we approached, we saw that it was an orange warning light. There was a large road grader sitting in the middle of the road. An automobile had hit this road grader and appeared to be seriously damaged. There were two policemen on horseback guarding the area. We parked with our lights directly on the accident site, and John and I got out of our vehicle along with our driver. We told them who we were, and they said they had been there on guard for the last two or three hours, waiting for someone to arrive.

As we peered through the windshield of the car which was lying on its side, we could see a man's body lying in the front seat area of the vehicle. One of the policemen said he had climbed up on the side of the vehicle, opened the door, and climbed inside. He said he found the man's wallet lying on the floor, retrieved his driver's license, and that he knew the man's name and that he was an American. He further said that he had checked the man and that he was not breathing, so he figured the man must have died on impact or shortly thereafter.

I asked the policeman how much money there was in the wallet, and he said it was empty. John then asked both of the policemen again if there was any money in the wallet or out in the vehicle. John gave me a strange look, and then he said, "Bob, don't you think it's unusual that this man wouldn't have money in his wallet?"

I replied, "Yes, John, I certainly do. Maybe it fell out somewhere in the vehicle during the crash."

John then climbed up on the side, opened the vehicle, climbed in, and checked the body, looking to see if he could find any money in the wallet or on the body itself. He said, "Bob, we just can't let this man stay here. Maybe the two policemen can help us right the vehicle back on its wheels."

I found a couple of ropes in our embassy vehicle. The two policemen tied these ropes to their saddles, and, with the help of their horses, we righted the vehicle back on its four wheels. John wrote out the document saying that we had authorization to unload the body and take it back to Baghdad. We asked the policemen if it was all right if we moved the man's body to the trunk of our vehicle so we could take him back to the city. They agreed and signed the paper authorizing transfer of the body. With their help, we loaded the body into the trunk of our vehicle. We wanted to push the vehicle off to the side of the road, but it was seriously damaged and would not run, so we had to leave it next to the road grader. We thanked the policemen for all their help. I did ask again if there was any money in the vehicle, but they said there was no money.

We drove to the small Christian hospital in Baghdad and asked to speak to the medical director. We introduced ourselves to the doctor, and he recognized me, as we had met before. We explained to him that we had the body of an American who had been killed in an automobile accident and showed him the papers signed by the two policeman.

I explained to the doctor that we had not been able to completely identify the man as his facial features had been so badly damaged in the accident.

The doctor had several of his attendants to move the body into the hospital, and together, we identified the man from the photo on his driver's license, and were shocked to see that it was Donald Stafford. I then told John that I knew this man and the situation with his young son.

John said, "That is terrible. We need to call the company he works for and see if that will clear up why he was in that part of the country."

John called the emergency number of Donald Stafford's company in Iraq, and talked to Director David Campbell on the phone to explain what had happened. Director Campbell said his office was about ten miles from where the accident had occurred. On the day of the accident, Mr. Stafford was at the office that afternoon to pick up money to buy air tickets for his wife's body, his son, and himself to return to the States. John asked him if he had any idea how much money Mr. Stafford would have had on him when he was killed. Mr. Campbell replied, "I do not know the total amount he had on him, but I do recall that I gave him six thousand dollars in cash to help him make the trip home, and he put the money in his wallet."

John told him that we had found his wallet but there was nothing in it. Director Campbell said he would talk with his boss to see if he wanted to pursue it, and then said, "But right now, the son is at the hotel alone. My wife and I will leave right now to bring him to our home to comfort him. We will ship the two bodies back to the States as soon as we can with a male and a female escort."

Two or three weeks later, I received a telephone call from Director Campbell saying that two employees from their company had taken Jacob, the young son of Mr. and Mrs. Stafford, back to the States, along with his parents' bodies. Mr. Stafford's brother and his wife had two sons and had taken over as guardian for Jacob. It was reported that they had always been a very tight family, so we were confident that Jacob would be raised properly. As the Staffords had very adequate insurance, Jacob would have sufficient funds to complete his education.

Director Campbell thanked me and John profusely for the service we had provided and mentioned that the loss of Mr. Stafford's money was still under investigation. Although I had felt sorry for the young boy, I was glad to hear he was being taken good care of, and I thanked Mr. Campbell for the follow-up call.

CHAPTER 18

Leaving Baghdad, Iraq

In late October 1954, the embassy received orders from the State Department that I would be transferred for my next assignment, which would be the State Department in Washington DC, in an appropriate finance position.

Before I left, I had one more short trip to make to Beirut, Lebanon, to wind up several contracts. I called the air attaché and booked passage for a couple of days later to travel to Beirut, complete the business, and return to Baghdad. As on previous trips, I checked into a hotel, and Betsey stayed with friends. Once our business had been completed, Betsey and I boarded the air attaché again and prepared to return to Baghdad. As with every other trip, we had parachutes assigned to all the passengers, and I was also handed a long-webbed belt to fasten Betsey to me in the event it became necessary for us to bail out together due to plane trouble.

When we arrived back in Baghdad, I told Betsey that would be our last trip by air attaché requiring us to be belted together on the flight in the event the plane went down. She said, "Daddy, are you saying that I will no longer be belted to your tummy?" I told her that was correct, and she said, "Daddy, I am disappointed, as I was looking forward for us to parachute out together and float down through the clouds to a safe landing."

This makes a person realize how much confidence children can have in their parents regarding their safety in case of emergencies.

In late November, I received travel orders to depart Baghdad in early December with a one-week consultation in the department, two months' home leave, and assignment to the Office of Finance as a Financial Management Procedure Advisor.

After a few farewell parties by the embassy group and Joint Administrative Services agencies, Betsey and I departed Baghdad on schedule. We were fortunate and flew to London, where we took the ship USS *United States* from Southampton to New York, arriving in New York in mid-December. We had a very nice crossing on the ship.

When we arrived in New York, disembarking went quite well; but we found that the baggage handlers were on strike, and there was no one to take our baggage from customs to the curb and reload it into a taxi. As we had four footlockers and several suitcases, a couple of other passengers volunteered to help us with our baggage to the ship's departure dock. We stacked our baggage on the sidewalk, and by the time all taxis arrived at the pickup point, they were engaged by other travelers.

After waiting for over an hour to flag down a taxi, I decided the only thing to do was for Betsey to stay with the baggage and for me to walk down the street a block or two to catch a taxi and bring it back to the loading dock. I did not want to leave my six-year-old child with the baggage, but it seemed that was the only option.

Betsey said, "Daddy, I will sit on top of the baggage, and if anyone tries to take any of them, I will hit them with my umbrella."

By this time, I was exasperated and decided it was the only thing to do. I helped her up on the stack of bags and headed down the street at a dead run, caught a taxi, and headed back to the loading dock. Betsey was still sitting on top of the baggage, swinging her closed umbrella.

Fortunately, the taxi was a large van and had room for all of our baggage, but the taxi driver said he was not allowed to move the baggage from the sidewalk to the taxi. I offered him an extra twenty-dollar bill as a tip, and he decided he could load the baggage after all.

The taxi took us to the train station, and we boarded the train with only a few extra moments to spare before its departure for Washington DC. When we arrived, we were met by friends. They had previously invited us to stay with them for whatever time we needed until we could get settled in an apartment. We accepted their invitation and stayed with them during my consultation week at the department.

Everything went well in Washington, and then we left for Missouri, where Charlotte's parents lived. We stayed a few days, visiting Charlotte in her hospital room. After our long separation overseas, Charlotte was not too receptive to our presence. Reverend Russell, her father, recommended that we go on to Leavenworth to spend Christmas and

New Year's with my family. It appeared that Charlotte would not be discharged anytime soon, so we took his recommendation.

The New Year came and went, and even though we wanted to stay in Leavenworth a little while longer, we had to get back to Missouri to spend more time with Charlotte and her family. After a couple of weeks in Missouri, the doctors told me that they did not plan on discharging Charlotte anytime soon. After a couple more weeks in Missouri, we bid Charlotte good-bye. As we were leaving Charlotte's hospital room, we did not realize this would be our last good-bye to her.

We decided to return to Washington, where we found an apartment and a public school nearby for Betsey. I arranged for a neighbor lady to pick Betsey up in the morning, take her to school, and then pick her up midafternoon, and care for her until I arrived home about 6:00 p.m. We developed friendships in the neighborhood and at church and tried to lead a normal social life.

One night, shortly after midnight, the phone rang. Answering it, I found that it was a devastating call from Reverend Russell, who advised me that he had just received notice from the doctor at the hospital that Charlotte had passed. As he was a Methodist minister, he would be making the funeral arrangements on my behalf, and they would let me know when the funeral service would be held.

The next morning, I had the very difficult task of telling Betsey that her mother was no longer with us. Betsey said, "Daddy, I heard the phone ring during the night, and I wondered who would be calling at that hour. A number of nights, I have heard the phone ring, and I have wondered if it could be the hospital telling us something about my mother as I have realized the serious situation of her illness. I know this is tragic for both of us, but I believe Mother will be happier where she has gone. Thank you, Daddy, for all the help you've given me in the past couple of years when it was just us. Now we will have to continue this way."

I further explained that funeral arrangements were being made, and we would shortly be going back to Missouri for the funeral service. At that point, I began making arrangements for Betsey and me to return to Missouri one more time for Charlotte's funeral.

CHAPTER 19

Short Stories

The following events took place while we were in Baghdad, and even though they are brief, I would like to relate them as they do reveal other instances that took place while we were in the Middle East.

THE CORONATION

The year was 1953. The embassy received an invitation for a limited number of their diplomats to attend the coming coronation of the new king, Faisal II. In 1939, when Faisal II was just three years old, his father, King Faisal I, was reported to have died in a mysterious vehicle accident. Faisal's uncle, Prince Abdullah, served as regent until Faisal came of age in 1953. During Faisal's early years, he was being groomed for the responsibility of being king. The coronation was scheduled for May 2, 1953, on Faisal's eighteenth birthday.

As I recall, Mr. Phil Ireland, Deputy Chief of Mission (DCM), called a small meeting, and five of us reported to his office. As the ambassador had been called to Washington, Mr. Ireland had been named chargé d'affaires. He advised us that we would be the five officers, including himself, who would be attending the coronation of King Faisal II. His first question was which officers of this group have formal diplomatic dress, which consists of long striped pants, a coat with long tails, a formal shirt and tie, and a top hat. Of the six of us, four including Phil raised their hands. Phil and one of the officers each had an extra set, which they offered to me and the other officer, so it looked like the six of us were all set to go.

As I recall, we were scheduled to leave the embassy shortly before 10:00 a.m. to go to the palace. We all arrived early and met in the (DCM's) office. The DCM said, "All right, let's stand up for inspection."

He checked each one of us and found that two or three of the ties were crooked. He started correcting everyone's formal dress attire, it was discovered that one of the fellows had forgotten his tie and had to rush back to his office to get his tie. We stood there getting everything in order, and as some of us had never worn formal dress before, we were all getting a little nervous.

As Phil came to me, he said, "OK, Bob, let's check you out." He did, and then he said, "Bob, where's your top hat?"

I replied, "It's right here on the chair." I knew what was going to happen when I put the hat on, as it was several sizes too large. As I previously mentioned, we were all getting a little nervous, so I decided to lighten up the situation. I put the hat on my head, and it slid down over my eyes to my nose. Then I said, "OK, men, who is going to lead me?"

Phil then said, "Bob, quit acting, and let's go. Just carry your hat!"

By then, we had all relaxed and were ready to go to our most anticipated occasion of the year—the coronation.

The palace was a most attractive building and was decorated with grandeur. The new king rode in his plush, colorful carriage dressed in his white field marshal's uniform.

The ceremony was to be conducted in a beautiful large hall, and as our group entered the hall, we were all seriously impressed with the formality of this affair. During the ceremony, I looked at the young king, and it was difficult for me to fathom the responsibilities that would be placed on such a young man for the ruling of the country of Iraq, even though he would have a prime minister as his guide. I was most honored to have been invited to such an impressive and historical event.

As it turned out, it was to be the only coronation that I was privileged to attend during my many years of diplomatic service. During my tour in Iraq, I did meet the king on a couple of other occasions, and to me, he appeared to have his country's best interest at heart.

Unfortunately, his reign as king lasted only a few short years. In 1958, during an uprising, he and some members of his family were assassinated in the palace garden. Faisal II was the last person to serve as king of Iraq.

THE NEW AMBASSADOR'S PRIZED DOG

As I recall, I had been in Baghdad approximately six months, and our former Ambassador had been gone possibly a month or two. The Deputy Chief of Mission (DCM) received notice that the new ambassador, Waldemar J. Gallman, would be arriving on July 2, 1954. The maintenance department was busy redecorating the ambassador's residence and office. As the chancery building was quite a large building, the ambassador's residence and the DCM's residence were both located on the second floor. Both residences were very spacious, as considerable entertainment was required by both officers.

The DCM had selected six or seven officers and their wives to go to the airport in Baghdad as a welcome committee to greet Ambassador Gallman and his wife. We formed a small group in the receiving lounge at the airport, and the DCM escorted the ambassador and his wife to the receiving group, where we all had a brief moment to welcome them. We had been made aware that the ambassador was bringing with him his prize dog, a Great Dane, which weighed well over a hundred pounds. It was a beautiful dog and had won a number of prizes in various dog shows.

The DCM handed one of the officers the claim checks for the Ambassador's baggage, which he needed to clear through customs and place in an enclosed van, which we had brought with us. He then turned and handed me a thick wallet-like accordion case, which contained the dog's birth certificate, all his licenses, and the listings of the many prizes he had won. He said, "Bob, this is Rex," and handed me the leash. "Bob, you get Rex through customs and meet us outside."

I was not familiar with the regulations concerning customs clearance for animals, but I turned and said, "Yes sir. I will take care of it."

At that time, the welcome group left and headed for the parking lot. I immediately went to the customs clearing desk to check Rex through so I could meet the others. One of the officers checked and signed the clearance documents for Rex. He commented on what a fine animal this was and then motioned me on through.

I was almost through the door, when the chief of customs called to me and asked, "Where are you taking that animal?"

I replied, "Rex has been cleared by your customs officer, and I am taking him to the parking lot where his master, the Ambassador, is waiting."

He said, "Bring that animal over here to my table."

There was a large table by a window that opened to the parking lot. The window was open, and there was a drop of five to six feet to the ground outside, then a four- to five-foot fence between the customs office and the parking lot. As I took a second look, I saw that the Ambassador and the walking group had arrived at the vehicles and were waiting for me to bring Rex.

The customs officer in charge reviewed Rex's papers and said, "We do not need any dogs this size in our country. I am canceling this entry permit. You will now have to return this dog to the States on the next flight out."

At this point, I offered the chief customs officer a twenty-dollar tip, which was the normal order of business, but he said, "Consul Day, a tip won't do the trick today."

I knew this could not happen and my job probably would be in jeopardy. I said, "Mr. Customs Officer, you cannot do this. This dog has been cleared by one of your agents, and this dog is the prize dog of the American Ambassador."

He replied, "Consul Day, this dog is not entering this country."

Just then, one of the other customs agents called his boss and said, "I need you here right away." The chief of customs turned to me and said, "Stay where you are. I will be back as soon as I can."

After he left, I wondered how to get out of this mess. Rex had been cleared; I had the signed papers. I decided that I would have to do something unethical. I looked at ole Rex, and he had spotted the Ambassador in the parking lot. An embassy station wagon was parked next to the embassy limousine with the back door open for Rex to jump into.

I took hold of Rex's collar, and, pulling him up close, I whispered in his ear, "Rex, there is your master. Go get him!"

I unhooked Rex's leash. He was all enthused and ready to go, and I tapped him on his rear end. He jumped onto the table, across about six feet to the windowsill, and then jumped out the window to the ground. I looked to see if he had broken any bones, but he was on his feet again and headed for the fence. By this time, he was really moving, and I wondered if he would be able to clear the fence. He got within jumping distance of the fence, and he was in the air. He sailed right over the fence, out of the customs lot, and headed for the open door of the station wagon. I thought he must have been doing sixty miles per hour when he went through that vehicle door, but soon he was at the back door, wagging his tail.

I then thought, *Uh-oh, he is out, but I am still here.*

The chief of customs returned and saw that Rex was gone. He asked what happened, and I replied, "He jerked the leash and jumped out the window."

He then said, "Consul Day, you can't do this."

I said, "Sir, I have authorized papers." And he said, "Where is my tip?"

I handed him the twenty dollars I had in my hand, thanked him, and walked out the door.

When I arrived back at the group standing at the side of the limousine, the Ambassador thanked me for taking care of getting Rex through customs.

The DCM said, "Bob, this took longer than I expected."

I said, "Yes, sir, it did. If it is OK, I will tell you about it later."

Then we all got in our vehicles and headed for the embassy.

A few weeks later, when I was called to the Ambassador's office, Rex met me at the door and walked me to the visitor's chair at the Ambassador's desk. Then he laid down. The Ambassador said, "Bob, you are the only man on my staff who Rex meets at the door and brings to the visitor's chair, which is most unusual. "Then he laughed and said, "I hope you are not trying to steal my dog!"

I replied, "No, Mr. Ambassador, I would certainly not attempt to steal this wonderful dog from you."

The ambassador had a soft pad on the floor right next to his desk, and whenever he was in his office, Rex was there, protecting him. Several times a month, I would be asked to come to visit the ambassador's office to brief him on something. Each time I arrived, ole Rex would meet me at the door, licking my hand. I am sure he was thinking, *Thanks, Bob, for getting me out of that mess at the customs office.*

THE UNFORGETTABLE COOK

We had been in Baghdad for less than six months and had employed at least three men who claimed they were very good cooks, but none of them were satisfactory.

I received a call from the personnel officer who said a man who said he was a cook had applied for a position at the ambassador's residence, but the position had been filled. She had heard I was looking for a cook and said this man appeared to be from India and had three very good references as a cook, but she was unable to contact any of the references. She wanted to know if I would be interested in talking with him. I replied that I would be interested in interviewing him to determine if he would meet our requirements. She sent the man to my office, and when he arrived, I saw that he was quite a tall man, a little over six feet. His name was Jeffer.

During our conversation, he mentioned that he had worked for a number of people and had never been fired. He showed me his three references, but I could not verify that they were authentic. After talking with him for a short time, I decided that I would at least give him a try for a few weeks, and he reported to my residence the following day.

For the first two weeks, he was very good, but in the third week, his quality of cooking started to go downhill. I asked him what the problem was, and he said, "There is no problem, Master. Sometimes I don't feel like cooking. Remember, I have never been fired."

I advised him that his cooking would have to improve, or I would have to let him go. Again, he said, "Master, I have never been fired."

I replied, "Jeffer, if you don't show some improvement in your cooking in the next few days, I may have to terminate your services, or in other words, fire you."

He replied, "I will try to do better."

By the end of the fourth week, his cooking had not improved, and I decided that after Sunday lunch, I would have to let him go. Jeffer had been so obstinate a few times that I did not know for sure how he would respond when I fired him.

After lunch on Sunday afternoon, I put two envelopes in my pocket—the first containing his last week's pay and the second covering the following week's pay. Then I unlocked my bedroom cabinet and slipped my .38 pistol in my jacket pocket. I told Betsey's nursemaid to take Betsey into the bedroom and lock the door if any disturbance erupted.

Walking into the kitchen, I said, "Jeffer, have you finished eating and cleaning up the kitchen?"

He said, "Yes, Master, I am finished, and I will be leaving for my afternoon off soon."

I replied, "Fine, Jeffer, but as we have talked a couple of times, your cooking has not improved, and I am going to have to let you go."

He said, "Master, you should not fire me as I will have to cut your throat if you fire me."

At that point, he reached in a kitchen drawer and drew a butcher knife three-fourths of the way out of the drawer.

I said, "Jeffer, here are two envelopes. One is for last week's pay, and the other is for next week, as I am not giving you any notice."

He said, "Master, I told you no one fires me. I will have to cut your throat."

I was standing approximately ten feet from him, and he removed the knife from the drawer. He repeated, "Master, I will have to cut your throat."

I said, "Jeffer, I do not want to shoot you, but if you move, I will have to shoot you."

He started to take one step forward, and I said, "Jeffer, stay where you are. Drop that knife! Pick up your money and go."

He was very angry. His eyes flared. Then he said, "Master, you cannot fire me."

As he slipped the knife back into the drawer, he said, "I quit. I do not like working for you. I leave tomorrow."

I replied, "Jeffer, you go to your quarters, pack your bags, and leave within fifteen minutes. Don't ever come back here again."

Jeffer picked up his money, walked out the door to his quarters, and within ten minutes, he was gone. When I saw him walking down the street, I turned and started toward the bedroom, and there was Thelma, standing behind the door with a hammer in her hand.

I said, "Thelma, what are you doing here?"

She said, "Mr. Day, I was listening and watching. I was going to give you help. I locked Betsey in the bedroom where no one could get to her."

I said, "As you could see, I did not need any assistance."

She said, "Yes, Mr. Day, but that was close!"

"Yes, Thelma, but he is gone now, and I am sure he will not be back."

A few weeks later, the personnel officer called me and asked if I had hired Jeffer the few months before. I explained that he did work for me for a short time, but he was gone now. She said, "Just a minute!"

I could hear her talking. When she came back on the phone, she said, "Mr. Day, I have two well-dressed men who are detectives in my office who would like to talk with you." I told her to send them over.

When they arrived, I asked them for identification. They provided it, showing they were not local police officers. They told me they were looking for Jeffer. However, Jeffer was not the man's real name. He had been employed by a European couple, and they had been found in their home dead with their throats cut. These men had heard that Jeffer was going to answer an ad for employment with the American embassy, and they were checking to see if he was still in this area. I explained to them my dealings with Jeffer, and they said that I was very fortunate to have been able to defend myself, as he was known to have some mental problems.

Thereafter, I was a little more careful in selecting my household help.

AN UNUSUAL ACCIDENT

One weekend afternoon, Betsey and I decided to take a drive up country for fifty miles or so just for a little outing. We drove north on a two-lane blacktop road, and shortly after we approached the main highway, we noticed that the vehicle directly in front of us was carrying a pinewood box on the large framework that had been constructed on top of the vehicle to carry large objects. Now it was carrying a pinewood box about six and a half feet long and two and a half feet wide, which was, in effect, a casket. The occupants of the vehicle were no doubt friends or family members who had come to Baghdad to purchase this box or have it constructed for a family member that had passed.

After a short time the vehicle in front of us stopped within the right lane of the highway to pick up someone on the side of the road who needed a ride. This blocked us and all other traffic behind it. Apparently, someone in the vehicle explained that all seats were taken but the hitch hiker could ride in the rack on top of the vehicle. Consequently, the individual climbed aboard, and the vehicle then moved on.

After a short time, it started to rain. The man riding on top raised the lid of the large box and, to avoid getting wet, climbed inside and closed the lid. A few miles down the road, the vehicle stopped to pick up a second person who wanted a ride, and this person climbed aboard on top of the vehicle and sat within the rack next to the pine box. He sat there dozing. A few miles up the road, the rain stopped; and shortly thereafter, the man who had climbed inside the box, or intended casket, raised the lid and partly stood up. The second man was surprised to see this man rising out of the box. He apparently thought a dead person had come alive. He was so frightened that he jumped off the roof of the vehicle, which was then moving about fifty to sixty miles an hour. Someone within the vehicle saw what had taken place, and the vehicle stopped suddenly; and those of us behind him quickly applied our brakes and came to a screeching halt.

The man who had jumped had severely injured himself and lay motionless on the side of the road. Soon there was a long conversation between several individuals in the vehicle in front of us and some of the drivers in the vehicles behind us. I remained in my vehicle, as I did not think I should get involved. The result of this long conversation was the soliciting of a taxi, which was in the midst of traffic. The man who had jumped, who was either injured or deceased was placed in the taxi, and a man from one of the vehicles behind us got in the taxi with the driver, and they headed toward the hospital. All vehicles then moved ahead, as did we. We did not hear anything further concerning the incident.

GIN AS A BAKSHEESH

One afternoon, our general service officer in Baghdad dropped by to brief me on a couple of outstanding items as he was taking leave for a week. I would be required to assume the responsibilities of his office while he was gone. One of the items he needed to tell me about was a small hospital that was holding the body of an American employee of one of the JAS agencies. It was quite possible that the local government would approve the shipment of this body back to the States within the next few days. As I had not been in Baghdad too long, he wanted to explain to me the procedure we needed to use to expedite the shipment of a body to the States. He explained in detail what I needed to do. He said, "I know this sounds very strange, but I have experienced this problem several times while trying to get a body onto an airplane for shipment back to the States. With the assistance of the airline, this procedure has been approved by the Deputy Chief of Mission. Otherwise, you might have the problem of not getting the shipment to move after you arrive at the airport."

Within a few days, I received a call from the local authorities saying clearance had now been granted for one of the bodies to be moved out of the country and back to the States. The following day, the driver of the embassy van and I picked up a pine box and a rubber transfer bag from the embassy warehouse. Then, I picked up the consular officer who had the required custom documents. We went to our commissary and purchased five one-liter bottles of gin. We drove to the hospital where they placed the body of the American citizen in the rubber bag and then placed it in the pine box. We then locked the one lock on the pine box securely and drove to the airport presenting the necessary papers to the custom authorities.

The custom authority checked the casket and approved it for shipment. He assigned four local part-time laborers from the airport to transfer the box onto an airport cart for loading onto the plane. The four men only loaded the casket onto the airport cart part way out of my large van. I had been previously told that this would happen. One of the four men threw up his hands and hollered something that I did not understand. The airport custom official then turned to me and said that they could not load the box as they had just learned that it contained the body of an American, and that spirits were coming out of the box, and they needed to stop them and gin was the only way to do that. I replied that I understood and handed the supervisor of the four men a bottle of gin. He removed the cork of the bottle and poured the gin on the box as the four of them danced around it until the bottle was empty. Then I showed the leader that I had four more bottles of gin for them. They then moved the box onto the cargo cart wheeling it into the airport shipping room. The four of them returned and I gave them each one bottle of gin. They bowed and said a short phrase and sat down in the back of the airport drinking the gin. The airport supervisor then said that they would drink the gin to kill any spirits that had penetrated their bodies and then they would be alright.

Subsequently, there were several other American citizens who died and this procedure was followed. We recognized that this could be the true feelings concerning the handling of the deceased. On the other hand, it could have been a ploy to gain a *baksheesh*, or tip for their services, which was a bottle of gin. We all considered this was a *baksheesh*!

A NEAR AIR CRASH

One morning, when I was returning to Baghdad, we were flying over a desolate area of the desert when we suddenly encountered an unexpected dust storm. Both engines started sputtering, as apparently, the gas lines had been clogged with dust. We began losing altitude very rapidly. I don't recall what altitude we were flying at, but it was probably around five thousand feet. The ground was coming up very rapidly, and the pilot was doing everything he could to get the engines started again. He gave us the word to prepare for a crash landing. At about one-thousand-feet altitude, both engines suddenly started again, but we were still going down very rapidly. The pilot pulled out of the fall about five hundred feet from the ground and regained normal altitude and control of the plane.

The pilot said, "Sorry, folks, for giving you that thrill, but we're in good shape now."

We continued on at our normal flying altitude and safely landed in Baghdad, our destination.

NEAR ESCAPE FROM DEATH

Shortly after my arrival in Baghdad, one of the embassy officers called me and asked if I ever did any hunting or was interested in doing some. I answered that I had done considerable rabbit hunting and bird shooting.

He said, "Sometime back, four of us organized what we might call a small hunting club. We now have a vacancy and are looking for a man to fill this spot, who knows his weapons and who would be interested in joining us. As none of us are fluent in Arabic, we have asked a local in your department, who has done a great deal of bird hunting and enjoys it, to join us as our guide. This way, we have a fifth hunter, Alex, who speaks Arabic fluently, who will be of assistance in the event we get into any kind of a misunderstanding with an outsider."

I thanked him for the invitation, and a few days later, we met for lunch, and I joined the group. For over a year and a half, I was a member of this little club, and we went hunting together about fifteen or twenty times. I enjoyed being with this small group, as we all knew gun safety and were very careful with our weapons. The local gentleman, Alex, was also a good hunter, was a real sportsman, knew gun safety and followed it, and was of real value with a few outsiders concerning our hunting.

We decided to go on one more hunting trip before my departure from the post and, in advance, had selected a spot very near the edge of the desert where a rather large bird, known as a small pheasant, frequented. Usually, each of us would get two or three of these birds during a two- to three-hour hunting trip. They would run out of foliage at the edge of the desert and go into the open area, which made them quite easy to shoot.

On the day of the trip, we met at our designated meeting spot about 6:00 a.m. and headed to where we intended to park our vehicles for a few hours near the desert. We checked our weapons, locked our vehicles, loaded the chambers of our weapons with our favorite shells, moved out in our agreed formation, and started hunting.

Within thirty minutes or so, we had shot three or four birds and were coming to a very desolate area at the edge of the desert. Suddenly, we noticed three men on camels coming toward us. It was still before sunrise, so we watched to see what their intentions were. They each raised their right hand, indicating friendship, and stopped right near us. At that time, we never knew if these desert people were friendly or otherwise. However, the few we had met were all quite friendly.

In one case, however, a few months before, we had met a man on a camel. His wife was walking behind him, carrying a rather large package on her head. As they traveled within thirty feet or so, I had raised my camera to photograph her, as she still wore her veil. When she noticed that I intended to take her picture, she dropped her veil, looked directly at me, and smiled. Her husband noticed this action. He hopped off his camel, grabbing his saber with one hand, and looked at me, moving one finger back and forth across his throat, and I lowered my camera. He indicated "No!" and turned to his wife and said some very sharp words to her. She immediately put her veil back on, and he hopped back on his camel and they continued on their way. As he had his back to us, she teasingly dropped her veil again, nodded, and smiled. We nodded and smiled as well, but no one raised their camera to photograph her. They went on across the desert, as she followed her husband, and we never saw them again.

When the three men on camels arrived, they had given their sign of friendship. Their leader stopped and gave their sign of friendship again. He spoke English very well and asked what size shot we were using in our guns to kill the birds.

At first, none of us replied; but then one of the four of us said, "As we are shooting birds, we are only using a small shot."

We held on to our guns, as they were all loaded. The leader said that he certainly admired our weapons, and then indicated that they were leaving and wished us good luck as they rode off.

Alex turned to the one who had told them that he had only a small shot in his gun and said, "Joe, you made a mistake."

Joe said, "As soon as I said that, I knew I had."

Alex said, "He is not afraid of a small shot, as I noticed he was carrying a heavy blanket which resists small shot. He can throw that around him to protect himself."

Joe said, "Yes, I apologize, fellows."

We started to spread out again to continue hunting. Meanwhile, several of us, including myself, had slipped heavy loads into our guns. Suddenly, we heard several camels running fast, heading directly for us. When they got within 100 to 150 feet, they opened fire. Our friend Alex hollered, "Men, hit the dust and start shooting!"

I had reloaded with pumpkin balls, and my friend had reloaded with 00 buckshot. When they were quite close, their leader shouted, "I have been hit!" All three of them made a fast U-turn and headed back across the desert.

Thinking they might return, we lay on the ground another five to ten minutes before we got to our feet. Alex asked if everyone was OK, and we looked around at each other and said that we guessed we were all OK.

Alex said, "Bob and John, take off your jackets!"

John said, "Alex, it is chilly out here."

Alex repeated, "Bob and John, take off your jackets."

As we took off our jackets, Alex pointed to the right shoulder of John's jacket, which had a bullet hole in it. The left collar of my jacket also had a bullet hole in it. Alex figured that John had been standing slightly in front of me, and either one bullet nearly took care of both of us, or it was two separate shots very close together.

All of us rechecked both jackets and agreed that just before we hit the ground, John was standing just in front of me, and his jacket may have caught the bullet before it hit my jacket. We all agreed it was too close for comfort, and we decided we had had enough hunting for the day.

A couple of weeks later, all five of us met for lunch, said our goodbyes, and agreed that we were all thankful that we had come through two years of safe hunting together. That was our last hunting trip in Baghdad and the last time I saw any of my hunting friends.

Arab feast (couzi) - Baghdad 1952

CHAPTER 20

Assignment: Washington DC

On March 1, 1955, I was assigned for two years to the Office of Finance in Washington DC as a financial management procedure advisor. As a staff officer, I was given the opportunity to take the Foreign Service officer examination. After passing this examination, I was sworn in as a commissioned Foreign Service officer, which made me a Consul and Second Secretary of Embassy in the diplomatic service. After one year in this position, my duties were changed somewhat and included traveling overseas to various US embassies investigating financial and management problems.

At this point, I decided that it would be more appropriate for Betsey to attend the Samuel Ready Boarding School for Girls in Baltimore, Maryland, and Betsey agreed that she would attend the school. This worked out quite well, as I would do most of my traveling during the week when Betsey was in school, and on Friday evenings, I would pick her up and bring her home to the apartment for the weekend. This would give us time to spend together and get her uniform and other items of clothing ready for the next week.

In November 1956, I met a very lovely lady named Dorothy Jean Lambert at a social affair at Betsey's school, and we were married the first of June the following year. Dotty had been widowed for six years, and she had a daughter, Shaula, who was one year younger than Betsey.

After two years in the Office of Finance, I was given the opportunity to transfer to the Bureau of Near Eastern Affairs, where I was Deputy Budget Officer but served frequently as Budget Officer due to the other assignments my supervisor was called on to perform. I reviewed the budgets of all US embassies in the Bureau of Near Eastern and South Asian Affairs and granted them the approved financial funding for their operations. This included working with other teammates justifying the Bureau of Near Eastern Affairs budget requirements to Congress.

During this period with the bureau, I was promoted and became First Secretary of Embassy based on my performance while on my two assignments in Washington. As I was nearing the completion of my four-year assignment in Washington, I was advised that I would soon be notified of the location and transfer date of my new assignment overseas.

I had enjoyed our assignments in Washington and working with the staff but we were looking forward to our new overseas assignment when announced.

Betsey and Shaula at Bob and Dotty's wedding - June 1, 1957

CHAPTER 21

Assignment: Tehran, Iran

When we received our assignment to Tehran, Iran, in March 1959, we discussed the living conditions, educational facilities, and embassy operations with several senior officers, who had served in Iran and were very pleased with their duty station. We started reading up on this post of assignment, and within a few days, we also became very enthused.

On the assigned date, Dotty, Betsey, Shaula, and I departed New York on the ship SS *Constitution* to a shipping port in Genoa, Italy. We then moved on by train to Rome, Italy. We were booked at a very pleasant hotel for two nights, and then late evening on March 7, 1959, we departed Rome by Pan American World Airways to Tehran.

We were met early the next morning at the airport by administrative officer Basil Capaella and his wife, Nan. They expedited us through customs and to our hotel, which was in downtown Tehran. This would be our new home until we could locate a suitable residence.

We had our baggage delivered to our two hotel rooms, and Basil said, "Bob and Dotty, this is your schedule. We are invited to go to the hotel dining room for breakfast. You may want to shower and rest a few minutes afterwards. We will pick the two of you up in about an hour and a half. I will take you to meet the ambassador at 9:00 a.m. Then you will meet the division heads, and I will introduce you to your staff. Later, Dotty will take Betsey and Shaula to the Tehran American School, register them, and they will be assigned to their classrooms."

"Then, Nan will take Dotty to the American commissary, where she can pay your membership fees, and you will be immediately qualified to start making purchases from the commissary. The four of us will then meet some of our division chiefs and then meet for lunch at the hotel. Then you will go to your office and go to work. Betsey and Shaula will be returned by school bus at 4:00 p.m. to the hotel. Nan and I, with our two children, will meet you at 7:00 p.m. for dinner."

"You will notice, by your engagement schedule, that there is a cocktail party tomorrow evening at six o'clock being held by the Ambassador to welcome you and your family to Tehran. This will be embassy officers and wives only. You will then have the next night off. The following evening, there will be another cocktail party given by the eighteen directors and executive officers of the Joint Administrative Services support group, each representing a member agency. From then on, you and Dotty are on your own."

After searching for about a month during our extra time, we found a new home in Shemiran near Mount Damavand on the western side of the Elburz Mountains. This kept us well up out of the heat of the city, where we enjoyed our private gardens surrounded by an eight-foot wall, similar to many found throughout the Middle East. The huge *āb anbār*, or water storage area, had been converted into a swimming pool, which was a center of attraction for many swimming parties for all members of the family.

During the four years spent in Tehran, Betsey and Shaula attended the Tehran American School and received an excellent education. Dotty worked at the American School as a secretary to the superintendent. Before Dotty and I married, she had worked as secretary to the superintendent of a large business firm in Baltimore. During the last two years of World War II, she served as assistant team captain for a prominent aircraft company on the West Coast as a test pilot for newly constructed airplanes as they came off the assembly line prior to going into action.

During this period, in addition to my regular assignment, I served as the Ambassador's representative and as financial advisor to the Tehran American School. I was also selected by the ambassador as one of the six embassy duty officers to be on duty one week every six weeks beginning at five o'clock in the evening until eight o'clock the following morning. This assignment was to basically take care of emergencies at the embassy. It did not necessarily require me to be at the embassy, but I had to be immediately available whenever the marines needed a person to respond to an American citizen who called for assistance or protection.

Special care had to be exercised at all times for personal safety. Iran was a country of disturbances and international intrigue. Parents and children alike were always on guard for the unexpected.

In my position, I had a wide range of contacts who were members of the various US agencies as well as the Iranian government. During my tour of approximately four years, I had a number of interesting experiences, and I have related some of these experiences in this memoir.

Bob's house - Tehran, Iran 1960

Bob's second wife Dotty in Tehran - 1960

Dotty, Bob, Shaula, Betsey, and dog Liza -
Tehran, Iran - Christmas 1960

Betsey in Girl Scout uniform
Tehran, Iran - 1961

Our dog Liza on the patio of our house in Tehran, Iran

CHAPTER 22

A Man In Distress

As I recall, it was a cool spring night in April of 1960 when Dotty and I went to the Tehran International Airport, which was located a few miles from the city, to say bon voyage to some close friends who were heading for the States on home leave.

As we passed the Pan American ticket counter walking back through the airport after our friends' departure, I noticed a well-dressed American man at the counter involved in a very heated discussion with the ticket agent. I said to Dotty that I recognized the man as Edward R. Murrow, the CBS television journalist, and we walked up to the ticket counter. I asked if he was Mr. Murrow, to which he replied that he was. Handing him my card, I introduced myself and asked if I could be of any assistance, as I knew a number of the Pan Am employees.

He said that he and his two associates had first-class tickets booked on the midnight flight to New Delhi, India, which the Pan Am ticket agent had canceled. The agent explained to us that he had sold the tickets to other passengers who needed them more than Mr. Murrow. There was no doubt that the ticket agent had received some *baksheesh*, or remuneration, for this transaction.

I asked the ticket agent again if he could arrange some way for Mr. Murrow and his two associates to have three tickets on the midnight flight to New Delhi, to which he declined. I then asked if I could use his telephone. He reluctantly handed it to me, and I called the Pan Am district manager, Jack Barr, whom I knew very well. I explained the situation, and Jack then asked to speak with the agent. They had a rather lengthy discussion, concluding with the ticket agent handing me the telephone. Jack thanked me for calling and said that even though it was nearly midnight and fast approaching the departure time for the flight to New Delhi, the situation had been resolved.

After the phone call, the ticket agent advised Mr. Murrow and me that he now had three first-class tickets on the midnight flight. After a brief discussion with his two associates, Mr. Murrow thanked the ticket agent for his assistance but told him that he had just received notice that he needed to delay his departure until the following evening. He then asked the ticket agent if it would be possible to book them on the same flight for the following night. The ticket agent agreed and changed their tickets accordingly. I also thanked the ticket agent for his assistance, and he assured me that Mr. Murrow's tickets would not be canceled for the following night. I offered Mr. Murrow and his associates a ride back to the hotel from which they had just checked out a few hours earlier. It was after midnight when we delivered the three of them to the hotel, and they thanked us most graciously for our help.

The next morning, at about ten o'clock, I received a telephone call at my office from Mr. Murrow asking if I would care to have lunch with him at his hotel. Unfortunately, I had to decline as I had a previously scheduled business meeting and luncheon.

Several weeks later, I received a letter from Mr. Murrow thanking me for my assistance in resolving his problem with the Pan Am ticket agent. Mr. Murrow was a CBS representative and broadcaster for a number of years. He was later appointed director of the United States Information Service (USIS) by President Kennedy. Mr. Murrow died in April of 1965.

CHAPTER 23

A Night To Remember

By the summer of 1960, I had been assigned to Tehran, Iran for approximately one year. Dotty, our two daughters, Betsey and Shaula, who were both early teenagers, and I had adjusted well to the Middle East. I had many official business and social engagements due to my position as Budget Management Officer for the American embassy and the Joint Administrative Services. Dotty was involved fulfilling her duties as a mother, embassy wife, and secretary to the director of the Tehran American School, which had an enrollment of approximately nine hundred to one thousand American children. Our two daughters were doing very well in school and had developed many friendships with other youngsters in the American community, including some young Iranian friends.

The Shah, Mohammad Reza Pahlavi, supported a pro-Western government, and most of the time, the political situation was quite stable. However, at certain times during the year, especially during Iranian holidays, there were demonstrations and other incidents that made one realize that a certain amount of caution was necessary.

The Tehran American School provided bus service for American students, but it was always necessary for parents or friends to transport their youngsters to various activities or social events within the community. Therefore, many evenings, Dotty, Betsey, Shaula, and I would have a round-table discussion to coordinate our engagements and transportation requirements for the following day and evening.

One Thursday night, in mid-summer of 1960, the four of us sat down to coordinate our activities for the following day, which would be the last day of school for the girls that week. It had already been a very busy week, and when we checked our calendars, Dotty and I saw we had a 6:00 p.m. reception at a US Foreign Aid senior officer's residence to welcome the new executive officer and his wife, who had just arrived in Tehran. At 8:00 p.m., we were due at the Economic Officer's residence to attend a buffet dinner in honor of the Minister of Finance. Shaula would be coming home after school to work on a special school project, while Betsey had a birthday party to attend at 4:30 p.m. in honor of one of her classmates, and then at 8:00 p.m., both girls would be going to a swim party at Beth Neuman's home. Beth was the daughter of Colonel Howard Neuman, US Air Attaché, and Mrs. Neuman.

We decided that Dotty would take Betsey to her 4:30 p.m. birthday party. Dotty and I would attend the 6:00 p.m. reception at the US Foreign AID Officer's residence, leave the reception about 7:15 p.m., pick Betsey up from the birthday party, and then pick Shaula up at home. We would deliver both girls to the swim party; then Dotty and I should arrive at the Economic Officer's residence at 8:00 p.m. on schedule.

Friday evening arrived, and Dotty delivered Betsey to her engagement. I arrived home from the office on schedule, and Dotty and I attended the reception for the US AID Executive Director as planned and enjoyed meeting the new Foreign AID Program Executive Officer, his wife, and many other friends. After leaving the reception, we picked Betsey up from her birthday party and started home to pick up Shaula. Everything was working out as planned, and we were on schedule for the evening events.

As we drove down Old Shemiran Road, a four-lane main thoroughfare, a large black sedan pulled up on the left side of our vehicle, and we moved along side by side for a short distance. I did not give it too much consideration until the vehicle moved ahead of our vehicle about eight feet and began edging toward our left front fender. I then noticed two men in the front seat talking very adamantly. Suddenly, their vehicle moved more into my lane, and to avoid colliding, I moved my vehicle further to the right side of the road and sounded my horn.

The black sedan suddenly turned completely into my lane and, with tires squealing, we both made a sharp right turn into a side street. The driver of the black sedan drove his vehicle into the left front fender of my vehicle and blocked the driver's door, preventing it from opening. I asked Dotty to immediately move into the rear seat with Betsey, lock the doors, and roll her back window down slightly so she could hear the conversation and know what was taking place. Meanwhile, I moved across the seat and got out of the passenger side of the vehicle.

The two men in the black sedan both got out and ran up to me, shouting, "Why are you trying to run us off the road?"

I told them they ran me to the side of the road and around the corner, which caused the accident. After a short discussion, they agreed to send one of the many bystanders that had gathered around the accident to a telephone to call the police and the American Embassy Duty Officer. It was embassy policy to report such accidents. I learned the driver of the black sedan was named Mustafa, and the other man was Jaafar. I wrote down their full names, description of the vehicle, and their license plate number.

By this time, approximately five hundred or more Iranians had gathered to enjoy the excitement. Mustafa climbed onto the hood of his vehicle and started giving a political speech against the local government and shouting that all capitalist Americans should be run out of the country. The man known as Jaafar told the people who had gathered to build a little rock wall behind my vehicle so we could not drive away, and they followed his instructions.

There we were, in a large crowd of people looking for excitement, with rocks stacked about two or three feet high behind our vehicle, blocking a retreat, and Mustafa enraging the crowd with his political speech.

I walked to one edge of the crowd to survey a possible exit from the area. The only possibility was to proceed straight ahead, as the street was clear, but there was a five or six-foot mud-brick wall blocking the way. I noticed that parts of the top of the wall had been broken off and the brick had fallen inside, making a small ramp.

From where I was, I could not see very much into the other side of the wall, but there appeared to be little traffic moving and not many pedestrians walking. A short distance up the street, there was a tea house with men sitting at an outside table having their late afternoon tea. I thought this would be difficult and risky, but it was something to consider. I walked along the edge of the crowd back to my vehicle and noticed the crowd did not pay much attention to me; they were concentrating on the speaker.

I was standing at the side of my vehicle waiting for the police and the duty officer to arrive when an Iranian walked up to me and said, "Consul Day, I am Omar Ferdowsi, and I work at the Iranian Ministry of Finance. I know this is not your fault, but you are in big trouble."

I recognized Omar as a senior employee at the ministry, but realized he was not in a position to control the crowd who had gathered and now were becoming a violent mob. My Farsi was fair, and I had been listening to Mustafa's speech for about fifteen minutes, but most of the time, he was speaking in an unfamiliar dialect.

Omar said, in a low voice, to me, "This mob is growing very angry, and the man you and Mustafa sent to call the police and the American duty officer just returned without making the calls. He has now been sent by Jaafar to get a can of gasoline as they intend to burn your vehicle with you and your family in it."

About this time, Consular Officer Charles Hunter pulled into the side street to render some assistance, but the crowd stoned his vehicle, and he backed out, speeding away.

Before departing, he called out, "Bob, we will send you some help." I thought to myself, *when would help arrive, and would it be in time?*

Omar then came very close and quietly said, "Consul Day, these are very bad men. They are not from this area. I want you, your wife, and daughter to come to my house for protection. I live just a short distance down the street."

I said, "Omar, this is most kind of you, but you know this crowd will follow us to your house and stone you and your family too."

He said, "That is probably true, but you must leave here soon."

Realizing I would not accept his invitation, Omar lowered his head and moved through the mob and on down the street.

I was unable to back my vehicle up because of the rocks stacked behind it, and most of the mob was on both sides and behind my vehicle. I thought, *with the short distance I would have to travel, could I hit the wall hard enough to go on through with my vehicle, or would I be stopped by the impact?*

By then, the people were shouting, "Kill them, kill them!" The mob was ready to strike, and they wanted to see blood. There was no other alternative than to head for the wall.

I had purchased the new white Ford sedan a year earlier in the States and had it shipped to Tehran. The post report had advised personnel being transferred to Iran not to ship any vehicle to Iran that had an automatic transmission, as repair and maintenance at that time were not available. When I visited the Ford dealership to purchase a new vehicle, this was the only vehicle in their inventory that had a straight-shift transmission. The vehicle had been ordered by a law enforcement agency and, for some reason, had not been delivered. The vehicle not only had the straight-shift transmission, it also had a large V8 engine, and the front bumper had been equipped with extra bumper guards. At the time of purchase, I had advised the dealer I did not need these extra features, but he was anxious to sell the vehicle. As we were scheduled to leave the States within a few days, a favorable financial arrangement was worked out. Now, I was thankful my vehicle had these additional features.

By this time, twenty minutes or so had passed, and Mustafa had inflamed the mob to the point that they were again yelling and chanting, "Kill them, kill them, kill them now!"

Dotty and Betsey, sitting in the back seat, had become extremely nervous, and I knew they completely depended on me to find a safe way out of this very dangerous situation. We had been through some tight spots before, but this was becoming very intense. I did not want to injure any of the bystanders or the mob, but this was the moment of truth, and I was ready to take whatever action was necessary to get us out of this serious situation.

I walked to the back door of my vehicle, where the window was down slightly and said, "Girls, are you ready for some action?"

They said, "Let's do it."

I said, "I will be getting into the vehicle shortly. Remain seated until I start the engine, then both of you hit the floor."

The only reply I heard was, "Hurry, Daddy, hurry!"

I looked around and saw Mustafa was still standing on the hood of his vehicle, shouting to the crowd in the foreign dialect and pointing at me. Jaafar came walking toward me out of the mob and stood about five feet from my passenger door blocking my way.

I said, "Jaafar, move aside, I am going to get into my vehicle."

He said, "No, you stay outside of the vehicle."

As I took one step forward, Jaafar's right hand shot under his coat, and then he withdrew it, lifting it high over his head. I saw the setting sun sparkling on a long curved dagger blade, known as a khanjar. He had a look of anger and terror in his dark eyes and was frowning as he yelled, "Now is the time to kill you."

When Dotty heard his threat and saw the knife raised over his head, she screamed, "Bob, he has a knife!"

Jaafar was startled by her scream and looked sideways at Dotty in the back seat of the vehicle; for an instant, his attention had been diverted. I knew that one of us would be going down, and I did not intend for it to be me.

I realized if Jaafar was experienced in the art of the use of the khanjar, with a twist of his wrist, he could drive the dagger blade through my left hand. I grabbed his right wrist with my left hand and held it very firmly to prevent him from stabbing me. With my right hand I grabbed him by the throat. I slammed his head hard into the solid door post of my vehicle. Then at the same time I drove my right knee with all my force into his groin, and he let out a piercing scream. When his head hit the door post, he became unconscious and fell to the ground, where he lay, shaking. Abruptly, the movement stopped, and I thought maybe I had killed him; but I could not worry about that now. I saw his head was near the rear wheel of my vehicle, and I pulled his body clear of the vehicle so I would not run him over.

Dotty had unlocked the front passenger door, and I bolted into the front seat, the door snapping shut behind me. I turned the ignition switch and heard the beautiful music of the engine immediately starting.

At the same moment, I heard Dotty say, "Bob, we are on the floor. Let's go!"

As I shifted into low gear and my foot hit the accelerator, I wondered if I had enough power to rip away the black sedan's fender and gain enough speed to hit the wall with the force needed to break through. I put more pressure on the accelerator. The engine roared, and I engaged the clutch. The Ford responded, and the rear wheels were spinning, throwing gravel and rocks into the mob. We were still hooked into the fender of the black sedan. I could hear the mob shouting, "They are getting away! Stop them!"

I could also hear the metal on the fenders tearing, but we were still stuck. I remember thinking, *we have got to get loose from the black sedan*. I started rocking my vehicle forward and backward by quickly shifting the gears. We were still stuck. As this was an emergency vehicle, it was equipped with red lights and a very loud siren, which I had never used. I turned on both of these switches, and I applied full throttle; and with a large bang, the vehicle shot forward, jerking his fender off and throwing it to the ground. My vehicle was speeding forward, and the crowd in front of the vehicle scattered, running for their lives as these two emergency features had certainly frightened the mob. It looked as though we had missed everyone in the mob; but suddenly, there were three bangs as some of the bystanders had run into the side of the vehicle, knocking themselves down.

We neared the brick wall, and I'm sure we were doing fifty to sixty miles per hour, and I was confident that my plan would probably be successful. I called to the girls to hold on, and we hit the broken brick that had formed a small incline up the side of the wall, which still left four feet or more of the wall to crash through.

Suddenly, there was a loud bang and a terrific vibration. Dotty called out, "Bob, are we going to make it?"

I answered, "Yes, Dotty. Both of you, hold on."

We hit the wall, which crumbled and flew in all directions. We were airborne and landed on all four wheels, possibly twenty to thirty feet or more beyond the wall. We were free. As there was no major traffic in the area, I slowed down.

From the back seat, Betsey said, "Daddy, can we now get up from the floor?"

Dotty said, "Bob, are you OK? What a ride!"

The vehicle was steering properly, the engine running fine, so it seemed there was no major damage to the working parts. I was starting to breathe a sigh of relief when suddenly, the black sedan appeared directly behind us. This time, there was only Mustafa driving the vehicle; no doubt Jaafar was still lying in the street where I dropped him. Mustafa was waving his arm and showing his fist out the window. I had nothing to use for defense and knew the only answer was to outdistance and lose him in the traffic. I had the advantage, plenty of power, and was now familiar with the area.

We lost Mustafa within a mile or so and then headed for home. I called in the report to the Embassy Duty Officer, who advised me that Consular Officer Charles Hunter had notified the police and was at his desk reporting what he knew of the incident.

By this time, we were close to an hour late for the economic officer's buffet dinner, so I called him and apologized for our delay. He explained that there was no problem, as the Minister of Finance had been called to the Shah's palace to discuss some urgent business, and that he had also been delayed for the dinner. Dotty and I freshened up, delivered the girls to their swim party at the Neuman's, and then went on to attend the dinner as originally scheduled.

The following day, an official report was made to the Ministry of Foreign Affairs with detailed information concerning the incident, including the full names of the men involved. Within a few days, Ambassador Tom Wailes's secretary called and asked me to report to the Ambassador's office for a meeting with a member of the Iranian Foreign Office and an investigator with the Tehran Police Department. The purpose of this meeting was for the Iranian government to apologize for the incident and to report on their findings.

According to their report, Mustafa and Jaafar were just two of the four men involved. The report revealed the other two men, known as Rishawd and Hassan, were engaged by a radical group to create an incident to embarrass the American Embassy. It was reported that the four men involved knew the diplomatic license plate numbers assigned to members of the American Embassy. Therefore, Mustafa and Jaafar were on Old Shemiran Road waiting for a vehicle to pass that had American Embassy license plates, and my vehicle was the one they selected.

However, the incident could have been more tragic, as it was discovered that Mustafa and Jaafar had instructions to pull a vehicle to the curb approximately one mile farther down the road, where the second two men, Rishawd and Hassan, were waiting. The four men had been instructed to kidnap the Americans whom they had selected. Fortunately, Mustafa and Jaafar had become confused about the meeting location and had stopped us too soon. It was reported that Mustafa and Jaafar did not have any weapons, but Rishawd and Hassan were well armed. It was further reported that all four men had been apprehended the following day and that they were wanted for other serious crimes. At present, the four men were in jail pending court hearing and trial.

According to subsequent reports received from the local authorities, all four men—Mustafa, Jaafar, Rishawd, and Hassan—were tried for various crimes, including assault and attempted kidnapping of a diplomatic officer, and found guilty. Each of the four received a sentence of ninety-nine years in prison without possibility of parole. Members of the mission felt much safer knowing these men were now in prison. To my knowledge, there were no repeat incidents such as this while I was living in Tehran.

I wish to mention that we found the Iranians to be most hospitable. We enjoyed their friendship and participated in the progress of the Iranian American activities. A number of former Iranian employees of the American Embassy now live in the United States, and I have communicated with some of them frequently. Looking back, even though we had a number of additional exciting events in Tehran, Iran, this trip was one of the most interesting posts of my assignments, and one of my favorites.

CHAPTER 24

R & R Trip To Paris

One afternoon, I was busy at my desk when my secretary buzzed me. She said that General Lindquist's office was on the phone and wanted to speak with me. General Lindquist was in charge of all American military forces in Iran. These military forces, along with many of his officers, were under the administrative support plan that provided some administration support functions. To my understanding, General Lindquist was well thought of and a real straight shooter in his operations. Our embassy offices had an excellent relationship with General Lindquist, as he heavily supported the Joint Administrative Services philosophy and the current operation of the American school system.

When I picked up the call, it was Colonel David Sanders, who was the top assistant to General Lindquist. I knew David quite well. He said he had just come from a meeting with General Lindquist, who had asked him to pass a message on to me. General Lindquist and I were business friends, and he wanted to know if Dotty and I would be interested in going along on his annual weeklong rest and recuperation, or R&R trip to Paris. There would be twenty-four military personnel with their wives, plus Dotty and me, and the aircrew on board for the trip. The first night, we would stop in Athens, Greece, and then arrive in Paris, France, the following day. The departing flight was two weeks away, on a Thursday, and we would return the following Friday.

Given that it was spring, the weather would be nice for such a trip, and I told the colonel that Dotty and I would love to go, but that I needed to check with the Ambassador to make sure nothing special was scheduled for me that week. The colonel told me to give him a call in the next day or two and said he hoped we would be able to go on the trip. He and his wife, Sally, were also invited, and it would be great for all of us to go together.

Later that afternoon, I called my supervisor, Basil Capella, to give him the message, and he said, "Bob, that's fine with me, but if you will, please call the Ambassador to get his approval, as I am tied up on another project."

I called the Ambassador's secretary, and she said she would call me back shortly. When the secretary returned my call later that afternoon, she said she had spoken with the Ambassador about the trip, and he said it was fine with him, as he had nothing special for me that week. He acknowledged that it had been two years since I had been out of Iran, and I was therefore deserving of a little R & R time.

When I told Dotty that the Ambassador had approved our R & R trip to Paris, she was delighted. Dotty and I arranged for an embassy couple that had just arrived in Tehran to live at our house during this weeklong trip and watch over our two daughters, who were in their early teenage years. The couple was delighted to move out of the hotel and be in our home for a week with our daughters, our German shepherd, our cook, houseboy, and a full pantry without obligations.

A couple weeks later, we arrived at the airport on Thursday morning for takeoff. We met General Lindquist and the aircrew planeside and were then introduced to all other passengers on our flight. Shortly thereafter, we boarded by protocol order the C-54, which was a four-engine air craft, a military transport with a crew of four and capacity for 50 passengers. The general and his wife had seating at a small table in the front of the plane on the left-hand side. Dotty and I were assigned seats on the right-hand side in the second row, with Colonel Sanders and his wife, Sally, in the two seats in front of us, so they were first across from the general, and we were second across. The general had a PA system in contact with the pilot and the copilot; therefore, we could clearly hear when they communicated back and forth.

We took off promptly and headed west, arriving at our assigned altitude of nineteen thousand feet. The copilot announced that passengers could move around as desired from seat to seat unless he announced that we were entering a bad weather area. The two seats directly across from the table of the general and his wife could be rotated, so the general had an opportunity to talk or play cards with all the passengers. At this point, Colonel Sanders gave us a short briefing of the scheduled trip, and another officer gave us a briefing in case of an emergency, which included safety operations and crash procedures.

Our trip to Athens was uneventful, and we arrived on schedule. There was an US Air Force bus waiting for us as we disembarked, which took us to a nice hotel where we all had reservations.

While we were in Paris, we all had a wonderful time as most of us traveled in small groups of two to four couples. We attended movie theaters, lunches, and dinners, which included dinner theaters. Some of our group, including Dotty and myself, went on sightseeing trips and other special-occasion activities. I am sure most, if not all, couples contacted their families back in Iran at times during the week to make sure everything was going well at home.

The day of our return to Tehran arrived sooner than we wished, and on Wednesday morning, the general announced at breakfast that the next day we would be flying out of Paris and would be arriving in Tehran sometime Friday afternoon or early evening. The US Air Force bus would be waiting at the hotel entrance at 7:00 a.m. and would depart at 7:15 a.m. As a final social get-together, we would all meet in the hotel dining room that evening at eight o'clock for cocktails and dinner.

When we were on the plane the following morning, Colonel Sanders gave us a briefing on our scheduled flight. He stated there was an unusually severe storm over the Mediterranean Sea. This meant that we would be flying directly south out of Paris at nineteen thousand feet, which was considered a safe altitude, crossing the tip of the Mediterranean Sea, making our way across Algeria to the capital of Algiers, and then turning east to fly across northern Africa. From there, we would fly on to Tehran. He said that despite the war taking place between Algeria and France, the Algerian air controller had given us clearance to fly at an altitude of six thousand feet across Algeria.

After we crossed Southern Europe and the Mediterranean Sea, we entered Algeria, and everything seemed to be going fine until we reached Algiers. Suddenly, the sky below us filled with puffs of black smoke. We knew this to be antiaircraft fire. General Lindquist immediately asked the pilot what was going on, and the pilot replied that they were trying to shoot us down; they were not following the clearance order they gave us. The pilot had suspected something might be in the works when Algerian air control told him to fly at six thousand feet, which wasn't an altitude that was frequently used, and so he had flown over Algeria at ten thousand feet instead. He was trying to get us out of the area as fast as possible, and then would go back to the original course, flying over the middle of the Mediterranean Sea instead of the North African route. Fortunately, we had not been hit by the antiaircraft fire, and we moved out of the area without any known damage.

As soon as we got back on our original altitude of nineteen thousand feet, it felt like we were on a roller coaster due to the storm. The pilot came back on his microphone and said, "Friends, I am sorry to be giving you such a rough ride, but it looks like this is the only course to take for now. I hope that it will be much smoother riding on up the line a little ways."

Sure enough, after another hour, the plane smoothed out somewhat, but it was still storming outside, with lightning, thunder, and torrential rainfall. Suddenly, there was a very loud clap of thunder, and lightning struck the far-right engine. A ball of fire came rolling down the right wing and hit the side of the plane just outside our window, startling Dotty and me. This caused the plane to go into a flat fall, doing a slow spin downward, known as the falling leaf. We went down, down, down; and I am sure many of us on the plane thought we were going to crash.

The pilot was able to gain control of the plane and moved it out of a flat spin by maneuvering into a power dive. This, however, caused another problem, we were headed straight toward the water. Now the pilot had the problem of bringing the plane out of the power dive before we hit the water. Again he spoke to us. "Folks, I'm trying to get us out of this dive, but just in case, everyone should prepare for a water crash landing."

I looked at Dotty, she looked at me and said, "Bob, we'll be leaving our two daughters alone in Tehran, but if we go down, we'll be together."

I replied, "That's true, but they'll be well cared for financially, and that will be our consolation." We then exchanged words of love and braced ourselves.

Somewhere around three thousand feet, the pilot began trying to pull us out of the dive and slowly, at around five hundred feet, we began to pull out. It was such a sharp pull out that the far-left engine was strained, apparently breaking the fuel lines and causing that engine to catch fire.

The pilot had been able to gain a little altitude. He came on his intercom and said, "Friends, we are flying at approximately five thousand feet altitude with two engines on fire, and we are over 150 miles from any airport where we could land. It looks like we are going to crash into the ocean. I will try to go in tail down, which will give a smoother landing. I just called a MAYDAY. I will keep you posted on our situation."

Soon he came back and said, "I have three ships responding to my MAYDAY, and they will come to the rescue if we do not stay in the air. We have recalculated, and if we do not lose too much altitude, we should be able to land in Athens at the airport where we stayed the other night. Thank you. Keep you posted."

Sitting by the window, I could see we were slowly losing altitude, and I was wondering if, by chance, we could make it to the safe-haven airport.

Dotty was holding my hand, and she turned to face me and asked if we were going to make it, worrying about leaving our girls without a mother and a father. I reassured her that the pilot was doing his best to get us all safely on the ground and on home.

The third engine sputtered. We heard the pilot tell his copilot to turn all the reserve tanks back on, as possibly, there was some fuel left. Shortly, the third engine started again, and we had more power to keep us in the air longer.

About that time, the pilot came on and said, "A new calculation shows we will be going down approximately fifty miles from shore, and if all goes well, we should be able to land on the water. Our lifeboats will be out, and we will have ten to fifteen minutes to get into the lifeboats before our plane sinks. The three ships standing by should be able to reach our pickup point. I will give the word when to take your crash positions, but meanwhile, I am nursing this baby for all it is worth, still hoping to stretch our gas supply out far enough to reach our safe-haven landing. However, as you can see by the smoke, the two engines are still on fire, and we are rapidly losing gasoline. We will keep you posted."

At this point, all passengers were trying to remain as calm as possible. However, I did notice some were biting their nails, and others were saying their prayers, as Dotty and I were. Suddenly, I thought I saw land in the distance. It was still raining but had slacked down considerably. At that same time, the pilot came on his intercom system and said, "Folks, we are just passing our landing point. The three ships are waiting for us. They have just advised me that if I continue straight ahead, they will follow in case we do go down. But we still have a little gas in our tanks, and I'm trusting that we are going to make it all the way in. We are going to try."

Shortly, the third engine coughed again. I knew what that meant: it was hungry for more fuel. The airport was now in sight, though still at a considerable distance.

Up to this point, the general had been speaking over the intercom to all the passengers in an effort to keep everybody in good spirits, but we had been watching the airport in the distance and saw it was getting closer.

The pilot said, "Folks, there is the airport. We still have a little gas, and we have five hundred feet altitude left. We will squeeze everything out as far as possible."

I am not sure how far we were from the landing strip, but suddenly, the fire went out in both burning engines, and all engine propellers stopped turning. The pilot came onto the PA system and said, "Friends, we are out of gas. The engines have stopped, and we are in a glide for the runway. I think we are going to make it. Everyone go into a crash position."

I raised my head for a minute to see where we were, and we were on our glide, but we still had a little distance to go. I glanced at Dotty; she was holding my arm tight, and I could see her lips moving.

The pilot said, "Folks, keep your heads down. I don't know if we are going to make it or not."

I thought, *how much gliding power does this baby have?*

I could now see the end of the runway coming up rapidly, but we were in a steeper glide now. Suddenly, the pilot said, "Friends, we have just crossed the end of the runway with about fifty feet of altitude. We will be hitting hard soon. Hold on!"

Then came a severe bump as we hit the runway. It sounded like the landing gear had folded up, but we learned later that it had held together although with some damage. We came to a sliding stop, and the pilot called out, "Friends, disembark immediately and get back from the plane. The engines are so hot I am afraid the plane may blow."

Someone pushed the doors open, and we jumped to the ground and ran some distance from the plane. The pilot and the copilot were the last out, and they joined us on the runway. The waiting firetrucks sprayed the plane with foam, and fortunately, there was no explosion.

The general was the first to greet the pilot and the copilot; and as he walked up to them, he shook their hands, gave them hugs, and congratulated them on their heroic actions. I was close by and heard the pilot say softly to the general, "We made it, General, but this was a very close one."

After the pilot and the copilot shook hands with and talked to the general a moment, all the other passengers congratulated them both. Afterward, we boarded the bus and headed for town. The general, the pilot, and the copilot stayed behind to inspect the plane and get an idea of when we would have another plane or have the current plane repaired.

After checking into the hotel, we all went to the dining room to have a cocktail and dinner while we waited for the general and the crew. When the general joined us a little later, most of us ordered another cocktail, and the general gave a little talk congratulating the pilots on their wonderful performance during this crisis, saying we would fly again because of their expert training and experience. Then he said they would need to change the engines on the plane and repair the landing gear, but that seemed to be the only damage to the plane, with the exception that the tail of the plane had a few pieces of antiaircraft flack. The pilot said we were extremely lucky that none of this flack had hit any wiring that controlled any sensitive parts to the tail of the plane. If this was true, the plane should be ready to take off and fly us back to Tehran by early morning.

At that point, the airport officer handed the general three small pieces of flack. The general looked at all three pieces of flack and then handed one to the pilot and one to the co-pilot and put one in his own pocket. Then he said to the airport officer, "I am sure we will all treasure these pieces of flack."

During the early-morning hours, the general received a call that the plane had been repaired, inspected, and a test flight had been conducted; and it was ready to go when he desired. Therefore, we were all alerted at 6:00 a.m. that we should have an early breakfast, and the bus would pick us up again at 7:30 a.m. for a ride to the airport.

We all met in the lobby at about 7:15 a.m., boarded the bus at 7:30 a.m. as scheduled, and we arrived at the airport at approximately 8:00 a.m. It appeared to be the same plane from the day before. After boarding, the general, along with an Air Force colonel, assured us that our plane had been repaired as needed, thoroughly inspected, and was ready to fly. Some of the passengers may have had a little doubt, but they did not express them, and we took off for Tehran in good style. It was still raining, but not like it had been the previous day.

Shortly after takeoff, I noticed the general left his seat and went into the cockpit. A few moments later, the steward came to our seat and advised me that the general needed to see me in the cockpit and led me to the door. After the steward tapped on the door, the general opened it and asked me to join them, then said, "Bob, as you are the Ambassador's representative, we have the Ambassador on the radio, and he would like to talk with you."

He handed me the microphone, and I said, "Good morning, Mr. Ambassador."

He said, "Good morning, Bob. Tell me, and give me the straight information. What is going on?"

I told him what had happened the day before, but assured him that we were all safe and on our way back to Tehran. He said that the general had given him similar information, and they were proud of the air crew and the repair crew for getting us back in the air so soon.

He was sending a message to the families of the crew and passengers, saying we would be a day late because of a small problem, but all was well. He wished us luck on the rest of the trip and then asked to speak to the general again.

The Ambassador said, "General, I would like for you to stop over at Nicosia, Cyprus. I hope all of you will have a little refreshment on me in the lounge, and tell Jonathan, the lounge manager, to place these refreshments on my tab. Good luck to all of you, and thanks for calling, General."

The general replied, "Thank you, Mr. Ambassador. Look forward to seeing you again before long."

The general and I then left the cockpit area, and then he made a brief announcement to the passengers that we would be landing in Nicosia, Cyprus, staying one night, and going on into Tehran the following day. He also mentioned what the Ambassador said about refreshments in Nicosia and other parts of the conversation.

Even though we had a considerable amount of rain most of the trip, we arrived in Nicosia that afternoon, checked into the hotel recommended by the Ambassador, and had refreshments. We departed Nicosia in the morning and arrived in Tehran midafternoon on Saturday.

After arriving in Tehran, all passengers shook hands with the general, Mrs. Lindquist, and the flight crew, and thanked them for the trip to Paris and for bringing us home safely. One of the senior officers gave a little tongue-in-cheek speech, saying, "Thank you, General, for an exciting trip. Not only were we nearly shot down over Algiers, our plane was struck by lightning and nearly went down, and we could have crashed as we landed if it had not been for the expertise of our aircrew."

CHAPTER 25

Hijacked

One afternoon, the Ambassador's secretary called and told my secretary that if I were free, the Ambassador would like to see me at three o'clock that afternoon. My secretary told her that I was free and would be there as requested.

When arriving at Ambassador Wailes office, and talking briefly, he told me he had a very special assignment and had been wondering, who was the best person to select for it. Part of the assignment dealt with finance work, along with other various subjects. After considering the entire package, he decided that I was one of the people most knowledgeable of those subjects relating to the American Consulates in Iran, which were Tabriz, Mashhad, Isfahan, and Basra. He wanted me to take this assignment in addition to my other duties, and said that the project was considered classified, and I was not to discuss the details of it with anyone else in the embassy. If I were to accept the assignment, he had a booklet with the required information that he would give me. He went on to say that I would be performing this assignment at the US American Consulates several times during the year to obtain the necessary information. I would be authorized to fly to each of these destinations via attaché service using a two-engine C-37 passenger plane, which carried ten passengers plus crew. At times, you might be the only passenger on these trips, and other times, there may be other passengers flying to the post for other reasons. At my request, Colonel Hunter, Air Attaché Officer (pilot), would fly me to these destinations.

Naturally, I accepted the assignment and, for over a year, traveled twice to each of these destinations and obtained the information to complete the report. At times, the air attaché would fly me to the post and then, the same day, fly on to another assignment, returning three days later to pick me up. If he did not have other assignments, he would park his plane at the airport and have his four military security men guard the plane until his return.

The time came for me to travel to one of the US American Consulates in the north to complete my semiannual report for the Ambassador. This would be an unusual visit to the Tabriz Consulate, as I would be going up by myself for my normal three-day visit, and the plane would be returning to Tehran. The Consul and his wife invited a VIP and his wife from Washington DC, plus Colonel Hunter, Captain Smith (co-pilot), and their wives, along with my wife and me to a dinner party. On the third afternoon, the plane would return from Tehran with the additional visitors.

I was completing my normal visit, and the attaché plane arrived at the very small airport in Tabriz with the VIPs and their wives after lunch on the third day for the evening dinner party. To my understanding, the Iranian lieutenant assigned at the airport told Colonel Hunter that he and his company of twenty soldiers had been ordered to guard the air attaché plane while it was parked at the airport. This was somewhat unusual, as normally, the four-man American security detail that traveled with us frequently to Tabriz would camp out and guard the plane. Previously, the same lieutenant was always very sociable when the air attaché parked his plane at the airport. But with this unusual statement from the Iranian lieutenant, Colonel Hunter decided to call the Iranian airport headquarters to verify that the lieutenant's order to guard the attaché plane until the next day was correct. Iranian headquarters confirmed that these orders were correct, and also said the Iranian lieutenant was honest, trustworthy, and would do a very good job. Therefore, Colonel Hunter proceeded accordingly, advising his four-person security detail that the orders were correct.

As Colonel Hunter and his security men, along with all his passengers, were leaving the airport by consulate vehicles, they noticed the Iranian lieutenant's men had formed a circle around the attaché plane and were setting up small tents.

After the VIPs' visit and a very appropriate dinner party, the visiting group, including myself and Dotty, was transported to the airport the following day for our return to Tehran. Upon our arrival at the airport, we were met by the Iranian lieutenant, and we all walked toward the attaché plane surrounded by twenty Iranian military security guards.

Our group was stopped a short distance from the plane by the Iranian lieutenant. Colonel Hunter shook hands with him and thanked him for his services.

Suddenly, the Iranian lieutenant said to our group, "You can go no farther as this is now my airplane."

Thinking he must be joking, I told the colonel we should move ahead, and the Iranian lieutenant then hollered, "Halt!" and shouted to his troops, "Men, fix bayonets!"

Colonel Hunter asked what he was talking about, and the lieutenant replied that the plane was now his.

"This aircraft belongs to the United States government," Colonel Hunter said. "How can it be yours?"

The lieutenant said, "We have now hijacked your aircraft."

I said, "Lieutenant, as you know, I am with the American Embassy in Tehran, and you cannot do this."

"Consul Day, we have just done it."

Colonel Hunter said, "Lieutenant, can you fly this plane? What are you going to do with it?"

The lieutenant said, "No, I cannot fly this plane, Colonel Hunter. You are going to fly it for me at gunpoint. We are revolutionists, and with your help, we are going to Tehran to bomb the Shah's palace." He explained that they had a stack of small bombs accumulated over in one of the hangars at the airport. The bombs were probably seventy-five to one-hundred-pounders. They would need us to fly them to Tehran and over the palace. He and his soldiers would release the safety on the bombs and throw them out the door.

Colonel Hunter said, "Well, friend, this is not the way you do a bombing run."

"Well, this is the way we're going to do it this time."

Colonel Hunter replied, "What we need to do is to go back to Tehran and get a small bomber and bring it back and load up these bombs in the bomb racks."

The Iranian lieutenant replied, "If you leave here, I'll never see you again."

Then, this started a long conversation about what we would be agreeable to do, knowing all the time that we would not be coming back to assist the Iranian lieutenant.

Finally, the Iranian lieutenant said, "I will agree with one thing only. If you will leave Consul Day here as a hostage with the promise you will bring back a small bomber for us to use, and you will fly it, I will agree to the plan. I will give you three days to return, and if you do not return on the third day, I will shoot Consul Day."

Colonel Hunter said, "Well, I think maybe we can arrange that. But, Bob, do you agree with this?"

I knew all the time that the colonel would not be returning with a bombing plane, but I considered, hoped anyway, that the colonel had some plan whereby I would not be remaining with this renegade group here in Tabriz.

My reply was, "Well, Colonel Hunter, if this is the only way we can settle this situation and get our wives and the VIP and his wife back to Tehran, then yes, I will agree to it."

The Iranian lieutenant said, "Well, all right, Colonel Hunter. You folks may board the plane, return to Tehran, and bring back the bomber."

The Iranian lieutenant turned to say something to one of his men, and Colonel Hunter turned to me, shot his fist into the air, and said softly, "Bob, I will give you the sign."

I had no idea what the colonel had in mind, but I knew his main objective was to get all the ladies on the plane with the VIP and to get the four security men, who I understood were also Green Berets, back to their weapons. I figured there would probably be a shoot-out in order to get me released, and I was ready to take defensive action.

Colonel Hunter and the others all boarded the attaché plane and taxied to within about seventy-five feet of where I was standing with the Iranian lieutenant and the twenty soldiers. Meanwhile, the lieutenant had removed his weapon from its holster, and he pushed his gun against my stomach. The attaché plane remained still; nothing was happening. As we stood, there was no movement from anyone, but I did know that

Colonel Hunter's objective was to get his group and the four security men aboard the plane.

Suddenly, Colonel Hunter came to the door of the plane carrying a bullhorn, and he shot his fist into the air. I thought, *what in the hell does he want me to do?* Then it occurred to me, *possibly a diversion.*

The lieutenant was watching the plane very carefully, and I said, "Lieutenant, you are a dog, and your mother was a dog," which is probably the worst thing you can say to a man of his station. He turned to me, forgetting about the plane, and said, "I can shoot you right now."

I said, "Maybe so, sir," and at that moment, Colonel Hunter shouted to the lieutenant and his soldiers on the bullhorn. At the same time, the four security men jumped out of the plane with their automatic weapons and spread out along the side of the plane.

Colonel Hunter said to the Iranian soldiers, "drop your weapons immediately, or be shot."

The Iranian lieutenant turned and saw that the automatic weapons covered his troops. Very surprised, the twenty soldiers immediately dropped their weapons. However, the lieutenant still held his weapon against my stomach.

Colonel Hunter hollered to me, "Bob, let's go! We're ready for action!"

I said to the lieutenant, "I'm going to walk to that plane, and you are not going to shoot me, because you will be a dead man within ten seconds. If you will look, you will see two sharpshooters ready to shoot you. They are going to shoot you with explosive bullets, and you will be a mess."

The Iranian lieutenant said, "I cannot die yet. Our mission has not been completed."

Then as I started walking toward the plane, I heard the lieutenant's revolver click. I thought he was going to fire and shoot me in the back, but I kept walking. As soon as I got near the plane, one of the security men helped me aboard, and the plane started slowly moving with the security men running alongside, still watching the Iranian soldiers to see if there was going to be any resistance. I looked back at the lieutenant, who was standing with his mouth open, his weapon still in his hand pointed toward the ground. He appeared somewhat dazed; he knew his plan had failed and the consequences he would face by his commanding officer.

Colonel Hunter took control of the plane, and we quickly took off.

The copilot, Captain Smith, greeted me. "Bob, I know that was a tough one. The diversion you provided was exactly what we needed. Job well done."

Putting his arm around my shoulder, he escorted me to my seat beside my wife. As I sat down next to Dotty, she threw her arms around me and started crying. Then she said in a low tone, "I thought the lieutenant was going to shoot you."

I said, "I did not know if he would shoot me or not. But I did know that I got you, the crew, and the others onto the plane safely."

After sitting with Dotty for a short time, I began to relax somewhat; then the copilot came back and said I was needed up front.

Colonel Hunter said, "Bob, I have the Ambassador on the radio, and he wants to talk to you."

As soon as I picked up the radiophone, the Ambassador asked, "Bob, are you all right?"

I told him I was a little shook up, and he said that was understandable, then asked me to tell him briefly what had happened. I told him that an Iranian lieutenant and twenty of his men, who apparently were renegades, hijacked the attaché plane because they wanted to bomb the Shah's palace; but fortunately, we outfoxed them.

He said, "OK, as long as everyone is all right. We'll see you at the Tehran airport."

Approximately two or three hours later, we arrived back in Tehran at the airport. The Iranian Air Force Commanding General was there to meet us, accompanied by a second general, who talked to Colonel Hunter, Captain Smith, and me, wanting the full story, which we gave him.

A few nights later, Dotty and I were attending a dinner party, and the commanding general was a guest. He came up, shook hands, and apologized again for what we had gone through at the Tabriz airport. I asked the general if he would tell me what had happened after we left.

"Consul Day, I would rather not talk about it. Just let it go."

I said, "General, I would not wish for you to reveal anything considered classified in your country, but I would certainly like to know what happened to the men in Tabriz."

He replied, "All right, I will tell you. We sent a small squad back to the airport that day to locate the lieutenant and his squad. They knew the penalty for treason, so they decided to try to escape, and there was a shoot-out. The lieutenant and all of his twenty men were killed. In addition, there were only a few airport buildings, and we checked out every one of them. We found quite a supply of small bombs and other weapons that had been accumulated. We had no idea that this group of men was trying to create such a problem within our government. We want to thank you sincerely for your help in aborting their planned action."

CHAPTER 26

Medical Attention In Tehran, Iran

One item I have not covered is medical attention for local embassy staff and employees at a local hospital.

There is one incident that took place in my office during a move of the administrative section from one area to another during the early months of my assignment. We had a moving firm performing the move, but a few local employees were assigned under my direction to advise the movers where to place the furniture. The movers were moving and placing heavy four-drawer file cabinets, and during this operation, one of my senior employees, Ali, had his hand caught between two of the heavy file cabinets. This seriously injured three or four of his fingers on one hand.

As I was tied up with the moving operations, along with four or five other American staff, I asked one of my local supervisors to take Ali to the nearby hospital for necessary medical attention. Ali said he would not go with the local supervisor because he knew that he would not be treated adequately. He wanted me, as an officer of the US Embassy, to go with him. As I considered his hand needed immediate attention, I decided it would be best that I accompany him and his supervisor to ensure that Ali received proper medical treatment.

I presented my identification card at the hospital, and we were ushered immediately into the emergency room, where two doctors examined his hand. After a long discussion between the two doctors, they said they could take care of this, and one of the doctors started drawing some marks around Ali's wrist with his pen. I asked the lead doctor what the marks were for, and he said that was where they were going to amputate the hand.

I said, "Doctor, there must be some other way to handle this situation without amputating the hand."

The doctor replied, "No, we do this all the time with bad wounds like this."

I said, "Well, Doctor, I have seen a number of similar incidents, and they just stopped the flow of blood, straightened out the fingers, placing them in small splints, and with medication, everything worked out."

The doctor replied, "Well, if you want us to do this, we will. But I am confident this man will be back here, and we will have to remove even more of his arm."

I said, "Doctor, I'm not a medical man, but let us give this man a chance."

The doctors followed my suggestion, and two to three weeks later, the bandages were removed, and it was clear the fingers were healing quite well.

Even though it was several years later when I departed the post, Ali came to me at the airport when we departed and, holding up his hand, said, "Mr. Day, if it wasn't for you, I would not have this hand. I want to thank you again very, very much for not allowing the doctors to amputate when I got my fingers smashed."

I thanked him for remembering and told him I was very happy to assist him. He gave me a big hug, and I could see the tears running down his face, showing just how grateful he was.

CHAPTER 27

A Lady Called Spider

My four-year assignment to Tehran, Iran, was completed in August 1962, and I had received orders for my new assignment. With Dotty, and our two teenaged daughters, Betsey and Shaula, we would soon be on our way to a new post. Our schedule provided for us to fly to Amman, Jordan; Tel Aviv, Israel; and Beirut, Lebanon. Afterward, we were to stay in London, England for a few days and then sail from Southampton to New York. From there, we were to drive on to Washington DC.

Prior to departing for my new post, in Madrid, Spain, I was scheduled for consultation in Washington and then six weeks' home leave. I did not realize that an interesting experience in Tehran had not ended and would continue for some time to come.

As my family and I arrived at the airport early in the morning in Tehran, we found many friends waiting to say good-bye. Many of the children, who were friends of our daughters, were singing farewell songs and crying at the same time. In many respects, it was a sad time because all of us had developed close friendships during our four years in Tehran.

When we disembarked from the airplane in Amman, Jordan, and started the long walk to the air terminal, a very attractive lady passed us. She slowed down, turned to me, looked me straight in the eye, smiled, and said, "Good morning, Consul Day."

She had steel-blue eyes, was probably in her late thirties or early forties, and was one of the most beautiful women I had ever seen. She radiated with perfume that was very intoxicating. I smiled and returned her greeting, and she nodded and went on her way without saying anything else.

When we stopped to readjust our luggage, Dotty said, "Bob, I saw that lady smile and speak to you, but why were you looking at her that way?"

I replied, "Dotty, I know I have met her somewhere, but I don't recall her name or where I met her. I will let you know when I remember."

That evening after dinner, Dotty and I were watching the news on television in our hotel room while the girls went swimming in the hotel swimming pool. A high-ranking government official was giving an interesting talk to a fair-sized group of people. I looked closely at the television screen and could not believe my eyes: there was the lady who spoke to me at the airport, standing in the crowd quite near the speaker. I asked myself, *what is she doing there, who is she, and where did I previously meet her?*

As I studied her, suddenly it all came back to me. The lady was Sylvia Gunter. She had changed her hairstyle and the way she dressed, but there was no doubt in my mind that she was Sylvia Gunter.

We had met Sylvia Gunter about two years earlier at a dinner party in Tehran, and I recalled the details of the meeting very clearly. George Nelson, a senior embassy officer, and I were leaving the Ambassador's office following an early-morning staff meeting. George asked me to stop by his office for a minute. It was somewhat unusual for him to invite me to his office because our duties did not overlap, but on several occasions, we had worked together on special assignments.

After arriving at George's office, we briefly spoke to his secretary, and then George invited me into his office and quickly closed the door.

George said, "Bob, I have discussed this case with the Ambassador, and he asked me to discuss it with you, and also said for you to watch your back. What I need to pass on to you is a very sensitive subject and should not be discussed with anyone while you are assigned to Tehran."

I replied that I understood, and George continued, "Bob, do you recall last evening at the dinner party given by the Minister of Finance when I introduced you and Dotty to a lady by the name of Sylvia Gunter?"

I replied, "Yes, she was a most attractive lady, but we did not meet her husband."

George said, "It is believed that she may be a foreign agent. They do not usually have husbands. Her nickname is 'Spider' or 'Spider Lady.'"

He went on to explain that they were not sure who she was currently working for, but in the last couple of years, it was believed she had targeted two men, and they disappeared without a trace. They just vanished, like they had been eaten up, like a black widow spider eats her prey. Last evening, after our talk with Sylvia, George had noticed her checking Dotty and me out several times during the evening. This raised a red flag with him because I was Director of Financial Management for the Embassy and for the Joint Administrative Services, which included eighteen other agencies. Because of this, I had a close relationship with the banks and was responsible for large sums of money, so he thought Sylvia might have something special in mind for me. However, to the best of our knowledge, she had never made a hit on any one of us.

George added, "We believe the local government knows of her activities, but apparently, they do not have evidence to prosecute her. They frequently invite her to official functions just to keep track of her and possibly learn of her next target."

Before leaving his office, I thanked George for the information and assured him I would be careful. It was difficult for me to realize that such an attractive lady could be a foreign agent, but I was aware that most foreign agents were very intelligent and difficult to detect. Because this was a confidential subject, I could not mention it to anyone, including Dotty.

I turned the television off and said, "Dotty, the mystery concerning the lady we saw at the airport has been solved. Her name is Sylvia Gunter, and we met her at a dinner party approximately two years ago in Tehran. I just had a flashback when I saw her on television. As I recall, George Nelson introduced us to her at a dinner party in Tehran."

Dotty said she did not remember her at all, and at this point, I considered the subject closed, for now.

The following day, we found new points of interest in Jordan and moved across the border into Israel, and then on to Tel Aviv, a city in Israel. The second evening in Tel Aviv, we were returning to the hotel room after dinner, and as we walked through the hotel lobby, we came face-to-face with Sylvia on the arm of her escort, who was a very distinguished gentleman, possibly twenty years her senior.

Once again, she looked me straight in the eye with her steel-blue eyes, smiled, nodded, and said, "Good evening, Consul Day."

I smiled and returned her greeting, and Dotty and I continued on to the hotel room.

Dotty said, "Bob, if we get the opportunity, please introduce me to her again. I think she would be interesting to talk with, but there is something about her that really spooks me."

I replied, "OK. Dotty, you have always been a very good judge of character, but I do not have any information to give you."

Dotty laughed, and I thought, *how close to the truth have you judged Sylvia?*

That evening, after I retired, I was having difficulty sleeping because I was thinking about Sylvia. I thought, *was her escort this evening a friend, a partner in crime, or possibly her target? If he was her target, what method would she use to accomplish her objective? Possibly a bullet in his heart, but more likely a little pill in his drink, and feed him to the sharks in the Mediterranean Sea or the Persian Gulf.*

The next morning, as the family was taking a short walk, we met Sylvia by herself walking back to the hotel. I saw the opportunity I had been waiting for and said, "Good morning, Ms. Gunter."

She smiled and said, "Good morning to you, Consul Day. I was hoping we would have the opportunity to visit a little while somewhere along the way. It is so good to see you and your family."

I acknowledged her greeting and introduced Dotty to her again, and then introduced Betsey and Shaula. The girls were quite fluent in French, and during their visit with Sylvia, they found that she also spoke French.

After saying good-bye to Sylvia, we continued our walk back to the hotel. Both of the girls thought Sylvia was very attractive and thought the way she spoke French and expressed herself was amazing. Dotty also mentioned that she was most attractive but withheld further comments. I could easily read Dotty in this respect and knew she was retaining certain thoughts and remarks regarding Sylvia's personality, which I could certainly understand.

When we got back to the hotel, we learned that airport transportation would be arriving soon to take us to the airport. We traveled on to Beirut, Lebanon, where we had reservations for two adjoining rooms at a modest hotel overlooking the Mediterranean Sea, and enjoyed several days visiting friends and touring various sites of interest.

Before long, the day arrived for our departure to London and then to the United States. We arrived in Washington DC for home leave and transfer. During my first week of consultation in the department prior to home leave, my next assignment changed from Madrid, Spain, to Munich, Germany, as an Administrative Officer.

During this assignment to Germany, at times I would travel to other posts in Europe to work on special projects. The children missed Tehran and all their friends, but it was exciting to be in Europe and making new friends.

I had been in Munich about a year and had settled in my new position very well when my office asked me to go to Paris for a week to work with a small team on a special project. The project was finished and approved by mid-Friday morning, and we received thanks for our assistance. We were ready to return home and decided to eat lunch together at a nearby restaurant before departing to our home posts. We had an enjoyable lunch together, said our good-byes, and I took a cab to the airport.

After checking in at the ticket counter, I found there were no earlier flights available to Munich, so I would depart at the scheduled time. I checked through security and called Dotty to ask her to meet me at the airport. We had a good conversation, and I suggested we eat dinner at one of our favorite restaurants in Munich. This suited Dotty just fine, and we ended our conversation.

I walked on and found a comfortable seat where I could watch the passengers arriving and departing from the various flights. Eventually, I noticed a lady who I thought I recognized but could not be sure due to the distance. *Who is this attractive lady?* Suddenly I recognized her. She had a big smile on her face and came directly toward me as if she knew I would be waiting for her. There was no question; it was Sylvia Gunter, "Spider Lady." She had spotted me before I had noticed her.

As she came closer to me, I stood up to greet her by shaking her hand, but she put her arm gently around my waist and gave me a short hug. This really surprised me because I was not expecting such a greeting from a possible foreign agent, and I tried not to act surprised, returning the light hug. We exchanged greetings and both expressed how surprised we were to see each other again. Sylvia mentioned she was on her way to get some coffee and invited me to join her. We located a table in a small restaurant in the airport, and Sylvia selected her chair. I assisted her as she sat down and sat directly across the table from her to watch my coffee closely in case she decided to drop any little knockout pills in my cup.

We talked briefly about Tehran, and then Sylvia mentioned she was working as an investigator for a law firm in Paris that required a considerable amount of travel. I told her I had been on a brief assignment in Paris and was on my way back to Munich. Sylvia mentioned the discussion that she had had with Dotty and the girls in Jordan and told me that I had a beautiful family.

Suddenly, Sylvia said, "Bob, I want you to know I like you very much."

Surprised by such a statement, I replied, "Sylvia, thank you for the kind words. However, as you know, I am married to a very lovely lady, and I would not do anything to damage our marriage. Dotty is a wonderful wife, and we have two great daughters."

Sylvia replied, "Yes, I know, Bob, but I just wanted you to know my feelings."

I decided it was time to slow the relationship down and said, "Sylvia, not to change the subject, but I just noticed that our flights will be departing before long, so we should leave soon for our gates."

Sylvia agreed, and I left a tip for the waiter and paid the check. As we prepared to leave, I noticed that Sylvia placed her purse strap on her left shoulder, even though she was right handed.

We walked out of the restaurant, and Sylvia turned to me and expressed her thanks for the coffee, then said, "Bob, I feel that I have known you for a long time."

Before I could respond, she slipped her right arm into my left arm and moved closer to me. I was surprised and somewhat concerned by this movement because I knew I might have some explaining to do if by chance I met someone I knew.

The main corridor was a short walk to where we would be departing, so I decided not to say anything further concerning our previous conversation. Suddenly, Sylvia quickly removed her arm from mine, swung her purse to her chest, and placed her right hand on top of the purse. I noticed she was looking directly at two neatly dressed men who were walking in our direction. As they came closer, one of the men flipped his jacket back and placed his right hand on his hip as if he was ready to draw a weapon. At this point, Sylvia thrust her right hand deep into her purse, and, because I was so close to her, I could see she was holding a weapon. However, her jacket concealed the weapon from any bystanders.

She watched both men very closely as they approached, ready to defend herself if necessary. I slowly moved a couple of feet to my right to avoid being in the line of fire in the event there was any shooting. Sylvia's sharp eyes followed every movement one of the men made as they approached. When they were twenty to thirty feet from us, the man removed his hand from his hip and flipped his coat back in place. Sylvia's hand remained in her purse. The men smiled at her as they passed, but Sylvia did not withdraw her hand until they were a good distance down the corridor.

I turned to Sylvia and asked what was going on.

She replied, "Mistaken identity, Bob. In my position, all the people I meet do not turn out to be my friends. Enough said."

I replied, "I think I understand."

As we reached the main corridor, we found our departure gates, which were in separate directions, so we stopped to say good-bye. I told Sylvia to be careful on her trip, and she replied that she had had problems before and always resolved them promptly.

Once again, I extended my right hand to her for a friendly farewell handshake, but instead, Sylvia said, "Bob, as a good-bye, I need more than just a handshake."

Quickly placing her arm around my waist, she gently pulled me very close to her, and even though it was only for a short time, I could feel her body trembling as she whispered in my ear, "Bob, we must arrange to meet again, and next time, it will be for dinner. I am sure we can find something to do afterwards. Thanks again, and I am looking forward to our next meeting."

I replied, "Sylvia, I have enjoyed seeing you, but for reasons that we have discussed earlier, I think it is appropriate that we do not see each other again, so let's make this our good-bye and best wishes."

Sylvia smiled and said, "Bob, we shall see. Bye for now, and good luck."

I watched her walking down the corridor and the other male passengers admiring her as she passed. After a short distance, Sylvia stopped, turned around, and waved. I returned her farewell gesture, then turned and walked toward my departure gate. As I walked, I thought to myself that even though Sylvia was a very attractive lady, I would never do anything to damage my marriage to Dotty or my position at work. I had a feeling she was trying to lead me on for some other reasons. I remembered what the Ambassador had said in Tehran several years previous: "Tell Bob to watch his back with Sylvia."

I walked on down the corridor and boarded my flight. As I sat thumbing through a magazine, I could not get Sylvia out of my mind. To me, this was a very strange chance meeting. I tried to analyze our meeting, with Sylvia coming out of a group of passengers with a big smile, just as if she was an actress coming out onstage. Could she have known through her intelligence facilities that I would be at the airport at a certain time? She was interested in seeing me again, but I wondered why she did not want me to escort her to her departure gate. Was she going to meet someone else? These questions would never be answered. I considered no harm had come of our chance meeting, so I would put the entire subject to rest.

I arrived in Munich on time, and Dotty met me as scheduled. We had a quiet dinner together at our favorite restaurant and discussed our schedule for the following day. I did not mention to her my unexpected meeting with Sylvia at the airport as I considered no harm had been done.

Approximately a year later, I was at the Department of State in Washington DC to attend a meeting and ran into George Nelson in the hallway on his way to lunch. We had not seen each other since I left Tehran. George had completed his tour in Tehran and was in Washington for consultation and reassignment, and we decided to have lunch together in the department dining room.

After talking about several subjects, George said, "Bob, do you remember Sylvia, 'Spider Lady'?"

I replied, "Yes, George, I certainly do. She was the attractive lady who used that exotic perfume. Dotty and I met her by accident in Jordan right after we left Tehran."

George said, "Shortly after you left Tehran, I met Sylvia at a dinner party. During our conversation, she mentioned she had not seen you for some time and asked if you were still in Tehran. I told her you had been transferred to Munich. As I recall, that was the last time I saw Sylvia."

George and I finished lunch, and as we both had meetings to attend, we said our farewells and left the dining room. As I walked down the hallway to my meeting, I wondered what really happened to Sylvia. She was a beautiful lady, and I had no doubt her looks assisted her greatly in becoming an expert foreign agent—if, indeed, she was in that dangerous profession.

Thereafter, Dotty and I traveled extensively in the Middle East, Europe, and Africa, but I did not see or hear anything about Sylvia again.

CHAPTER 28

Assignment: Munich

Even though Tehran was rated as a hazard duty post, I enjoyed my assignment there due to the significant and various responsibilities my office carried. My wife and my daughters also enjoyed our assignment there because there was always a lot of activity going on at the embassy or socially for the family.

In August 1962, we received transfer orders and departed Tehran, Iran, on September 29, flying to Southampton, England, and then taking the ship SS *Constitution* to New York. Prior to departing the post, we attended several farewell cocktail and farewell dinner parties held by embassy officers or Joint Administrative Service officers.

When we finally arrived in Washington DC for home leave, we felt we were ready for a little vacation and were looking forward to seeing friends and family members. My orders provided for a one-week assignment in Washington DC for debriefing on Tehran and a briefing for our new post in Madrid, Spain, where I was scheduled to serve as budget management officer for a three- or four-year tour.

After my one-week assignment in Washington was completed, our first visitation would be with Dotty's parents in Baltimore, Maryland, for about a week. Afterward, we would then travel on to my folks, who still lived in Leavenworth, Kansas.

While in Baltimore, I received a call from the desk officer for Germany asking me if it was possible to come back into the department for a few days to discuss a special subject. I replied to the affirmative, and they suggested I come in on the following Monday for an all-day meeting. After I completed the call, I told Dotty that due to this Monday meeting, we would be delayed a few days for our travels to Kansas.

I recall she said, "Bob, what do you think this meeting is all about?"

I said, "Dotty, to me it sounds like a change of assignment to our next post."

When I arrived at the Office for European Affairs, we chatted a little while with the desk officer, and he said, "Bob, let's move down the hall to the farthest conference room." This officer was required to approve all assignments of personnel to Germany.

As we entered the room, I saw there were several other officers coming into the conference room as well, and we were all introduced to each other. Then one of the officers said, "Mr. Day, I engineered your transfer from Tehran to Madrid as we had a new spot coming up for a new budget management officer. We thought this would be an excellent assignment for you, after two budget management office assignments, on which, according to reports, you have done a fine job.

"However, the Bureau of European Affairs considered they would like to have you moved to the position of Administrative Officer to the Consul General in Munich, Germany. Of course, he operates under the American Embassy in Bonn, Germany. It is believed this would be an excellent opportunity for you to move in as Administrative Officer and move up the line in the field of administration."

I told the officer that before accepting this proposal, I would like to discuss it with my wife to see how it may affect my two daughters and their schooling assignments and activities. Dotty and our two daughters, Betsey and Shaula, had been very interested in spending a few years in Madrid. However, thinking it over, all three of them decided that Munich would be just as interesting.

The following day, when our group met again at the Department of State concerning my next assignment, I advised the group that I would accept the assignment to Germany, hoping that the home leave and arrival date were the same as Madrid. This would allow us to continue with our home leave for about another six weeks before reporting to our new post. After a little conversation, we all agreed to this arrangement.

Therefore, as scheduled, we drove on to Kansas to spend a couple of weeks with relatives and friends. We returned to Maryland afterward, where we had previously rented a furnished apartment for two months. We also made several other trips in the Baltimore area to visit friends.

We enjoyed our home leave and purchased some new clothing and a number of other items for our new post. Before long, our departure date arrived, and it was time to move ahead. We departed Washington as scheduled, with tears and sadness, as we did not know for sure when we would see some of our close relatives and friends again.

We departed New York by airline to Paris, France, with a transfer to Munich, Germany. Upon arriving in Munich, we were greeted by the Deputy Chief of Mission, Neil Ruge, and his wife, Helga, and a few other officers of the post. We were escorted to our new living quarters, rented and furnished by the American Consulate. Our quarters were in a new apartment area containing approximately twenty-five residences leased by the Consulate and occupied by Consulate General officers and staff. The apartment complex was located a few miles north of the business district.

The following business day, I met the American Consul General and many of the other officers of the post, and most of my staff in the administrative section. During the next few days, my wife and our two daughters visited the Munich American High School. The girls were promptly enrolled and seated in classrooms. They were anxious to become involved in activities that were provided by their school or by the embassy activities council. During the first ten days, we attended a number of cocktail and dinner parties, and met many new friends and officials with whom I would be working while at this post. In addition, Dotty attended a number of teas and luncheons to meet the wives of prominent individuals of the community. We went to the American military commissary and officers' club to establish our membership.

I had been assigned to Munich as Administrative Officer to replace an officer who had died unexpectedly of a heart attack. He had been highly respected by many of the American staff, leaving me with some big shoes to fill; but the consulate staff welcomed me, and within a few months, I had settled in and earned my own respect. By this time, our family was involved in the study of the German language, but I am afraid our daughters were learning much faster than Dotty and myself.

At previous post assignments, there was frequently a problem in obtaining food products at a reasonable price. We did not have this problem in Munich as all American Consulate General officers and

American employees had the authority to attend the American military commissary, Post Exchange, and officers' club.

Munich was known for its many cultural activities, such as the opera, Fasching, Octoberfest and its many fine restaurants and hotels. My office was frequently called upon by officers of other American embassies in Europe for assistance in obtaining tickets and hotel reservations for many affairs. One advantage to this arrangement, which had been previously established, was developing good public relations with various local business associations.

Shortly after I arrived in Munich, a new ambassador was assigned to Germany and stationed in Bonn. He developed many business contacts in the Munich area that required him to visit Munich on frequent occasions. At this time, the Consul General assigned me as control officer to the Ambassador for his trips to Munich. This assignment required me to meet the Ambassador at the airport on his arrival, take him by embassy limousine to his quarters, and escort him to his various appointments and evening arrangements for the Ambassador and his wife. Frequently, my wife and I would escort them to their social affairs of an evening. I accompanied and assisted him on these business and social engagements.

After the Ambassador's first visit to Munich, I asked him how we might improve any item of his visit. Although he seemed pleased with the arrangements I had made, he suggested that we expedite the procedure though customs. Consequently, after obtaining the necessary permission from the local officials, I arranged to pick him up by our limousine at planeside with a police escort and take him directly into the Consulate General's facilities, where I had assigned him to a furnished apartment with amenities for him and his wife's stay during their visits. On his next visit to Munich, he told me how much these few changes had improved his visits to the various meetings, and over time, we developed a very good friendship.

I was the third-ranking officer at this post, so if the Consul General and his deputy were not available, I then served as chargé d'affaires, which was a most interesting assignment. I was one of four officers designated by the Consul General to serve as duty officer from 5:00 p.m.

to 8:00 a.m. to assist, handle, and investigate any unusual incidences of American citizens having problems. During my service overseas at the embassies and at the US Consulate General, I had many interesting and most unusual experiences as duty officer.

CHAPTER 29

The Rescue

Late one Sunday afternoon, while I was on assignment as duty officer, I received a call from the marine on duty at the US Consulate General Building that an American senator had a problem and was calling for assistance, and I was to call him at a given telephone number in Germany. I called the senator, and he said that his life was in danger, and he needed assistance immediately to rescue him. He gave me the address where he was, which was about thirty miles south of Munich, and said there was a shooting in the area, and he was the target. I told him I would be there as soon as I could.

I called the marine back and asked for an official vehicle with a driver to report to me at my residence as soon as possible. As I was waiting for the vehicle to arrive, my supervisor, Senior Officer Neil Ruge, came by for a quick visit. My wife invited him in, and he asked if I was home. Dotty replied that I was, but that I was getting ready to leave on a mission. I greeted Neil, told him I had just called for a vehicle and was getting ready to leave on a mission that sounded most serious. He asked if it would it be alright for him to ride along, thinking he might be able to give me some help. I said that it would be fine and told him we would be leaving shortly.

About that time, the vehicle arrived. I told the driver where we wanted to go, and that it was an emergency, so to speed it up. He was driving one of our special Mercuries, and we headed for the small town south of Munich.

I explained to Neil what I knew as we drove, and as we approached the town, he suggested that we might need some extra assistance. I told him I had planned on stopping by the local police station, as there had been a shooting reported in the area. We soon arrived at the station. I explained our problem and they got two police officers ready to go.

When we arrived at the address, which was an apartment complex, I told the driver to sit with the engine running in case we needed to get out of there in a hurry. Everything was quiet, so Neil and I cautiously approached the front of the building.

We rang the doorbell, and a well-dressed gentleman came to the door and said, "Where in the hell have you been?"

I told him that we had gotten to his apartment as quickly as possible and asked him to explain what the problem was. He relaxed somewhat and said that somebody had been shooting at him when he was outside a short time ago. He pointed out the two bullet holes in the glass in the front door. The police officers examined the front door and then took off to search the neighborhood.

I asked him first for identification to make sure he was an American citizen. He gave me an ID card, and Neil and I both noticed that he was carrying a card that referred to him as a US Senator. I asked if he was still a US senator. He replied that he was previously a US Senator but that he was now a state senator. But at times he used his US Senator ID for more prestige. I told him that we didn't appreciate him saying he was a US Senator when he wasn't, but regardless, we would do what we could to assist him.

I proceeded to ask him what he was doing here in this little town south of Munich. He replied that he had met two very attractive German ladies in Washington DC a couple of weeks ago, and even though he was married, he escorted them around and spent some private time with them. After several days, they left Washington for home and invited him to visit them in Germany. His wife was away, visiting family, so he decided to make the trip to Germany and had been visiting with the girls the last few days. Now someone was shooting at him.

I told him I thought it was time to get him out of there in a hurry and on a plane back to Washington. He agreed, so I told him to grab his bag so we could go, but then he abruptly changed his mind and decided to stay.

At this time, the two police officers rang the doorbell and said they had searched the neighborhood but could not find any suspicious individuals who may have done the shooting. We thanked the police officers, and they left but stated they would cruise the area frequently to keep an eye out for trouble.

Senator Smith said, "That confirms it for sure. I'm going to stay."

I told him he still needed to leave, and that we were ready to take him back to Munich and get him on a plane to the States, but he insisted that things would quiet down, and everything would be all right. Neil and I both once again tried to convince him to leave, but he still insisted on staying, so we said there was nothing else we could do to help him. He said he would be OK, so Neil and I said good-bye to Senator Smith and the two girls, and we returned to Munich.

When we arrived in Munich, I dropped Neil off at his house, and drove on to my house a short distance down the street. My wife was standing on the front porch and said, "Bob, hold the driver, the senator's on the telephone."

I rushed in and picked up the phone. It was Senator Smith, and I could hear gunfire in the background.

"Consul Day?" he said. "They are back, and they are shooting at me! They have already broken one window out. You get yourself down here and rescue me."

I reminded Senator Smith that we had been there to rescue him, and he did not want to return with us. I knew that I would return and continue the rescue operation, but wanting to scare him a little, I replied, "Senator Smith, we were there, and we coaxed you, but you wouldn't come back with us. I don't think I had better come back."

He said, "Please, Mr. Day, come and get me out of this mess! I've changed my mind. You've got to come back."

I replied, "Senator Smith, I will come back and pick you up, but you are to be inside the door with your bag, ready to run for the vehicle."

He responded, "I will, I will, I will, but hurry!"

I ran back to the vehicle. As it was getting late in the evening, I decided not to call Neil, as he had expressed earlier that he had been out on another mission and was rather tired. The driver and I wasted no time getting back to Senator Smith's apartment, and upon arriving, we drove up the street a little ways to survey the area. All was quiet, so we returned to the apartment.

We pulled up and stopped, and I told the driver to leave the back door open and the engine running so we could be ready to take off. I stepped from the vehicle and cautiously headed for the house.

I ran up to the front door, which opened quickly, and Senator Smith said, "Thank you, thank you for coming back. We are ready to go."

I asked, "Senator Smith, what do you mean 'we' are ready to go?"

He replied, "The girls and I."

"Sorry, friend, but I am not taking the girls. They are German citizens. I cannot rescue them. Senator Smith, I think it is time that we get something settled right now. I am rescuing you from this situation you have gotten yourself involved in. Please understand, both of our lives are in jeopardy, and I am giving the orders. If you don't want to abide with them, you can stay right here in Germany. In all probability, whoever is shooting at you are friends of the girls. Are you ready to go now?"

Senator Smith replied, "Yes, yes, yes, I agree! I'm sorry. I am ready!"

I grabbed his bag and said, "We're going to make a run for the vehicle. You get in the back seat, on the floor, fast."

About halfway to the vehicle, the shooting started again. It appeared that one person had a shotgun, and he was shooting over our heads, blowing the leaves off the trees; the other person must have had a revolver shooting blanks. We ran as fast as we could to the vehicle, and I pushed Senator Smith into the back, hopped in myself, slammed the door, and we took off.

A couple blocks down the street, a vehicle pulled up behind us and fired several shots. I told the driver to take the Autobahn, as it was closer. We were moving fast by this time, and I heard a siren somewhere behind us, then a second siren. We caught the Autobahn and picked up even more speed. Then, even though we were doing close to ninety miles per hour, one of the vehicles was moving up on us.

The driver said, "Hold on, Consul Day! When he gets alongside, I'm going to run him off the road."

I thought, *Uh-oh, what will happen now?*

As the vehicle was pulling up alongside of us, the driver suddenly turned on his siren and his blue light, and I saw we had a friend. We slowed down and pulled over, and it turned out to be the police who had escorted us to the apartment to start with. He asked where we were going, and if we wanted an escort, to which the driver replied, "Sure. It is certainly good to see you. I'll bet we were going close to ninety miles per hour when you pulled us over."

The policeman replied, "You were going over 100 mph, and I was reading your mind. I knew that as soon as I pulled up a little farther, you were going to run me off the road, so I decided it was time to pull you over."

I told the policeman that we wanted to go to a certain hotel in Munich, and he said, "Good. Just hold on."

He took us for a fast ride to Munich and up to the hotel. I got out of the vehicle with Senator Smith, telling the driver to sit tight and wait. I then approached the police vehicle and thanked the officer again and asked, "What happened to the fellow who was shooting at us?"

He said, "He's probably in jail now. That was my partner in the other vehicle who pulled him over."

I thanked him again very profusely and took Senator Smith into the hotel. I suggested to him it would be wise to register under an assumed name to protect himself if anybody came asking for him. He paid for a room for the night, and I walked with him to the room. Once he was inside, I told him that I would be back at eight o'clock the next morning to take him to the airport for his 9:30 flight. I would make sure he got on the plane and told him to call me once he reached Baltimore so I would know he arrived safely.

I gave him my card and then said, "Do not open that door until I pound on it in the morning. Do you understand me?"

"Yes, yes, yes," he said. "Thank you very, very much, Consul Day. You sure scared the hell out of me tonight."

I said, "I didn't scare you. You scared yourself."

He said, "Well, thank you. Thank you again."

I left the hotel, and the driver took me home, arriving around 2:00 a.m. Later that morning, at eight o'clock, I went to the hotel, and knocked five times on Senator Smith's door. He cautiously opened the door and was ready to go. I drove him to the airport and walked with him to his terminal gate.

Before we separated, I said, "Senator Smith, I want you to know that I'm pleased that I could help you, but for your own safety, I suggest that you do not return to Munich to visit the girls again."

"I won't, I won't," he assured me.

As I left the airport, I said to myself, *Please, Senator Smith, do not come back to Munich to visit the girls again.*

I drove to the office, knowing it was going to be a busy morning. About 11:00 a.m., my secretary came in and said, "Mr. Day, there are two men wanting to see you."

"Who are they?" I asked.

"They just said they want to see you about what happened last night."

I told her to bring them in, and they each handed me their card, and then said, "Consul Day, we are very angry with you."

I replied, "What is the problem?"

The lead man explained that he was Detective Sam Goodman, a private detective from the Washington DC area, and had been hired by Senator Smith's wife to obtain evidence to prove he was stepping out on her. The other day, I had been waiting for Senator Smith to leave home, supposedly for work, but instead, he went directly to the airport and purchased a ticket for Munich. In order to follow him, Detective Goodman purchased a ticket to Munich on the same flight, and when they arrived at the airport in Munich, there were two attractive ladies waiting for Senator Smith. The girls took the senator home with them, and Detective Goodman followed, gathering more information for several days. When the opportunity presented itself, he left Senator Smith to hire a German private detective, Mr. Browning, to assist him as he was not familiar with German laws on surveillance. Detective Browning and Detective Goodman had been together when the shooting started the night before.

Mr. Goodman said I spoiled his investigation by rescuing the senator. He understood that the girls' boyfriends just intended to scare him for coming to Germany to visit their girlfriends.

After talking over coffee for a little while, I explained to them that I was doing an official rescue, and it would not be legal to file any lawsuit against me. They understood my position, and we shook hands, and they cordially left.

Approximately a year after this incident, my secretary came in one morning and said there was a couple outside asking to see me. The gentleman said he knew me, and my secretary gave me his card, which said his name was Senator John Smith. Looking at his card, I remembered who Senator Smith was and the incident the year before, and asked my secretary to show them in.

As they entered my office, Senator Smith said, "Consul Day, it is so good to see you again. I want you to meet my dear wife, Mary Sue."

I shook hands with them and asked them to sit down. We talked a short time about current events, and then I asked him what he was doing in Munich. He told me that Munich was such a beautiful city that he wanted to bring his wife over for a little visit.

After talking a little while, he said, "Consul Day, if your schedule is open, I would like for you to join my wife and me for lunch today."

I accepted his invitation, and we went to a well-known restaurant in the neighborhood. As we were winding up our lunch, his wife excused herself and headed for the ladies' room.

Once she was gone, I asked, "Senator, it may not be any of my business, but what is going on with you and your wife?"

Senator Smith explained that they had decided not to divorce, but instead had chosen to regroup and enjoy life together. He added that he had broken off his relationship with the two German girls and had not seen either of them since the incident. At that moment, his wife was returning to the table, so our conversation on that subject ended.

I picked up my check so I would not be obligated to him in any way, and as we left the restaurant, he thanked me again for assisting him in his previous travels.

A few weeks later, I received a short letter from the senator, thanking me again for all the assistance I had provided him during his first visit to Munich, and apologizing for his actions and the problems he may have caused me. He wished me the best for the future and signed off. I have not seen the senator since, but I hope that everything worked out between him and his wife.

During my four-year tour in Munich, I served as duty officer every fifth week many times and had many interesting experiences during this period. It was surprising how visiting Americans could have so many emergencies requiring assistance, but I consider we served them well, and most were very appreciative of assistance rendered.

CHAPTER 30

A Lucky Miss

One morning, I was sitting at my desk working on a paper concerning a proposal to revise a program in our administrative section. I received a call from my secretary, who said the Consul General's secretary had just called saying the Consul General needed to see me immediately. I told her to let the secretary know I would be there shortly.

As the project I was working on was classified, it could not be left unprotected on my desk while I was absent. I took a short time to gather together all the papers, place them in my safe, and lock the cabinet door. About that time, the Consul General's secretary called again and said I was needed right away. I returned to my desk and quickly checked again to make sure there were no documents marked classified, told my secretary where I was going, and headed out down the hall.

I was only about twenty feet down the hall when there was an explosion. I immediately returned to my office, and my secretary said, "Mr. Day, please do not go into your office. A bomb went off!"

Even with her caution, I opened the door very slowly a couple of inches and did not see any smoke. Pushing it open farther, I discovered that the window behind my desk had closed and shattered, spreading glass all over my office. To explain, my office was a corner room on the third floor. It was a bright, cheerful room, and there were two very large thermal-paned windows about seven feet wide and ten feet high behind my desk, and two identical windows down the side of the room. As the building was not air-conditioned, the windows could be opened from the bottom outward to a maximum of two feet to get a little fresh air, and was held open by a secure rod that was fastened to the windowsill.

There were a number of large shards of glass-like spears, perhaps fifteen inches long, protruding from my desk chair, through the back and coming out the front six or eight inches. The front door to my office was directly in front of my desk, approximately fifteen feet from my desk chair, and hundreds of glass shards had not only run through my chair and were sticking out, but they had formed an outline of my chair on my front door. If I had remained sitting in my chair for another two minutes, it was clear that I would have been stabbed forty or fifty times.

After seeing what had taken place in my office, I reported to the Consul General's office as requested and relayed what had just happened downstairs. He said he had heard something like an explosion but was waiting for me to arrive to advise him what had happened.

We then proceeded to take care of his questions to his satisfaction, and then he said, "Bob, I'm going to walk with you back to your office. I want to see with my own eyes what took place."

Upon arriving at my office, we saw that the chief of maintenance was there, inspecting the window lock. He explained that the wind was so strong it had jerked the window and broke the lock, allowing the window to open wide and then slam closed, shattering the glass and sending it flying through the office.

He said, "Mr. Day, if you had been sitting in your chair, unfortunately, you would not be alive this minute, due to the amount of glass that was flying in this room. With your permission, I'll notify the company, and we will have them inspect every window in this building so an incident similar to this will not occur again."

Before leaving, the Consul General said, "Bob, I am deeply grateful that my secretary called you when she did. Otherwise, I'm afraid my chief of maintenance would have been correct when he stated that this incidence could have been fatal to you."

I thanked the Consul General for giving me an immediate call to his office; otherwise, I would have never gone home that evening. I thought to myself, *it looks like I still have an angel sitting on my shoulder.*

A few days later, two inspectors from the company arrived and inspected every window in the building. Based on this incident, they had the window lock redesigned and reinstalled on all our windows.

Consulate General building - Munich, Germany 1964
(note the windows)

CHAPTER 31

Celebrations In Germany

Fasching is the German carnival season, which is seen as a chance for people to have some fun before Lent starts on Ash Wednesday. The festivities start on the eleventh day of November at 11:11 a.m., and most of the hotels in Munich provide festive entertainment during this time. The festivities continue for a week. This has been a German tradition for many years.

My wife and I would attend dinners and formal activities during the celebration. We were fortunate one year to have our pictures taken with other couples on the dance floor for *Time Magazine*, which was a real honor. Consequently, our picture was on the cover of the magazine.

During one of these Fasching events, prize tickets for various gifts were handed out free to the purchaser of the admission tickets. My wife won a very expensive baby carriage for twins during one of these occasions; however, at our age, we were not interested in increasing our family. Right after my wife was presented with the gift, we had several couples rush up to our table wanting to purchase it. Everyone was in a party mood, and it turned into a sort of raffle. One couple said they would give us three hundred dollars for it. At the same time, two other couples joined our group and said they would raise the bid to six hundred dollars. Then the third couple said they would raise it to nine hundred dollars, and so right then and there, my wife sold this beautiful baby carriage for twins for nine hundred dollars.

Oktoberfest is a large celebration of the harvest, with festivities lasting approximately two weeks. It is attended by millions of people from around the world. They celebrate not only with carnival activities, including amusement rides, but also beer tents with one or more bands in each tent holding five thousand or more people. They serve beer by the liter, and German meals, which are extremely tasty. Each year, the Consul General's American staff would attend in groups.

One year after the Oktoberfest, I asked several of my employees if they enjoyed the occasion of the Oktoberfest. They replied that they would love to go with their wives but were unable to afford it, and this got me thinking. I made a number of inquiries from other German staff, and their reply was the same. This was a big occasion for Germans, and I decided that I would try to correct this problem.

I discussed the situation with the Ambassador and the Consul General and received their approval. They agreed that we would solicit donations from our American Officers and Staff to provide funds to have an Oktoberfest night for the local employees, and during the year ahead, we would receive quite a sum from our American staff. The invitation that went out to the German staff included a statement that this celebration of Oktoberfest was being financed by contributions from the American officers and staff. These contributions enabled us to have a large number of seats reserved for our local employees. The ticket included a delicious meal and two one-liter steins of beer. The few American supervisors who attended with their spouses were required to purchase their own tickets.

The two bands in each tent played all the time, alternating back and forth, and many people danced on the large dance floor. For an additional sum, one could purchase a special ticket to conduct the band for about twenty or thirty minutes.

The German staff learned that I was the person behind this celebration, and about halfway through the evening, four senior members of our staff unexpectedly came to my table and said that I was being honored by the German staff for orchestrating this wonderful evening, and that they were there to accompany me to be the conductor of one of the bands.

I rose to my feet, and the four men escorted me to the podium of the larger band, which consisted of about seventy-five musicians. The bands were on a stage probably twenty feet above the tables. A ticket was presented to the conductor of the band, we shook hands, and he told me his name. He then said, "Consul Day, what do you wish to play?"

I had been thinking during our short trip to the podium what two pieces would be appropriate. I said to him, "Mr. Conductor, first we will play "The Stars and Stripes Forever," and secondly the German national anthem."

I recall he said, "Very well."

After announcing that the first song would be "The Stars and Stripes Forever," he marched over and sat down with his band. I turned to the band, raised my right hand, and tapped the baton several times on the music stand. The band then started playing "The Stars and Stripes Forever." I kept the beat with my baton to the music as if I were directing the band, and it went well. When this piece was finished, the conductor announced on the PA system that the second piece would be the German national anthem.

After tapping the baton three times, the band started playing once again, and I kept the baton moving with the beat of the music. When this piece was finished, I took a deep bow to the audience, and the crowd went wild in response to the music. My honor group came to the podium and ushered me back to my seat. The crowd was still clapping and shouting as I returned to my table, and they continued clapping for four or five minutes.

For a few minutes, I sat at the table, thankful for the opportunity to make not only our staff but also the crowd pleased and happy with the music I was so honored to conduct.

The following workday, many German employees came by my office and thanked me for initiating the Consulate General's night at Oktoberfest. Many of them said that nothing like this had ever been provided for them. I was very pleased and honored that the American staff had provided this special evening for the German staff. During the following two years I was there, the same special event was held, and it was well attended and appreciated.

CHAPTER 32

A Tragedy To The Nation

On the evening of November 22, 1963, Dotty and I were scheduled to attend a dinner party, which later in the evening was canceled. However, prior to the dinner party, we decided to go by the US Marine house for a short cocktail. The marines of the American Consulate's Marine Security Guard always had open house on Friday evening, and if possible, we tried to attend to support them.

The Consul General was on an assignment out of the country, so Consul Neil Ruge was chargé d'affaires. He was there with his wife, as were several other officers and their wives. As I recall, we arrived at the marine house at about 6:00 p.m. and were talking with friends when the marine sergeant called for everyone's attention, stating that there was an announcement coming in concerning a shooting involving President John Kennedy.

Everyone came closer to the television in complete silence. Then, it was announced that the president had been shot at a parade in Dallas, Texas, and was being rushed to a hospital. We were all awed, as I know the nation was, that our very well-thought-of president had been shot. As we all stood there, listening, the announcer said that the president was in his vehicle at the time, and the FBI driver had immediately driven the vehicle to a nearby hospital with a police escort. Within a short time, it was further announced that the president had not survived the shooting.

As Neil Ruge was in charge of the Consulate General, he stated that all officers should immediately report to the US Consulate General Building. He arranged to have all the wives in attendance at the marine house, including mine, taken to their homes.

As third-ranking to the Consul General, I immediately went to the Consul General's office as instructed and assumed charge until Consul Ruge, who had been delayed due to communicating with Washington DC, arrived. After arriving at the US Consulate General Building, we received an alert that we may be attacked by some unknown source. I immediately notified the marine house that all marines should report for duty at their emergency posts, ready for appropriate action.

Shortly, several newspaper reporters came to the locked front door and asked to see the man in charge, and I went to the door with a couple of marines. I was asked by the reporters to let them come into the office and do a reenactment concerning receipt of a message from the Department of State in Washington regarding the shooting. I declined this request. They then requested that I do a reenactment with them photographing it through one of the large windows. I again declined, and the newspaper men unhappily went on their way.

By that time, Consul Ruge had arrived at the building. He reported that there was a large group of individuals coming up the street toward the Consulate General Building, but he did not know who they were or what their intent was.

When they arrived at the entrance of our building, Consul Ruge, escorted by two marines, went out to talk to them. By that time, there were several thousand individuals. As he was fluent in German, he found that these individuals were all friendly residents and had come to express their sincere condolences. He then returned with the marines back into the building, and shortly thereafter, as I recall, these individuals started singing various songs in sympathy to our nation's great loss. We stayed on duty for about two hours, and then Consul Ruge suggested we all return home. He went out again and talked to the group, thanking them for their sincerity. They left, saying they would return the following day.

Early the next morning, we set up a memorial inside the Consulate General Building entrance area with a black tapestry and a book to be signed by those people who wished to express their condolences. As I recall, the security officer posted marines at the door and in the lobby to expedite the movement of the individuals in and out of the lobby.

We kept this memorial open for several days from 8:00 a.m. to 6:00 p.m. each day, until all who wished to sign the memorial book had been given the opportunity. During this time, a large number of memorial books, each containing a couple hundred pages, were signed by sympathetic individuals.

A few days later, after President Kennedy's services had been completed, the Consul General asked for suggestions as to what type of memorial could be presented in honor of President Kennedy. I suggested we take a collection from our American staff who wished to contribute and plant a large tree on the lawn of the Consulate General Building in memory of President Kennedy. This suggestion was accepted, and within a few weeks, a beautiful tree was planted prominently on the lawn with a plaque.

As this incident occurred over sixty years ago, I wonder if that beautiful tree still stands in memory of President Kennedy.

CHAPTER 33

Leaving Munich

My four-year assignment in Munich was ending, and I was subject for transfer. I wondered where I would be assigned next. In a couple of weeks, I received notice from the Department of State that I was being considered for assignment to Reykjavik, Iceland, as Administrative Officer. I was not sure that I really wanted to go to a cold country, as I had experienced a case of double pneumonia during my last winter in Munich after standing for two hours in zero-degree weather for the dedication ceremony of the new bridge across the Rhine River, in memory of President Eisenhower. The double pneumonia was so severe that I did not want to chance going through that again.

Then I received information from Administrative Officer Basil Capella, Bonn, Germany, that I was also being considered for a position at the American Embassy in Bonn, replacing him as he would probably be retiring within the next year. After arriving at home, I explained to Dotty the possible change in assignment, and she was delighted that we would possibly be going to Bonn. A week later, the Ambassador received notice that another officer had been assigned to the position in Bonn and would be arriving within the next few weeks. At this late date, his transfer to Bonn could not be canceled. That ended the possibility of my transfer to Bonn, leaving the possibility of my transfer to Reykjavik active.

Our summer vacation was coming up. The previous year, we had spent our vacation relaxing on the beautiful sandy beaches in the Italian Riviera, which offered small towns with lots of shopping for tourists, including the famous glass blowing and art studios, fine restaurants with delicious Italian cuisine, and of course, authentic Chianti wine.

This year, Dotty and I decided that it would be interesting to spend a week with our girls, Betsey and Shaula, in the Italian Riviera and then drive on to Switzerland, where the girls had reservations at the International Summer Camp Montana for a three-week camping experience. This camp was located in the town of Crans-Montana, Switzerland, in the French Alps. The girls participated in many of the activities offered at the camp. One of the most outstanding was horseback riding. The campers learned to ride on former Swiss Army horses, which were very large animals that were trained to stop immediately if their rider fell off. Campers also learned how to stand up in the saddle and ride the cantering horse around the ring while standing and holding only the reins. The girls enjoyed this immensely and became very good riders. The camping experience also included excursions riding the cable train up the side of the mountain to the rooftop restaurant that overlooked hundreds of miles of the French Alps. To this day, Betsey says this was the most beautiful, breathtaking view she has ever seen in all her worldly travels.

After their day of arrival at camp and getting them settled, Dotty and I spent a day at one of the beautiful resorts in the area and then drove back to Munich. Three weeks later, the girls returned home by air. When we met them at the airport in Munich, they were still basking in the joy of their wonderful summer in the Riviera and at camp.

Before long, the time came when we would be leaving Munich, with two months' leave in Washington DC, after four years in Germany, and then on to our new post of assignment to Reykjavik, Iceland. Dotty, the girls, and I attended several good-bye parties held for us. It was difficult to say good-bye to the many friends we had met and known over the past four years. It was the same for Betsey and Shaula, as this was a major time in their teenage years; Betsey had just graduated high school in Munich, and Shaula had completed her junior year at the same school. Betsey intended to enroll at the University of Maryland in College Park, Maryland; and Shaula would be attending the Samuel Ready Boarding School for Girls in Baltimore for her senior year of high school.

CHAPTER 34

Assignment Change

At the end of June 1965, we left Munich and flew to London. Within a couple of days, we moved on to Southampton, England, where we boarded the ship SS *Constitution* and sailed to New York City. Once there, we rented a vehicle and drove on to Washington DC, where we had an apartment rented for two months. The first week in Washington was spent being debriefed on Munich, Germany, and then being briefed on Reykjavik, Iceland. We began visiting Dotty's family with the intention of leaving for Kansas in ten days to visit my family and friends.

During this first week of home leave, I received a call from the Executive Director of European Affairs asking me to come back for a consultation. I advised them that I intended to leave the next week for Kansas for two or three weeks, but they said they needed to see me right away, so we delayed our travels west so I could go to the Department of State for a couple of days.

When I arrived at the department, I reported to the Executive Director for European Affairs. He said he had set up a meeting for that morning in about an hour that included the Executive Director for African Affairs. After talking a little, we moved to the conference room down the hall. There were a couple of officers from the European Affairs office and a couple from the Office of African Affairs, including the executive directors.

After introductions were made, the executive director from European Affairs said, "Bob, we are in a discussion concerning your proposed transfer from Munich to Reykjavik. The Ambassador desires your transfer, and at the same time African Affairs wants you on an assignment in Africa. The assignment to Reykjavik would be as a budget management officer, and the assignment to Africa would be as an administrative officer. Going to Accra, Ghana, in West Africa would place you in a different category, and hopefully thereafter, you may move on up the line in the management field."

After a discussion on this subject, the two executive directors suggested it would be better career-wise for me to accept the African assignment instead of going to Reykjavik. This was a tough decision for me to make, and with their permission, I asked to be excused from the meeting for a short time to call my wife and discuss the proposed change of assignment.

For either assignment, the girls would not be affected as Betsey would be going to the University of Maryland, and Shaula would be going to the Samuel Ready Boarding School for Girls, then on to a university. As we had a number of close relatives in the Baltimore area who were willing to assist and guide the girls in our absence, we decided, overall, it would probably be best health wise and career-wise for me to accept the African assignment. This meant that our family of four would be facing a long separation for the first time, which would be a very difficult situation.

When I returned to the meeting in the conference room, I told them that I talked with my wife and we decided that even though it would cause a number of changes within our family, we would accept the transfer to Ghana, West Africa. The meeting adjourned with the understanding that we would be leaving for Africa after our two months of home leave.

When we advised our daughters of this major change, they had some mixed feelings, as there were pros and cons to this situation. However, after we told our daughters they could come to Africa each year for their summer vacation, they agreed that it was a good idea.

We left Washington for a few weeks to visit family and friends and returned to the Maryland area in time for both girls to settle into their new locations.

CHAPTER 35

Assignment: Ghana, West Africa

Early in September of 1965, I departed for Ghana alone. Dotty remained in Baltimore for another month to make sure that Shaula was satisfied with her new school facilities at Samuel Ready Boarding School for Girls, where her grandparents and other relatives lived. Betsey was satisfied as a boarder at the University of Maryland and was settled in for college life.

Upon my arrival in Ghana, a political officer by the name of George Whitefield met me. We drove into town, and he took me to my new home, which was in a large compound with three other residences of the same design and size. These units were very spacious and comfortable, with flat roofs, so there was a large outside area for chairs and lounges in which to relax. There was a small front yard with a two-vehicle garage and a very nice back porch and lawn for entertaining. An eight-foot brick wall with broken glass embedded into the concrete surrounded the four-unit area to prevent unwanted individuals from crawling over the wall; this was a normal protective device throughout Africa and the Middle East.

After placing my suitcases in one of the bedrooms, George and I moved into the living room, where we sat and talked. Around 11:30 a.m., he suggested we go to his house for lunch, where I met his charming wife, Mary Lee, as well as two other embassy couples. We had a very nice lunch together, and it was good to meet others with whom I would be working with on my new assignment.

After we ate, George, Mary Lee, and I went for a ride around Accra, which was located on the Atlantic coast. After the tour of the city, we drove north on a blacktop road through the jungle, and saw many snakes on the road, monkeys playing, and other small animals. There were few restaurants, so we ate dinner that evening at what might have been the top restaurant in the area. I was tired, so he drove me back to my house to turn in early.

The following day, I met all my staff and the other officers at the embassy; and during the week, there were a couple of welcome parties for me.

I settled into the operations of the embassy, and a month later, my dear wife, Dotty, arrived at the post. As she had never been to Africa before, she was somewhat surprised by the culture of the people, but was delighted with our residence where we would spend the next two years. We had one houseman who did some of the cooking and a part-time gardener. A couple of the officers and their wives gave a little welcome dinner for Dotty, which she and I appreciated. It appeared now that I had been welcomed by my staff and officers, and Dotty had arrived to perform as an embassy wife. We were now both settled in to perform our required duties.

Bob's house - Accra, Ghana 1966

CHAPTER 36

The Ambassador's Get-Acquainted Visit

A few months later, a new ambassador arrived, and some of the officers and their wives, including Dotty and I, met him and his wife at the airport. This was his first appointment as an ambassador.

Shortly after his arrival in the early fall of 1965, the Ambassador decided he would like to make a week's tour around the country meeting some of the dignitaries of four fair-sized cities. He selected one other officer and me, including our spouses, to accompany him and his wife. This trip would be accomplished for the Ambassador and his staff by the air attaché service, but we needed good ground transportation at the four cities when we arrived, so we selected two vehicles that could withstand the rough roads.

One vehicle left two days before our first stop. A couple days later, our second vehicle left for our second stop. After finishing our first stop, the first vehicle went ahead to our third stop; and likewise, after finishing our second stop, then that vehicle went on to our fourth and last stop. After finishing visitations at the third and fourth stops, both vehicles returned to Accra with only their drivers. This worked out quite well, and we had good transportation at each location.

We were royally entertained at each of these four locations by a local political figure, who also provided lodging for the Ambassador and his wife, while the other officer and I, with our wives, stayed at hotels. After a few days, the other officer and his wife had to return home because of an emergency, leaving Dotty and me to stay alone at the selected hotels. At each location, the Ambassador gave a talk about his position as the new Ambassador, and how he intended to work with the political figures to cultivate improved relationships with the country. Afterward, I was introduced, and I made a short speech promoting education and presented the city with a set of one hundred reference books on various educational subjects. These books were gifted to various cities by the United States Information Service (USIS) program. In response, the principal political figure of the area gave a short address and was very thankful for the books provided.

In the evenings, we were always entertained by a local political figure, one of which Dotty and I would remember for a long time due to a special event that took place at our last and fourth stop. We were having a cocktail at this very fine residence prior to dinner. I was in conversation with three or four guests at the party when I suddenly noticed something running across the floor. It was dark in color, about four inches long, and its tail was curled up over its back. It was moving toward a group of ladies who were in conversation.

After seeing several of these little insect-like creatures moving very rapidly, I asked one of the gentlemen in our group what they were. He watched for a minute, and then he saw two of them running in different directions. Rather than discuss it with us, he left our group and walked quickly across the room to our host, who was in deep conversation with our Ambassador. The host seemed surprised, but then immediately disappeared into the large room where we were going to have dinner. By this time, there were any number of these creatures moving into the room.

Suddenly, the host said, "Ladies and gentlemen, we are going to move into the dining room now for dinner."

As each person moved into the dining room, the houseman was sweeping what appeared to be the same little insect-like creature away from the doorway, being very careful to make sure that none of them entered the dining room.

After everyone was in the dining room, the door was closed and a carpet was placed under the door to prevent any of the creatures from coming in. As we were seated, the host said, "Ladies and gentlemen, I apologize for this quick entry into the dining room, but we have been invaded by a couple thousand scorpions who are moving across the country. Apparently, this house was recently built on their cross-country trail. When we finish dinner, my workers will escort you all to your vehicles accompanied by men with brooms to keep you safe."

We had a delightful dinner, wondering if some of the women were trying to figure out how they were going to get to their vehicle in scorpion country. As we left and said thank you to our host, Dotty and I did not realize that we had one other event in store for us later that evening.

The Ambassador and his wife were staying at one of the local residences, but Dotty and I had been booked at what we understood was the only five-star hotel in town. As we checked into the hotel, the manager greeted us and told us we were being assigned to the best room—the bridal suite.

As we checked into our private room, we noticed that there were two straight chairs, a dresser with a washbasin, a pitcher of water, and two towels on the dresser. There was a double bed with a gallon can of kerosene under each of the four legs, giving the room an interesting aroma.

I asked the bellhop about it, and he said, "Oh, that is something special the manager has provided to keep the bugs from crawling into the bed."

We undressed and put on our nightwear; then we carefully moved our suitcase to one of the chairs and hung our clothes on the back of the chair. We moved our house slippers to the chair as well. We noticed that the wallpaper had been torn loose from part of the wall but was still in place.

The big question was, who was going to turn off the wall switch, which was across the room. I told my wife I would be chivalrous and hop out of bed very fast, flip the light off, and get back in.

She said, "Thank you. You are a gentleman!"

As we lay there, trying to doze off, Dotty touched me on the shoulder and said in a whisper, "What is that scratching sound?"

I said, "I don't know. But let's try something."

Once again, I crawled out of bed, turned on the lights, and the scratching sound stopped. I stood there by the light switch and turned the lights off. The scratching sound started again. I quickly flipped the light switch on and saw what was causing the scratching sound. Behind the torn wallpaper were large water bugs (roaches), probably an inch and a half to two inches long. They were ripping the wallpaper loose from the wall and eating the dried paste.

I decided at that point that there must be a better way of turning this light switch on and off. I quickly looked through my suitcase, as I always carried a number of small items to use for emergencies, and I found a large piece of heavy twine. I tied this to the light switch, found that the twine was long enough to reach the bed, and tied that end to the rod at the head of the bed. That way, I could turn the switch on and off by just pulling on the string. After I got in bed, I pulled on the string, the lights went out, and the string pulled loose from the switch.

I told Dotty, "The string has pulled loose from the switch. What do I do now?"

She laughed, "That is simple, Bob. You are the adventurous type." She then suggested that I jump out of bed in the dark and go fix the string on the switch.

I slipped my slippers on, hopped out of bed in the dark, and headed for the light switch. After two or three steps, there was a *crunch, crunch, and crunch*; and by the time I got to the wall and got the light on, my slippers were slick, and I knew what had happened: I had been stepping on and crushing large water bugs.

After I fixed the string and headed back to the bed, I slipped and caught myself, preventing a fall. As I reached the foot of the bed, I thought, *Oh hell, I sure don't want to fall here among the water bugs.*

I got in bed, and Dotty asked what the crunching noise was. I explained that I was stepping on the backs of water bugs, and she said, "If you talk like that, I won't be able to sleep a wink tonight."

As I hung my house slippers on the foot of the bed to dry, I turned the light switch on again; the floor was covered with water bugs. I told Dotty that the only way to get some sleep would be to leave the light on during the night, and she said we could just cover our heads with the sheet, and that is how we slept that night.

As soon as it was daylight, we were dressed and out of there to a small restaurant in the hotel. When we finished breakfast, we had the driver go by and pick up the Ambassador and his wife, as the attaché plane was due in to pick us up at 9:00 a.m. This was the last stop on our trip. Apparently, the Ambassador had a different experience with his sleeping quarters; he and his wife both said they had a comfortable night.

We were all tired of traveling, so we welcomed the pilot and the copilot, but the Ambassador said he wanted to take the host, his wife, and two other local couples for an air ride over the countryside. We were flying in a C-37, which was a very comfortable plane similar to the C-54 we had used on our R & R trip to Paris; but the C-37 had only two engines. I had flown hundreds of miles in this type of aircraft in the Middle East and never experienced any difficulty. We flew about 1000 to 1,200 feet above the jungle so our honored guest could see many of his constituents waving at him. We were enjoying the flight when, suddenly, one of the engines coughed several times and the propeller stopped turning. As we were just above the treetop level and everything below was trees, trees, trees, we all thought we were going down. I know we were wondering where we would land as there was nothing but jungle below us, which would mean a crash. We were rapidly losing altitude. I could see the copilot rapidly adjusting some of his instruments. Suddenly, the engines started again, and for the time being, we had recovered and all could, hopefully, continue to enjoy the flight. The pilot said, "Sorry, friends, it looks like our fuel had some moisture in it and gave us a little excitement there for a short time. Everything is now fine."

The flight lasted for about an hour. Our guests said it was their first air trip around the country and were happy to see some of the villages from the sky.

At the airport, we all said our good-byes and re-boarded our plane. At our last stop, the Ambassador had purchased two wild canaries at a bazaar as a gift to Dotty for making the trip with us and for assisting in conversing with the local dignitaries: we made sure the two wild canaries in a cage were safely aboard. The embassy driver then told us good-bye and headed back to Accra. By plane, we would be there in a couple of hours, whereas it would take the embassy driver probably two days of hard driving to return to the embassy.

Upon arriving in Accra, we thanked the pilot and the copilot for their fine service and picked up our vehicle at the airport. We were very happy to be back home. As it was Sunday morning, the first thing we did was to take a good warm shower and have lunch at home, where we had a very restful afternoon.

CHAPTER 37

Rescue of The Monthly Food Shipment

Early Monday morning, I had my regular 9:00 a.m. staff meeting, which lasted about forty-five minutes. As we finished the meeting, my General Service Officer (GSO) said he needed me to sign some papers to get our monthly food shipment cleared through customs.

As we did not have any good local food markets available, we had set up an ordering procedure for embassy officers and staff to order food shipments from a wholesale grocer in the United States. These orders were individually packed for each family with their name on the large package but recorded as a large food shipment for American Embassy families for clearance through the Ghanaian Customs Office. This meant that each family who wished to obtain food through this manner had to submit an order through the GSO every month, and it would not be received for ninety days, so we had to plan ahead to have our food shipment in the food line.

Normally, we did not have any problem with the custom officials in clearing these food shipments, which arrived in two or three large shipping vans. These food vans would be unloaded and placed on the docks for the embassy to submit the proper documentation, then would be loaded onto embassy trucks, and the packages would be delivered to each resident.

That morning, at about eleven, the GSO called me and said he was unable to get authorization from the new customs director to have these food shipments released to the embassy. The GSO did not know what was causing the delay, but the shipments were now sitting on the docks in 110-degree weather, waiting to be loaded onto embassy trucks. I asked him what the problem was, and he said they were just telling him they did not have the papers and they would not release the food shipments until the customs officer had signed the papers. The GSO had called the customs office to find out what the problem was. All they could tell him was that the papers were not signed and, therefore, could not be delivered to him.

I immediately drove to the Director of Customs Office, which was located near the docks, and went to the director's office.

The male secretary said the director was out and did not know where he was or when he would be back. As the door to the director's office was slightly open, I decided to knock on the door.

The secretary said, "You cannot enter that office."

I explained to the secretary that I heard someone cough in his office and thought that he had returned by the rear entrance. The secretary opened the door briefly, looked in, came back, and said, "No, no one here."

He sat down and put his feet up on his desk, and I said, "Sorry. I guess I was mistaken."

I then went over, sat down in one of the visitor's chairs, and thought, *what am I going to do now?*

Those frozen shipments sitting on the docks thawing were probably worth twenty thousand to twenty-five thousand dollars. *Bob, you must do something.*

I decided that drastic action was necessary, even if it was completely undiplomatic; so when I saw his secretary engrossed in something he was reading, I stood up and quickly walked to the director's office. I quietly opened the door, walked in, and saw the Director of Customs sitting at his desk looking at a newspaper.

He jumped up, saying, "What are you doing here?"

I replied, "Pardon me for disturbing you, sir. Mr. Director, I am Robert Day, First Secretary at the American Embassy, and we have a shipment melting on your docks. We need your clearance to rescue that shipment before it melts and becomes contaminated."

He said, "Consul Day, when I receive and get ready to sign that document, your office will be called."

As I was standing directly in front of his desk, I noticed a few papers lying in front of him. I scanned the papers lying on top of the pile and noticed the custom papers for the American Embassy among them.

I said, "Mr. Director, you said you were waiting for the papers to arrive, and apparently, you had not noticed, but the papers I'm looking for are right on top of this pile. Would you be so kind as to sign these papers so I can get that shipment loaded on our trucks?"

He said, "Consul Day, when I get ready, I will sign those papers."

At this point, I decided what I was doing was certainly not diplomatic, but I had to get those papers signed.

I said, "Mr. Director, I think we have a problem here that you and I need to talk about."

He said, "Yes, Consul Day, there is. Sit down, and I will tell you."

I thought, *At least I am breaking the ice.*

He said, "Consul Day, I am new here as Director of Customs. I was previously Consul General in one of your East Coast cities in America. I was seriously offended by the American owner of a very prominent restaurant on the East Coast. I decided that one day when I had the opportunity, I would retaliate."

I said, "Mr. Director, whatever this was that happened on the East Coast, was I involved?"

He said, "No, Mr. Day, you were not."

I said, "Then why are you retaliating against the American Embassy here when we had nothing to do with your problem in America?"

He sat back with a cigar and said, "I think you have a good point."

I said, "As you are new here, and you have just become Director and I'm with the American Embassy, I think you and I should have a cordial relationship."

He said, "Yes, I think so also."

I replied, "Mr. Director, my wife and I are having a cocktail and dinner party this Thursday evening. There will be several Ministers or department heads from the Ghanaian government attending, and I think this would be a great opportunity for you to meet some of these officials. I would like to invite you and your wife to our party this Thursday evening. I will send you a written invitation."

He looked at me and said, "Thank you very much, Consul Day. I accept."

He reached over, picked up the top packet on his desk, signed the papers in question, and handed it to me.

He then said, "Consul Day, I look forward to meeting your wife and the others this Thursday evening."

We shook hands, and I left his office with the signed papers. I went directly to the dock, where my GSO was still waiting with the trucks. I handed him the papers, and he presented them to the customs officials who were waiting. After completing the transaction, while they were hoisting the shipments onto our truck, the GSO turned to me and said, "How in the hell did you do that?"

I just said, "My friend, you have the papers. We will talk about it later."

Thursday evening prior to his departure from our dinner party, the Director of Customs said he enjoyed it very much; and during the remainder of my time at that post, we were at his residence several times for various engagements, and he attended a number of parties at our place. This action restored very good public relations between the Embassy and the Director of the Customs Office. Thereafter, we received excellent service from the customs office.

CHAPTER 38

The Revolution

In February of 1966, I had been in Ghana, West Africa, a little less than a year. During that time, there had been some rumors about a revolution, but most of us considered this idle talk.

One Sunday morning, just at sunup, I was awakened by machine gun fire. I sat up on the edge of the bed and listened, realizing it was not too far away.

About that time, there was pounding on the front door. Not having any idea who it might be at this hour, I grabbed my weapon, ran downstairs, and hollered, "Who is it?"

A male voice answered, "Bob, American Embassy."

I slowly opened the door and, recognizing the man, immediately invited him in. He said, "The revolution has just started. The Ambassador's orders are that you stay at home, activate your emergency phone, and keep in touch with the operator. There is too much shooting on the street right now for you to try to get to the embassy, where you will soon be needed. Alert your three neighbors and tell them to stay put and inside their residence. As you know, President Nkrumah's palace is about a mile from here. At the present, some armed force is surrounding the palace, and we do not know who they are. There is no doubt there will be a lot of gunfire, so be sure to stay in your residence until told to do otherwise. You are safer here than anywhere. That is all for now, so keep in touch."

He jumped in his vehicle with the driver, and they were gone. I went out and knocked on the front door of each of the three other residences that housed officers from the embassy and passed the message along to them.

This was the beginning of the overthrow of President Kwame Nkrumah. To my understanding, he was the first president of Ghana since it had received its independence from Great Britain seven years prior. President Nkrumah was presently out of the country on a diplomatic mission to one of the other countries, and apparently, the revolting force had taken this opportunity to revolt.

During my brief meeting with each of the three neighbors, I advised them to pack a small bag for each member of the family and be ready to leave the country by air sometime during the morning, if authorized. In addition, I advised them that these homes had been built with two-foot concrete walls and there was a six-foot secure layer of earth on top of the flat roof. This six-foot roof was designed to keep the house cool during the hot summers, but it also provided a safety net from gunfire coming from the air.

I immediately returned to my own residence and asked Dotty to prepare a small bag for us, in case we were authorized to evacuate later that morning. Abruptly, I remembered there was one other item I needed to mention to the officer who lived directly across the street, so I ran across to his home to deliver the message, and then hurried back to my house.

As I crossed the street to my residence, an armored vehicle pulled up outside my wall, turned its machine gun directly at me, and the man inside the vehicle hollered, "Halt!"

I stopped at my door, and I saw him take the safety switch off his gun, which was pointed at me. There was one man sitting on a small tower in the back of the armored vehicle, with a mounted machine gun, ready for action. I saw that he was one of four uniformed men riding on or in this vehicle.

I said, "This is a diplomatic residence area."

He replied, "Yes, I know." Then he asked, "Do you like Ghanaians?"

I said, "Yes, I do."

Even though I did not smoke, I always carried several packs of cigarettes in my jacket, so I told him I was going to give him something from my pocket and then flipped him two packs of cigarettes. He gave one pack to the soldier next to him and opened the other pack, took out a cigarette, and lit it. The man with the machine gun asked for one, so the first man lit another cigarette and handed it to his friend with the machine gun. This man immediately put it in the corner of his mouth, reminding me of a movie star I had seen recently sitting in the war zone, bent over his machine gun and grinning, with his cigarette hanging out of the corner of his mouth. As I think back, I can still picture that soldier very clearly bent over his gun, grinning, with the cigarette hanging out of the corner of his mouth. He did not know this would be his last cigarette.

Suddenly, his attention shifted to something at the end of the street. There I saw that a Ghanaian army tank had just come around the corner and had stopped at the intersection. I did not know if either the armored vehicle or tank was pro-Western or otherwise, but then the gunner on the machine gun rack swung his gun around, pointing it directly at the tank. I immediately figured they were not friends and it was time for me to leave in a hurry. I considered that I did not have time to go into the house, so I jumped from the steps to the ground and rolled up against a built-up flowerbed. At that moment, I heard the tank fire, and there was a terrific explosion just beyond the wall. Some of the wall shattered and heavy bricks fell in all directions.

Even though I was lying on the ground, the explosion bounced me around like a football. I lay there, stunned, and wondered what had happened in my house where my wife was. I stayed in place for a short time until I considered it was safe to move. As I slowly got up, I could see through the shattered wall that the armored vehicle had been blown to pieces, and the body parts of the four military men were lying in the street.

I moved quickly into my house, with my ears still ringing, and found Dotty in the dining room, sitting dazed on the floor, stunned by the explosion. I sat down and comforted her for a few minutes and found that apparently, she was not injured but was badly shaken up. Dishes from the china closet lay shattered on the floor near her. I helped her to her feet and into a chair at the table. She then called the houseboy and asked him to clean up the broken china. He did not respond to her call, so I went looking for him, and found him lying on the kitchen floor. I called to him, and he sat up, and I helped him to his feet. He sat down in a chair, and I asked him if he was all right, and he nodded his head. I asked him to go help my wife in the dining room when he felt like it, and returned to the dining room, where my wife and I sat for quite some time prior to moving around to check the rest of the house.

Early in the afternoon, the embassy called to say that they were sending a vehicle for me. I passed the message on to my neighbors that, as of now, they should remain in their houses until further notice. Dotty was invited by the next-door neighbors to stay with them until I returned from the embassy.

When the embassy vehicle arrived, I got in and met the political officer, Jack Jeffery. We proceeded to the embassy by a different route than was normally used, and during this trip, some of the people involved in the riot threw several bricks or rocks at the vehicle.

After several hours of emergency work, the ambassador said, "While the gunfire has slowed down somewhat, I think you fellas should return home."

As I was also security officer, I volunteered to stay with my marines, in case the embassy itself was invaded, and we had to take appropriate action. We stayed at the embassy all night, and during this period, everything was quiet.

Late in the afternoon of the previous day, the military commander had sent four military tanks to the embassy. As the embassy compound covered about one square block, one tank was posted at each corner of the square, ready to open fire on any intruders. This additional protection continued for over a week, but in that time, to my knowledge, they did not have to defend the embassy.

The Ghana Air Force consisted of only a small number of fighter planes at that time, and during this week of waiting, they would fly directly over our housing area, opening fire on the palace. The revolutionaries had taken refuge in the palace while the president was out of the country, and the planes attacking the palace would open fire with their machine guns. Some distance out from the palace, our compound was sprayed with bullets. However, we felt quite safe with the thick walls of concrete and the thick roofs.

After a few weeks, the Ghana Army, which was larger than the invading forces, had resolved the differences, and the revolution ceased.

A couple of weeks later, a man from Washington visited the embassy for a few days on a security matter, and he asked the Ambassador if I would be permitted to go to the American Embassy in Nigeria with him to work on a project. The Ambassador agreed, so we left the next day on the noon plane for Nigeria. On the plane, there were two men from a foreign embassy in Europe sitting across the aisle from us, and we talked with them during the flight.

When we arrived, we found that there was also an active revolution in Nigeria. The embassy vehicle was waiting for us, so after retrieving our suitcases, we left the airport for the embassy, which, as I recall, was about ten miles away. As we left the airport, we noticed that the two foreign embassy men were leaving as well.

On the way to our embassy, we passed through three checkpoints, which required us to stop at gunpoint by a detail of five or six men at each checkpoint, show our diplomatic passports, and wait until the men at the checkpoint were satisfied. Then they waved us through with their weapons cocked and pointed at us. This was not a very comfortable feeling, as usually, there were small arguments between them as to whether approval should be given, and as evidence, there were usually two or three vehicles parked at the checkpoint, waiting to receive an answer as to whether they could move ahead.

Things went well for us at the first two checkpoints, but when we arrived at the third checkpoint, the men had apparently been arguing about a vehicle they had just waved through the checkpoint. Earlier, I had noticed these two men, who were assigned to this other foreign embassy, were in an embassy vehicle directly behind our vehicle.

Finally, after a long discussion at the third checkpoint, the military types decided that it was OK for us to pass through, and we slowly moved forward. Then two other men stopped us and asked us several questions about where we were going and what we were doing. While we were sitting there, we noticed that the security men were arguing about a vehicle they were now checking; it was the embassy vehicle holding the two foreign embassy men with whom we had previously talked.

Finally, we were given the sign to move on out. Apparently, our driver did not understand, or was slow in moving. At the same time,

I was watching the vehicle behind us. One of the checkpoint men motioned to the vehicle behind us that he was cleared, and to move on. As he started forward, one of the other checkpoint men hollered for him to halt; apparently, their driver did not hear, so the checkpoint man opened fire with his machine gun, riddling the other vehicle with bullets.

I tapped our driver on the shoulder and told him, "Move on! Let's go!" And he took off with his wheels spinning before another checkpoint man could tell us to stop.

When we arrived at our embassy, I called the other foreign embassy and told them what had happened. They thanked me, and a couple of hours later, they called and thanked me again and told me that their two men and the driver had been killed in the incident. We considered ourselves very lucky that we moved through those checkpoints without difficulty.

After three days of work at the embassy in Nigeria, I returned to Accra, and was happy to be out of the rioting areas for a while.

CHAPTER 39

A Shocking Story

One Saturday afternoon in early May of 1966, my wife asked me if there was any way we could get electricity out to our back patio, where we had some lounge chairs. Dotty and I would frequently sit on the back patio after dinner if we did not have any other engagements. We enjoyed watching the banana bats coming in of an evening and sucking the juice from the heart of the banana trees our gardener had planted in our backyard.

I said, "Well, let me check to see what we have out there in the way of any electric plugs."

I checked for any electric outlet on the back patio that might be suitable to use to plug in outside lighting. Sure enough, there was an electric box just about where we would want a light. I explained to Dotty that I could easily open up this one electric box and install an electric plug for a floor lamp. She said that was great but reminded me that I would be dealing with 240 volts of electricity and not 110 as was standard in the States. I told her that I remembered and promised I would be careful.

I then went to the garage, pulled the switches on all power, and removed the six safety fuses that also cut off all power. Certain that I had cut off all power for the house, I felt confident as I went back out on the porch. I sat down on the tile floor and, using a safety screwdriver with a rubber handle, I opened the switchbox's small door. Seeing the two wires on a small plug, I placed my screwdriver into the box to loosen the wiring so I could connect my small plug into that area. As soon as the screwdriver reached the screw that would loosen the plug, there was a large bang and a flash of fire. It felt as though someone had hit me in the chest with a ball bat, and I went sailing backward off the porch about twenty feet.

Stunned, I lay there for several minutes. Dotty came running out of the house, grabbed my arm, and then fell backward. Apparently, I still had enough electricity in my body to give her a good shock. She slowly got up and came back over to me and, without touching me, said, "Bob, can you get up?"

I shook my head several times to clear it, and then slowly got to my feet. We sat on the porch while I tried to regain my bearings, and after a short time, we went back into the house and lay down for a while.

The following day, I called the maintenance supervisor at the embassy and asked him if he would check to see what the problem was. After investigating things, he called me and said that the embassy had leased these four residences for several years. He had now checked the other three in our compound, and they did not have any changes to the electric system; but sometime prior to the embassy acquiring these four residences, someone had wired the power around the meter in our house, which would allow the occupant of the house to use power without it being recorded in the meter, and thus without paying for it. He said the embassy electricians had removed the extra wiring, and now all power was routed through the meter, which eliminated our problem. He said I was very fortunate there was not moisture on the porch or I would have been electrocuted. I was very thankful that the porch had been dry at the time. They installed the plug for me, and we then had power on the porch for lamps, which we used frequently.

CHAPTER 40

Hunting In Africa

When I was in Baghdad in 1954, and later in Tehran, I did a considerable amount of hunting of a bird called a pheasant. It was not what we would call a pheasant in America—it was more like a prairie chicken. We would go out for three or four hours in a group of four or five men from the embassy, and each of us would come back with at least a half dozen pheasant. The meat was very good, and we would often invite a few of our friends and have a delightful dinner.

Upon learning I would be assigned to Africa, I had hopes that hunting for birds or small animals would be plentiful; but after arriving in Ghana, I found, through experience, this was not the case.

One of my American employees was known to be quite a hunter, and one Saturday, he invited me to go hunting with him. He had a 12-gauge shotgun, and I had a Winchester 12-gauge, which, as I recall, held about eight shells. In addition to small-pellet ammunition, we also carried a number of heavy buckshot and a larger shell called a pumpkin ball that was a large pellet-like marble.

We decided to take my vehicle, and as we drove out into the country, he said, "Bob, this is known as turkey and snake country, so you want to be prepared for either."

I loaded my gun with 00 buckshot, keeping some lighter and heavier ammunition available. We slipped on our snake boots and started into a desolate area that had a few trees but was mainly brush with a wide path through it.

We had not gone fifty feet when my friend Joe spotted a turkey sitting in the low trees. He fired one shot, and the turkey fell to the ground, but as we walked toward it, he said, "Bob, something has already claimed our turkey."

I looked and saw a large cobra, who must have been watching the turkey in the tree. As we slowly walked forward, the cobra grabbed the head of the turkey in his mouth. I guess he was indicating that he had claimed this bird, so Joe and I decided to let the cobra have his lunch.

Backing off, we moved on down the way, and within a few minutes, there was a second turkey sitting in a tree. Joe said, "Bob, this is your bird."

I raised my gun and fired, and Mr. Turkey came out of the tree, falling to the ground about sixty or seventy feet ahead of us. We slowly walked toward it, watching for any other snakes. Arriving at the turkey, I told Joe that, in view of the fact he lost his turkey, he should take this one. He felt that I should take the turkey but as my cook was off that day, I did not want to dress it. So I insisted that he take it and he agreed. He put the turkey in his hunting bag and threw the straps over his shoulder.

We walked farther through the area and probably traveled at least half a mile without seeing any more turkeys. We saw a number of small animals, but Joe said they were not good for eating, so we did not shoot.

After a little while, we decided we weren't having much luck and started to go back to the vehicle.

As we turned around, Joe said, "Bob, we are blocked in! Look about seventy-five feet ahead."

I looked, and there were two black mambas coming at us at full speed. Joe quickly said, "You take the right one, and I will take the left one."

By that time, the snakes were within forty feet of us. I shot the snake directly in the head with the buckshot, and Joe shot his slightly below the head with a pumpkin ball. Fortunately, both snakes dropped immediately and were dead. We could not measure the snakes because we did not have any measuring device, but we estimated that both snakes were approximately seven feet long.

Joe said, "Bob, do you realize that if either of these snakes had bitten one of us, we would only have had time to sit down and say a short prayer? They are that poisonous."

I replied that I had heard they were very poisonous but did not realize how much.

As we reached the vehicle, Joe said, "Bob, I think we have had enough hunting for today. Let's go home."

Joe was transferred a few weeks later, so that turned out to be our one and only hunting trip together. Not long after, on a Sunday afternoon, I decided to drive out near where Joe and I had hunted previously to see if I could find any turkeys. I invited Dotty to go with me, and she agreed, but said she was going to stay in the vehicle.

When we reached a likely spot for turkeys where we had been before, I stopped and got out of the vehicle. I loaded my gun with 00 buckshot and a few pumpkin balls. I put on my snake boots, told Dotty that I would only be gone a short time, and to be sure to lock the doors. She said, "Bob, I will lock my doors, but you should know I brought my .38 along just in case I need it."

I replied, "Good girl. See you soon." I did not realize at the time how quickly "soon" would arrive.

I walked down through a weeded area about a city block with very few trees. Suddenly, something came over me. I definitely felt I was not alone. I stopped and looked around, looking for an animal of some type. None was to be seen. I felt my hair was standing on end. I looked again. Scanning the tall grass all around me, I expected to see a lion, a tiger, or maybe a wild boar with his head sticking out of the grass.

Suddenly, I saw a green mamba snake coming up behind me. I swung around with my semi-automatic shotgun and opened fire. I fired at least three or four times with buckshot, and the snake dropped twenty-five or thirty feet from me. I said to myself, *Dear Lord, thank you for giving me that warning signal. I should not be out here by myself looking for wild game.*

I looked at the snake and saw that this one was also about seven feet long. With my shotgun, I had blown him apart from the head down about a foot. He was still wiggling.

At that time, I decided there were better things I could do on a Sunday afternoon, and so I returned to the vehicle. Dotty smiled at me and jokingly asked, "Where's all that wild game you shot?"

I replied, "I shot one green mamba who was charging me, and then decided I would not disturb any other creatures on a Sunday afternoon."

CHAPTER 41

My Dad's Passing

One morning in March of 1966, when I arrived at my office, I was advised by my communication officer that I had received a personal telegram during the night.

I sat down at my desk and opened the envelope, seeing it was from my mother back in Kansas. In the telegram, my mother explained that since I had been so busy and out of town for a while, she had not let me know that my father had been ill the last few weeks. We had visited my folks a little over a year ago, and he seemed to be in quite good health at that time, but he did have emphysema from smoking most of his life. He was eighty-nine years old, and in fairly good health, but recently, he had been spending some time in the hospital due to his emphysema. Within the last few days it became much more serious, and the previous day he had died during his afternoon rest.

As I sat there at my desk, it was very difficult for me to believe that he was now gone, and to know that when I went home again, he would not be there to exchange stories. My dad was a great storyteller, and many times when we would travel together when I was in my early to late teens, and on cold, snowy evenings at home, he would tell me stories of when he was a younger man.

After reading the telegram, I went to the Ambassador's office and informed him that my father had died. He said he was aware that a personal telegram had come in for me during the night, and he was always concerned about families overseas losing their loved ones back in the States.

I was undecided whether to return home for the funeral and spend a few days with my mother during this crisis. I mentioned that I was the only boy in the family, but I did have three sisters. Therefore, I was asking for time to go home and talk to my wife as to whether we should return for the funeral.

The Ambassador said, "Bob, by all means, go home for a few hours and discuss it with Dotty, and if you and your wife decide you need a week or two of leave for this purpose, you go ahead."

I thanked the Ambassador, drove home, and told my wife the bad news. She said, "Bob, I think you should go back to Kansas and help your mother for a few days. How does our checkbook look?"

I said, "Well, not too good." We had spent a considerable amount of money getting our daughters enrolled in college and paying the educational fees while we were on home leave. Dotty said, "Well, Bob, I loved your dad like my own father. He was a great man, and I miss him already. I consider it a must that you go, but I will stay here and wait for your return, as it would be quite costly for me to fly from Africa back to Kansas on short notice."

Having reached our decision, I called the Delta Air Lines manager, who was a good friend of mine, and asked him if he could get me one or two tickets, hoping that he might have some discount tickets available. He replied that he had only one ticket available for the next forty-eight hours, and that ticket was for the midnight flight out that night. He gave me the schedule for that flight, which would take thirty-seven hours, including a number of layovers, and had me arriving back in Kansas City the night before the funeral.

That settled our dilemma, as there was no chance of getting a seat for Dotty. He issued the ticket to me, which would take me out of Accra on the midnight plane, flying directly east to Lagos, Nigeria, then heading north across Central Africa, crossing the Mediterranean Sea on to Rome. I would transfer in Rome, then on to London, landing in New York and transferring to a flight arriving in Kansas City. An old friend would meet me in Kansas City and drive me to my parents' home in Leavenworth, Kansas, which was about thirty-five miles from Kansas City.

I returned to the embassy and advised the Ambassador of my plans, and he said that he had already notified the Department of State, and I was to contact them after arriving in Leavenworth, as they had a message for me.

I then went to my office and cleaned up a few small items on my desk, told my staff what had taken place, and drove home, arriving about lunchtime. I spent the necessary time that afternoon packing and getting ready to leave. Hearing the news that my father had passed, my three neighbors came over and spent a good share of the afternoon with me, promising they would take good care of Dotty while I was gone.

That evening, two couples and Dotty took me to the airport prior to midnight to board the outgoing flight. I did not like leaving my wife in Africa, but I had two live-in servants to assist her as needed, and my neighbors and other friends said they would keep watch over Dotty all the time while I was gone. Dotty was an excellent markswoman, and we always kept our own weapons handy, so I felt that she would be safe with the neighbors' assistance while I was gone. As the plane took off, I was very sad—both over the loss of my dad and for leaving Dotty behind, as we were very close.

I knew it would take approximately an hour for the flight to Lagos, Nigeria. However, about fifteen minutes before landing in Lagos, the pilot came on the over the speaker system announcing that there had been a change in landing as a revolution had broken out in Lagos. We would be landing at the end of the runway, turning around, dropping off any passengers who wanted to get off and picking up any who wanted to get on, and then taking off in five minutes to avoid being at the airport during the revolutionary shooting.

He announced that any passengers who wished to get off at the end of the runway without their baggage should let the crew know immediately. After this announcement, three of the six passengers who had planned to disembark in Lagos decided they would remain on the plane and go on to Rome.

As we went in for a landing, the copilot announced that the revolutionary group with heavy weapons was only about a mile from the runway, so we would remain on the ground for only three minutes before takeoff.

We came in and landed as planned at the end of the runway. After we turned around, three passengers exited the plane and boarded an airport bus that was waiting to take them to the terminal. No one boarded the plane. The revolutionary group was rapidly approaching, and the pilot took off at full power back down the runway and put the plane in a steep climb to avoid the revolutionists' gunfire.

Soon the pilot said, "Friends, I think we have avoided the gunfire." We reached Rome on schedule. As we landed, the pilot said, "Whether you are scheduled to disembark at this location or not, everyone should get off the plane. We believe that some of that gunfire may have hit the plane in non-vital zones, so it'll be thoroughly inspected before it can move on to any farther flights. We will keep you advised."

As I was in no hurry to disembark and other passengers were anxious to get off the plane, I stayed in my seat. When all the passengers had left the plane, I disembarked at the same time as the flight crew. As I knew the pilot and the copilot, we talked briefly. As we got to the bottom of the exit steps, several mechanics arrived to check the aircraft. They pointed out to the pilot three bullet holes near the top section of the tail of the plane, and told the captain that they would need to give the entire plane a good check to make sure everything was OK, so the captain and I said our good-byes and I entered the terminal.

During this layover in Rome, I took the opportunity to call my mother and tell her that I was on my way. I also asked her if she had a Masonic funeral service planned for my dad. She said that she had been so upset over his death that she had not even considered such. I mentioned to her that since my dad was a fifty-year Mason, I thought it would be most appropriate for her to contact the Masonic Lodge and make arrangements. She took my suggestion and immediately called the Masonic Lodge. During that short period, they arranged a Masonic funeral. This type of funeral was most inspiring, and we all appreciated the Masonic Lodge arranging the service for my dad, which we knew he would have appreciated.

My flights from Rome to Kansas City were all on time, and my friend was at the airport as scheduled to take me on to Leavenworth. It was good to see my mother and the rest of the family. We had dinner together, and then one of my brothers-in-law said, "Bob, since you won't have much time tomorrow before the funeral in the afternoon to spend with your dad, I've called the funeral home. They said to come down and spend as much time as you wish with your dad. There will be an employee at the funeral home all night long."

Even though it was ten o'clock by then, Ralph, my older sister's husband, drove me down to the funeral home and told me to give him a ring at any time when I had finished visiting with my dad so he could come pick me up. Despite the late hour, I spoke with the manager, and he ushered me to the room where my father was waiting for me. I sat with him for well over two hours and then said my good-byes. Then I called Ralph and told him I was ready to be picked up. He took me to my mother's home where I immediately turned in as I was exhausted. I was most thankful that I had a safe flight and arrived in Leavenworth in time to be with my dad before he was buried at the family plot in the cemetery, where I would also be buried one day.

During the next week, I helped my mother make sure that her bank accounts were well in order, as she now had full control over their life savings. I also called the State Department in Washington. They expressed their condolences for the death of my father, and then they requested that after leaving Leavenworth, I report to the department for a week on a special assignment.

After completing this weeklong assignment in the department, I flew back to Accra. My wife was at the airport to greet me and we returned home to discuss what had gone on for us, both in Accra and back home in Leavenworth, over the past two weeks.

CHAPTER 42

What Price My Daughter

In late May 1966, Betsey and Shaula, both having grown into very attractive young ladies, arrived in Accra, Ghana to spend their summer vacation with us, anxious for new experiences in another foreign country. The summer passed quickly as they went sightseeing, shopped in the bazaar, and attended social functions as well as beach swim parties. They accompanied Dotty and me on two official visits—one to Tamale, the second to Agona, where I delivered a graduation exercise talk to the Akim Swedru Secondary School and presented the school with a large set of reference books made available under a USIS program.

Eventually, with only about two weeks' vacation days remaining and a desire to expand the girls' already-fluent French vocabulary, we set out for a short visit to Togoland, a French-speaking country bordering Ghana on the east.

Lomé, Togoland, was approximately two hundred miles from Accra, and required a drive of three to four hours on the two-lane blacktop road. Approximately halfway between the two cities, where the very wide Volta River flowed into the Gulf of Guinea, people had to cross the river on a ferry. With four nights reserved in a first-class beach side hotel in Lomé, our family set out midmorning on Wednesday carrying a picnic lunch. Traffic was light and the drive uneventful, with the exception of seeing a number of large monkeys playing on the road. Just west of Ada, we enjoyed our lunch in a nice shady spot, and then boarded the ferry.

The ferry, with a capacity for twelve to fifteen vehicles, plus passengers and farm animals, required all but the driver to leave the vehicle before boarding. Dotty and the girls walked on and found seats along the side of the ferry. I drove our vehicle aboard, parking it about mid-ship, and then sat on the front fender.

Eventually, Shaula joined me on the fender of our vehicle, and as we sat there talking, I noticed two black limousines parked two or three vehicles behind ours. Three or four very attractive Ghanaian women, all dressed in white including their duku headgear, got out of the two black limousines. It was rather unusual to see such ladies out in public without their veils, but I dismissed it from my mind.

As Shaula and I discussed our scheduled visit to Lomé and the beach, a man, probably in his late twenties or early thirties, suddenly appeared. He was dressed in a beautiful white native robe, or aba, with a headdress trimmed with thick twisted gold cord, which designated a member of the royal family. As he walked toward us, I noted his skin was very smooth and a light brown color. Two men accompanied him, one on each side, both dressed in black abas.

When they were within six feet of me, the man dressed in white said, in excellent English with a slight British accent, "Well, I do believe it is Consul Day from the American Embassy in Accra."

I said, "Yes, I am Robert Day from Accra."

He then introduced himself as Prince Mohammed Fayose and said the two men with him were his bodyguards. He held out his right hand, and we shook hands as I said it was an honor to meet him.

The two men in black did not offer to shake hands, just nodded, and then opened their abas wide, so that I could see their concealed weapons. Each man was carrying four pistols in addition to four long knives in a vest-like jacket. They closed their abas, nodded again, and stood at attention near the prince.

Prince Mohammed said, "I see you have Miss Shaula with you today as well as Mrs. Day and Betsey in the bleachers."

I said, "Yes, Prince, I do. Let me introduce my daughter Shaula to you."

They both nodded, but neither offered to shake hands. I immediately knew that I had been cased in Accra and had no doubt that the prince knew more about my family than what I knew about him.

We engaged in small talk for a little while about the ferry and the river crossing. Then suddenly, he said, "Consul Day, I am a very honest man and want you to know that I am not on this ferry today by accident. In fact, I am here to negotiate the purchase of your daughter Shaula."

I looked at Shaula, her face had turned red, and her eyes were larger than I had ever seen. I told the prince that Shaula was not for sale; she was just visiting for the summer and would be returning soon to her college in the United States.

The prince said, "How can you say she is not for sale when you have not even heard my offer?"

I repeated, "Prince Mohammed, Shaula is not for sale regardless of the offer."

The prince said, "Consul Day, I will trade you one hundred fine steers for your daughter."

I countered, "Prince Mohammed, I cannot accept your offer. As I said before, Shaula is not for sale, so let's not discuss the subject any further."

Prince Mohammed confidently upped his offer. "Consul Day, I was told by a person in Accra that you were a very tough negotiator and it would be most difficult to make a deal with you. Therefore, I am going to raise my offer to an amount you will not be able to resist. Consul Day, for your daughter Shaula, I am offering you one hundred fine steers and fifty thousand dollars in gold coins. How does that sound?"

"As I said before, Prince Mohammed, Shaula is not for sale. We do not sell our daughters, therefore, she is not for sale."

I did not want to offend the prince, because I was well aware that he had the upper hand when it came to overpowering me if it should reach that point. I had noticed that there were two police officers on board the ferry, but I had to consider they were probably friends, or possibly relatives, of the prince.

By this time, Shaula had become quite nervous and told me, "Daddy, I would like to go sit with Mother and Betsey for a little while."

I was concerned that if she left my side, she would be more vulnerable to the prince or his bodyguards, so I told her to stay with me until we docked.

At this point, the prince appeared to become somewhat exasperated, and he said, "Consul Day, you do not seem to understand the situation, and that is, what Prince Mohammed wants, Prince Mohammed usually gets."

Before I could say anything, the prince clapped his hands three times, and two women in long black native robes escorted a very attractive girl, possibly fourteen or fifteen years of age, dressed in a beautiful white gown with a gold-threaded white shawl covering her.

The prince said, "It is true, Consul Day, you drive a very tough bargain, but I will make you one final offer. I will give you one hundred of my finest steers, fifty thousand dollars in gold coins, and my sister."

Without smiling, the young girl looked me straight in the eye for only a moment, and then lowered her gaze.

The situation had become very serious with the prince's desire to purchase Shaula, and I needed to sidetrack the prince immediately without dishonoring him in front of his family members and bodyguards. I did not know what action or risks the prince was prepared to take.

Making every effort to keep my voice at a gentle and quiet tone, I said, "Prince Mohammed, I am honored with the offer you have made to purchase my daughter, especially the fact that within this transaction, you would include your sister, whom I know you dearly love. However, as I said to you previously, Shaula is not for sale at this time, because she must return to the States for college at least one more year. I am confident that you will agree that Shaula will make you or someone else a much better wife if she has at least one more year of college education. I know you are aware that a wife with a college education is much respected. I will make a deal with you: if Shaula returns to Accra next summer, I will meet with you in Accra and see what kind of arrangement we can agree on, provided you are still interested in purchasing Shaula for a wife."

Prince Mohammed paused for a moment and, with a very stern expression, said, "Yes, I agree with you, Consul Day. Shaula will make a much better wife if she has additional college education. In fact, I currently have four wives, and by waiting one year, it will give me time to rearrange my family, whereby Shaula will become my first wife. Consul Day, I will agree to your proposal, providing you will shake hands on this arrangement."

The prince may not have understood my condition—*if* Shaula returns—but he smiled, and we shook hands.

He immediately turned to his bodyguards and said, "We will take no further action today." Then he quickly turned back to me and said, "Consul Day, what are your travel plans? When do you plan to return to Accra?"

Immediately, a red flag went up in my mind, as I wondered why the prince would want to know our travel plans: "*What was his strategy. Was he thinking about meeting us somewhere on our return trip to take further action?*

Even though we had definite plans to return to Accra sometime Sunday, I decided it was time to circumvent his question, so I told him, "Prince Mohammed, to the best of our knowledge, we will be returning back home to Accra sometime Monday morning."

The prince said, "Thank you, Consul Day. I will see you at a later date."

I wished him luck on his travels, and by that point, the ferry was docking. The prince, with his two bodyguards and his family, moved off the ferry toward their vehicles. I told Shaula to get into the vehicle immediately, and we drove off the ferry.

When Betsey and Dotty joined us, they were quite curious about the long conversation with the man in the beautiful white robe. At the first opportunity to pull off the road, I stopped and briefed them about the bizarre discussion with the prince wanting to buy Shaula. We were apprehensive about continuing with our plans for our mini vacation; but after discussion, we decided to drive on to Lomé. Our visit was pleasant, and we enjoyed our time at the beach and meeting friends with whom the girls managed to expand their French vocabulary.

After breakfast on Sunday, we packed our vehicle and headed back to Accra. It was only a few miles to the Togo-Ghana border crossing. As we waited in the customs clearance line, we noticed that about four vehicles behind us was John Ambrose, who was my counterpart at the British Embassy in Accra. He and his family had stayed at the same hotel we had stayed at in Lomé. We presented our passports and automobile registration to the Togo customs officials, who seemed satisfied, raised the border gate, and waved us through into Ghana, where we again presented our passports and vehicle documents.

We noticed quite a number of military personnel standing guard with their automatic weapons, in addition to the Ghanaian customs officials. Our passports and auto documents were carefully checked, and we were asked to move our vehicle forward about twenty feet to allow another vehicle behind us to pass through the entry gate, and the gate was closed again.

As we sat in the new location, the customs officials continued carefully reviewing our documents. Without returning our passports and other documents, they said, "Everything looks OK." But we could not move on until they returned our papers.

Not understanding why we had not been cleared, I said, "Officer, we have diplomatic passports—is there a problem?"

He answered, "No."

At that point, I noticed that there were several military personnel nearby watching the process, and they were rather nervously clutching their weapons. Suddenly, we heard three shots fired nearby, and one of the military men near the side of my vehicle fell to the ground. As he lay there, I could see his uniform on his left shoulder turning a bright red, and I knew immediately that he had been shot.

Someone near the border gate shouted, "Nkrumah is coming!"

The Ghanaian customs officials quickly handed me all our documents and yelled, "Go! Go!"

I hit the accelerator, and we took off. It seemed the vehicle next in line was instructed to do the same, because they were right behind us for several miles until they turned off on a side road.

Our trip on to the Volta River crossing was uneventful, but we noticed we were the only vehicle on the road heading west. After crossing the Volta River by ferry, we ran into some traffic. We traveled back through Ada, and we were the only vehicle on the road.

Suddenly, several large black sedans passed us, going very fast. The windows of the vehicles were dark, and we could not see the occupants. We were traveling a safe distance behind one of the black sedans when the vehicle suddenly stopped in the center of the road, directly in front of us.

I thought, *what is he doing—is this a holdup, or could this be Prince Mohammed up to some trick?*

The road was blocked, and we stopped a reasonable distance behind the black sedan. I was prepared to take some defensive measure if necessary until I saw why the driver had stopped; there was a large king cobra starting to cross the road. The snake was enormous and appeared to be at least fifteen to twenty feet long. Its body was eight or nine inches in diameter, and its head, with hood extended, was three to four feet above the pavement. Looking closer, we noticed a family of small monkeys playing in the trees in the direction the snake was traveling. The king cobra was probably planning to have a monkey for lunch. The snake seemed to take its time crossing the road into the dense forest, but after it had safely crossed into the bush, we traveled on to Accra that Sunday afternoon to end a most exciting and eventful weekend.

I arrived at the office early the next morning, and around noon, John Ambrose telephoned me, wanting to know if we had arrived home safely. He brought me up to date on what had taken place on the Lomé–Ghanaian border on Sunday morning. Authorities had received information that Nkrumah was going to return to Ghana, so the military was on alert. One of the guards on duty had released the safety on his automatic weapon, to be ready for Nkrumah's arrival. Somehow, the guard fell over an object on the road, accidentally shooting one of the other guards in the shoulder. Before the border reopened, Ambrose and his family sat in line for six hours with the other vehicles on the Togo side of the border while an investigation took place. The military man who was shot was not seriously injured.

I consulted the Ambassador about our experience on the Volta River ferry, and he suggested that I try to learn more about Prince Mohammed and emphasized a point I already knew—my daughters would never be able to return to Ghana.

A brief investigation indicated that Prince Mohammed Fayose claimed Ghanaian citizenship and may have claimed citizenship in other nearby countries. He traveled frequently, spending considerable time in bordering countries.

He was back in Accra the week after our meeting on the ferry, which caused some uneasiness on our part. Betsey and Shaula were not scheduled to leave Accra for another seven days. All flights on Pan American World Airways were booked solid, so we decided to keep the same reservations. I hired two local armed guards who were reported to be very reliable, and until the girls could leave Accra, they stood watch at our residence around the clock.

Likewise, both Dotty and I were well trained and experienced in the use of firearms, so during the following week, there was always a weapon well within our reach. We told Betsey and Shaula that they must be with one of us at all times until they boarded the aircraft for the United States, which was a direct flight to New York. Even though their final week in Accra was somewhat restricted, with Dotty or I constantly at their side, they still managed a few social activities and departed Accra as scheduled, arriving safely back in the United States.

In early 1967, I received notice of my reassignment. I arranged to meet with my ambassador, and found he had received similar notice of my transfer. My replacement had been named, and he would be arriving at post shortly after my departure. I advised the ambassador that I would be phasing down my operations and would also be preparing information on embassy operations for administration and security, which would bring the new Consular of Embassy up to date on the workings of our embassy.

As my departure date of March 25, 1967, arrived, there were several farewell parties given for Dotty and me, which we enjoyed. We left Ghana on schedule and arrived in Washington DC, where we stayed for one week on consultation and debriefing before going on one month's home leave.

It was now August of 1967. The girls had been back in the States for a year, and Dotty and I were now stationed in Washington. I was still receiving letters from my replacement in Ghana, James Smith, concerning some long-term projects, and it was probably his last letter to me when he told me that he received a visit from a man who said his name was Prince Mohammed Fayose. He came to the entrance of the embassy and said he wanted to see Mr. Day, but the marine told him

I'd been replaced and had transferred back to Washington. The prince then said he wanted to see my replacement, and the marine told him he would be happy to escort him up to the office, but he would have to remove the saber he was wearing. The prince complained but finally took it off and left it in his limousine. The marine escorted him up to the office, where the prince asked where I was.

Mr. Smith told him I was back in Washington. The prince asked where Shaula and her sister were, and Mr. Smith told him he didn't know but assumed they were back in the States somewhere. At this point, the prince became very agitated and reached for his saber handle, as if he intended to use it on Mr. Smith, and shouted that he had a deal with me, and if I was not going to honor our agreement, he was going to come get me. Mr. Smith called for the marines, and the prince was escorted back to his limousine, where the marines suggested the driver take the prince home. Mr. Smith said he had not seen the prince since that incident but advised me to watch my back for a while and wished me luck.

Not knowing what the prince was going to try to do, if anything, I did take necessary precautions for several months but never heard anything from the prince again.

CHAPTER 43

Assignment: Washington, DC

Because of my longtime experience in budgeting, I was assigned as a Deputy Budget Director to the central office. Now I was told that I would become a Deputy to the Department Budget Director and would be allotting funds to all the five bureaus responsible for authorizing funds to American embassies worldwide.

Additionally, it would now also be necessary for me to attend budget hearings with Congress for the funds being authorized. This was a very demanding position, as you never knew the questions the congressmen would ask during these hearings, so it always required a great deal of prior study and research to be able to respond to their questions.

I was pleased with this new assignment, as my immediate supervisor would be William Meek, whom I had known for a number of years. He had visited my posts of assignment several times to discuss special programs. Bill had five assistants, including myself, and as mentioned previously, my area would involve the funding for operating our embassies around the world, and the other four deputies would have a large program involving other operations for which the Department of State was responsible. During the four years I was in this position, I traveled to a number of the embassies overseas to review certain operations.

I had been in Washington DC probably about a year when riots erupted in many large cities throughout the country, including Washington. Dotty had been employed by Comcast Corporation as secretary to the director. After most communication satellites were launched, they were turned over to this company for control and operating, and it was a very sensitive part of many of our communication projects at that time. Her office was on the other side of the District of Columbia and approximately two miles from my office at the Department of State.

Due to the riots that had erupted in one section of the city, buildings were being burned. It was an extremely bad situation. One afternoon, I had just returned from lunch, and all offices received an emergency flash that we were to evacuate the building within the next thirty minutes, as they had received word that bombs had been set in the building and were scheduled to explode in one hour. We had no more than received this directive when my wife called me and said that they had received a similar notice and that they would be evacuating immediately. She had our vehicle that day, so she said she would pick me up within the next fifteen minutes.

At that moment, my secretary said that my daughter Shaula was on the phone, and she sounded distressed. I told Dotty I would call her back and picked up my other phone.

Shaula was attending modeling college right at the edge of where the riots were in progress, and that day, unbeknownst to us, the riots had expanded outward to include her area.

Shaula said, "Daddy, we have to evacuate our dormitory building immediately, and I don't know what to do. All of the girls have left except three others and me."

I asked her where she was, and she said the three other girls were with her in her dormitory room. I told her that Dotty and I would be leaving our offices very soon and that we would come by and pick her and her friends up. I told her that she and the other girls should wait in the lobby with one overnight bag each, and we would be there as soon as possible. Shaula said that we would not be able to get in front of her building, as it was now being blocked by fire trucks. I told her not to worry, that we would get there some way, and she asked me to hurry and thanked me for including her friends.

Shortly after, Dotty picked me up at the entrance downstairs, and she slid over to the passenger seat so I could take the wheel. We drove to within about four city blocks of Shaula's location and had to stop as traffic was backed up. I was able to move another two blocks and was lucky to find a place to park. I asked Dotty to take the wheel and said I would be back as soon as I could, suggesting that she leave the engine running so we could move out of there as quickly as possible.

As I started to leave my vehicle, I thought, *I am defenseless if someone attacks me,* which I saw was taking place on the street, so I grabbed my ball bat, which I always carried in the back seat of my vehicle. I jogged up the sidewalk to my daughter's dormitory and saw the four girls standing inside the door, waiting.

Along the way, people were breaking store windows and carrying out all kinds of appliances. They were knocking each other down getting out of the stores, but so far, I had not encountered any problems. I rushed to the door of the dormitory, told the girls that we would be jogging back to the vehicle in single file, and to follow close behind me. We started out.

Suddenly, a man called out, "Fellas, look at the good-looking girls! I'm going to get one!"

As he rushed toward us, I swung my ball bat, catching him directly in the chest, and he went down. About fifty feet down the way, a second one made a similar statement. As he rushed to us, I saw he was carrying a piece of two-by-four. He swung it to hit me in the head, but I ducked and caught him just below the knees with my ball bat. He also went down. We had no further problems getting to the vehicle and driving to our home in Maryland, which was just outside of the District of Columbia.

The riots continued for several more days, and Shaula's friends stayed with us for the three days until their parents could come to pick them up. As I recall, their college was closed for about ten days until the police ended the disturbance and then the girls could return to school.

Both Betsey and Shaula went on with their education and settled in their chosen professions. Some years later, Shaula came to Dotty and me to tell us that her friend John had proposed and she was asking for our permission to accept his proposal. After Dotty expressed her approval, Shaula asked me, "Daddy, what do you think?"

Smiling, I said, "Shaula, my first question is, does John have fifty thousand dollars in gold to present to me for your hand in marriage?"

With a twinkle in her eye, she replied, "Daddy, John doesn't have one hundred fine African steers, fifty thousand dollars in gold, or a beautiful sister to trade. I know you love me very much and you would never have traded me to Prince Mohammed, but I sometimes wonder where I would be today if you had accepted the bounty the prince offered."

CHAPTER 44

Retirement

I enjoyed the assignment in Washington, but after four years in the State Department as Deputy Budget Director, I retired on June 30, 1971, with what was described as thirty-two years of loyal and devoted service to the US government.

After retirement, I moved to Florida, where I was employed by the State of Florida in senior management positions for the next twenty-four years. I was appointed by the president of the Florida Senate to serve approximately eight years on the Senate Ways and Means Committee, then four years as District Administrator for Health and Rehabilitative Services. Also, I was appointed by the governor for a one-year term as a commissioner of the Florida Real Estate Commission, and also appointed by the governor for approximately eleven years on the Florida Board of Professional Engineers. Simultaneously, I served on the National Board of Professional Engineers in Clemson, South Carolina. I did some volunteer work with several associations in senior management operations. I did some volunteer work with several agencies in senior management operations.

During my twenty-four years in Florida, I had some most unusual experiences. Two of these events took place several months before I left the assignment as a member to the Florida Board of Professional Engineers.

One day, the Board had dismissed the monthly meeting around 2:00 p.m. until the following day. I returned home and was having a cup of coffee with Dotty, when I received a telephone call from a dear friend of mine who was around seventy years old. He said he needed me to come to his house, but when I asked what the problem was, he just said I would see when I arrived and suggested I call for an ambulance.

To save time, I hung up and called emergency for an ambulance, then got into my vehicle and drove to his home, which was about a mile away. I entered his home through the back door and found him standing alone in his kitchen, wobbling and ready to fall forward on his face. As I grabbed him to hold him upright, I noticed he had a long pair of scissors sticking in his chest.

I asked him, "John, what happened?"

He mumbled, "I stabbed myself, but I do not know why."

At that point, his legs gave out, and he started to fall forward. I knew that this would be the end of John if he fell forward as the scissors would penetrate his heart. John weighed close to two hundred pounds, but I was somehow given the strength to pick him up and lay him down flat on his back on the kitchen floor, placing a pillow under his head.

I asked him where his wife, Mary, was, and he said she was at the food store, so I called Dotty to ask her to go get Mary and bring her home right away.

At that time, the ambulance pulled up near the kitchen door, and the driver and his assistant rushed in. They looked at John lying there with the scissors projecting from his chest, bleeding profusely, and then looked at me.

The driver, Mac, and I knew each other, so he said, "Bob, we may need your help."

I said, "I served as an ambulance medic early in my career, so I will do what I can."

Rather than attempting to remove the scissors which, would have caused severe hemorrhage, we started packing the wound with gauze to slow down the bleeding.

About that time, a sheriff's vehicle pulled up in the driveway and the deputy, who I also knew, rushed in, asking what was going on.

Mac replied, "When I arrived, this man was lying on the floor, and Bob was here."

The deputy knelt down over John's face and said, "Mister, what is your full name, and who did this to you?"

John replied, mumbling his full name and said, "I don't know why, but I did it to myself."

The deputy asked him to repeat that, and John said his name again, and then said loudly, "I did it to myself. I don't know why!"

The deputy stood up, came over, and put his arm around me and said, "Bob, I am sorry I had to consider you as a suspect under the circumstances. This is what was required. You are now off the hook."

I said, "I came to help my friend."

The deputy replied, "I now know you did, but you were the first one here, and I am glad we got this clarified."

About that time, the emergency helicopter landed in the street in front of the house, and the medic ran in and helped Mac finish packing the scissors, and the external bleeding slowed down. The medics rushed John onto the helicopter and rushed him to the hospital for surgery.

Mary and Dotty arrived, and we took Mary to the hospital. We sat outside of the emergency room for what seemed to be a very long time. Finally a surgeon came out and told Mary that the scissors, which were a quarter of an inch from his heart, had been removed from her husband's chest, and that he was going to live. He stated that whoever cared for this man before the medics arrived should be commended, as well as the medics who slowed down the flow of blood.

The surgeon said, "If he had fallen forward when he was by himself that would have been the end of John. We are checking now to see what caused him to do this to himself, and this is all I can tell you for right now."

John was hospitalized for about two weeks and was discharged in fair condition. I was advised that he had contracted salmonella, which had caused John to stab himself with the scissors. John lived for several years after this incident and led a fairly normal life. John always contended that I had helped save his life by taking care of him prior to the arrival of the medics.

I have wondered many times why the board meeting I was attending adjourned early that afternoon, which was most unusual; but it allowed me to be home at the time of John's call for emergency assistance. The answer to this question will never be known.

The second incident also occurred at John's residence about six to eight weeks after the prior incident. Mary, called me one afternoon when I was off work and said, "Bob, can you come over immediately? John Jr., our son, is in the master bathroom with the door locked. I can hear the water running in the bathtub, but John Jr. will not answer my call. I am afraid he may have fallen."

I asked Mary if she could get the bathroom door open, and she replied that John Jr. had locked the door. I told her I would be there in five minutes.

At the time, John Jr. was probably thirty-five to forty years old. When I arrived, Mary was pounding on the bathroom door, but there was no response from John Jr.

I told Mary I would have to break the lock or the door, and she said, "Break it down, Bob!"

I backed up to the opposite wall and slammed my foot into the door as hard as I could. The door broke open, and as I entered the bathroom, I could see John Jr. lying on his back in the bathtub. His eyes were closed, his mouth open, and the warm water was rushing into his mouth. He appeared to be unconscious.

I immediately turned off the water and lifted his 180-pound body out of the bathtub, laying him on his stomach on the bathroom floor. Remembering what I had learned as a Boy Scout, I immediately started administering CPR, straddling him and, with his head to the side, started pumping his lungs from his back; But he did not expel any fluid.

I called to Mary and found her standing in the door, crying, with her hands held tightly to each other. I told her to call emergency and ask for an ambulance, and I started pumping his lungs again. Suddenly, water started gushing from his mouth. With each squeeze of his lungs, more water rushed out of his mouth onto the bathroom floor; but John Jr. remained silent. He was not responding as I wanted him to do.

Suddenly, two medics rushed into the bathroom, opened up their equipment, and the head medic, a man I knew named Joe, said, "Keep pumping! We are going to change positions!"

As he directed, I slid off of John Jr.'s back and Joe slipped on and continued pumping. The second medic said, "I have the hospital on the line."

The medics decided it was time to use the electric paddles, and Joe rolled John Jr. over on his back and placed the paddle on his chest. Then we both stood up and backed away from his body. The hospital then authorized the medics to activate the electric paddles.

Immediately, there was a bang, and John Jr.'s body bounced upward off the floor and dropped back down but there was no response. Both medics shook their heads, and one spoke into the phone.

"No response!"

The hospital said to apply the paddles again, and there was another bang, and John Jr. bounced again. They waited a few seconds, but there was still no response. They shook their heads, and then the leader shouted into his phone, "No response!"

The attendant at the hospital said to try again, and there was another loud bang. John Jr's body bounced a third time and then fell to the floor, but there was still no response.

The medics turned to Mary and said, "Sorry, Mrs. Thompson. We have done all we can."

She was weeping, and I asked Joe to try one more time.

"Bob, he is gone!"

"Joe, please apply the paddles once more."

He said, "OK, Bob, but I don't think it is going to do any good."

The medic said to the hospital, "We are going to try once more."

John Jr. bounced high and fell limp to the floor. His mother was still weeping, and tears came into my eyes as we looked at John Jr.'s limp body lying on the floor. Suddenly, there was movement, and John Jr. started gasping for breath. The men quickly used CPR to help get his lungs moving a little easier. The medic shouted into his phone, "He is back!"

The medics started treating him, and his breathing became much stronger. One of them motioned to me, and we rushed out to the other room and brought in a gurney. We placed John Jr. on the gurney and rushed him out to the emergency helicopter that had just landed in the street.

As we placed him in the helicopter, one of the medics moved into the pilot's seat, and the helicopter headed for the hospital.

Before John Jr. left the hospital, the doctors asked him what had happened. He stated that he had slipped and fallen into the tub onto his back, knocking himself out; and the water ran into his mouth, and he began to drown. To my knowledge, his testimony was never contradicted.

About a week later, John Jr. was discharged from the hospital with no after effects, and after a few more days he returned to his employment as an office manager.

John Jr. gave precious thanks to the medics for saving his life. He and I continued our friendship for a long time, and he thanked me profusely for my part in saving his life. This incident took place a number of years back, and the last I heard, he had married and was doing well.

I joined a group of the Foreign Service retirees upon arriving in Tallahassee in the early 1970's. Together, we started meeting about every other month for a couple of days, further developing our Foreign Service relationships. We decided to form an association to be known as the Foreign Service Retirees Association of Florida because some other states had developed a similar organization. I was one of the original group; and for many years now, the group has met every few months to further develop old and new friendships of officers and staff who served in the Foreign Service. At various times, I have held positions in this group, from budget representative to vice chair.

In recent years, I have been unable to attend these luncheons and affairs due to my health, but I wish to say that I have enjoyed the friendships of these officers and the stories we shared about our experiences, relating to our longtime service abroad, which were most unusual.

While I worked for the State of Florida, my dear wife, Dotty, developed cancer and died after twenty-eight years of a wonderful marriage. Some four years later, I met a very attractive lady by the name of Eloise, who was related to a neighbor of mine; and after a courtship of about three years, we were married, which also developed into a wonderful marriage of twenty-four years; and then, most unfortunately, she passed as a result of a heart problem. As previously mentioned in this book under the chapters about Baghdad, my first wife, Charlotte, passed after a short marriage of eleven years due to injuries sustained in an automobile accident.

Now as I sit here in Florida, I think of the long life and the good times I have shared with these three intelligent and wonderful ladies. I have been blessed and most fortunate to have had three wonderful marriages. In addition, I have also shared my life with two great daughters, Betsey and Shaula, and their husbands, Jack D. Leonard, II, and Dave Noonan, and my grandson, Jack D. Leonard, III, along with some wonderful dear friends.

Earlier in this book, there is a photo of my mother and father, my three sisters, (Hazel, Bessie, Frances) and myself. My mother and father were great parents and were both extremely hard workers and guided us during our growing years. I am proud to have had them as my parents, then and now. Also I am proud to have had my three sisters as we shared life together during all those years, which included the Great Depression.

I cannot close this book without mentioning our little friend, Angel, who was our friend and companion for 17 years for Dotty, Eloise, and myself. She was a very important part of the family during her lifetime.

Bob with third wife Eloise

Our dog Angel in Tallahassee, Florida